# THE CENTENARY WAY

**Published by** Sigma Leisure - an imprint of
Sigma Press, Stobart House, Pontyclerc, Penybanc Road
Ammanford, Carmarthenshire SA18 3HP

**British Library Cataloguing in Publication Data**

A CIP record for this book is available from the British Library

**ISBN:** 978-1-910758-28-1

**Typesetting and design by:** Sigma Press, Ammanford, Carms



The sponsors of the Ordnance Survey copyright fee: Warwick Castle

**Cover photograph:** The distant Meon Hill taken from Sun Rising Hill

**Printed by:** Akcent Media Ltd

**Disclaimer:** The information in this book is given in good faith and is believed to be correct at the time of publication. Care should always be taken when walking in hill country. Where appropriate, attention has been drawn to matters of safety. The author and publisher cannot take responsibility for any accidents or injury incurred whilst following these walks. Only you can judge your own fitness, competence and experience. Do not rely solely on sketch maps for navigation: we strongly recommend the use of appropriate Ordnance Survey (or equivalent) maps.

# THE CENTENARY WAY

## 100 MILES OF LINEAR WALK OR
## 209 MILES OF 32 LINKED CIRCULAR WALKS

# THROUGH WARWICKSHIRE

STEPHEN CROSS

SIGMA Leisure

## MAP KEY & WAY MARK INDICATORS

- (1) Centenary Way and text section indicator
- (A) Circular return route and text section indicator
- Dual carriageway
- Main road
- Secondary road
- Lane
- Drive or track
- Other path or track
- Railway line – (Disused)
- Wooded area
- Pool or Lake
- River or Canal
- Stream
- Field boundary lines
- Towns & Villages

Centenary Way direction indicator

Centenary Way
Devised and promoted by
Warwickshire County Council

Footpath direction indicator

Public Footpath
Warwickshire County Council

N

SPC

Grid North

Car Parking
Indicated at user risk and discretion

P Car park   P Lay by   P£ Car park - pay   8 Kerbside or verge (indicative)

PC Public convenience   8 Visitor Information Centre   M Museum   Viewpoint

Pub   Café   Places of worship   Transmitter mast   Bridge

Buildings   Old Colliery Site   Site of battle   Golf Course

095 Ground height   Tree   Start GR:SP398834 National Grid Reference

1000 metres 0 Kilometres 1

1000 yards 0 Miles 1

# CONTENTS

*Dedicated to my grandchildren*
*Antonia, Harriet, Jasper, Reuben and Ruby*

# INTRODUCTION

The seed of *The Centenary Way* guide book, that I unwittingly sowed, commenced its germination in April 2012. That event celebrated the publication by Sigma Press of my guide book to *The Heart of England Way* long distance footpath. I had been a committee member of the Heart of England Way Association and edited their newsletter for many years. In that time I had written a number of articles which fulfilled my enjoyment of describing my discoveries of people, places and history along the 100 mile route. Having decided to take early retirement I determined to write the book; it also provided the easy answer to the much asked question; 'What will you find to do?'

That question naturally changed to; 'What are you going to do next?' I have to admit that one of the potential answers would have been to tackle the circle of Warwickshire and explore the Centenary Way. However this question answered itself when, having by chance met our prospective Member of Parliament, I became involved in local politics and was elected as a Warwick Town and District Councillor in 2011. My election for a second term has pushed me up the ladder of succession to become the Mayor of Warwick in 2017. What better way to extend my community service by promoting the joys of Warwickshire via a new Centenary Way guide book. The proceeds from the first book still provide a useful input to the funds of the Heart of England Way Association but the proceeds from this book will be held by Warwick Town Council for charitable distribution to local youth organisations.

The Centenary Way and my circular routes follow footpaths and bridleways, which are all Public Rights of Way and Warwickshire County Council is responsible for ensuring that they are not obstructed. The County web site, **www.warwickshire.gov.uk** has the facility for members of the public to report obstructions.

It is intended that, as necessary, any update information will be available on the Warwick Town Council web site at www.warwicktowncouncil.gov.uk

This guide to the Centenary Way also, like my *Heart of England Way* guide givesthe opportunity to expand your enjoyment of the region by following my circular walks.

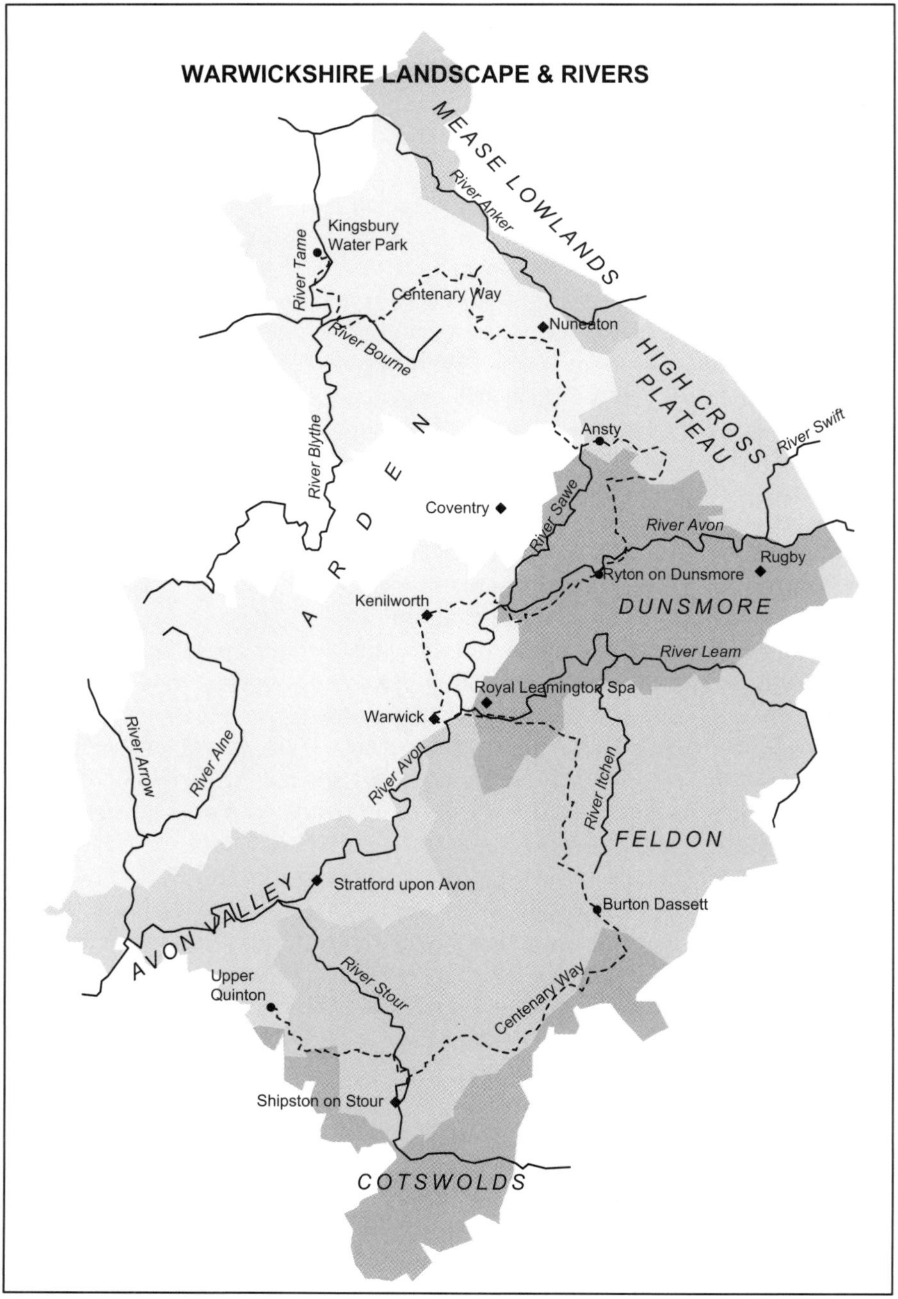
WARWICKSHIRE LANDSCAPE & RIVERS
MEASE LOWLANDS
River Anker
Kingsbury
Water Park
River Tame
Centenary Way
Nuneaton
River Bourne
HIGH CROSS
PLATEAU
River Swift
River Blythe
A R D E N
Ansty
Coventry
River Sawe
River Avon
Rugby
Ryton on Dunsmore
Kenilworth
DUNSMORE
River Leam
Royal Leamington Spa
Warwick
River Arrow
River Alne
River Avon
River Itchen
FELDON
Stratford upon Avon
Burton Dassett
AVON VALLEY
Upper
Quinton
River Stour
Centenary Way
Shipston on Stour
COTSWOLDS

## The County of Warwickshire

Motorway signs at the Warwickshire County boundaries announce that we are in 'Shakespeare's County'. Indeed the 100 mile, or potential 209 mile, circumnavigation of the County will prove that William Shakespeare was fortunate to be born here, even though we will not visit his home town. Our tour will thread its way through a complete cross section of Warwickshire's landscape, nature, history, culture, buildings and people.

The Warwickshire Centenary Way (the 'Way') was established to celebrate the first 100 years of the County's transition from a purely historical county to a local government administrative authority. This followed the decision of the Government, through the introduction of the Local Government Act 1888, to overhaul the delivery of the nations second tier governance and administration. The 'Way' was officially opened on 13th July 1991 by Sir John Johnson, the then Chairman of the Countryside Commission.

In most other counties, the county town was already the economic centre but, for Warwick's prominence, we must thank Æthelflæd, the Lady of the Mercians. It was she, in 914, who directed that Warwick should be the site for one of her burghs, a fort to keep out the Danes. Thus Warwick was effectively put on the map and its strategic importance through many centuries of power broking continued.

However, in civil engineering terms, it was the Romans who left the oldest, longest lasting feature still in use today, their roads. The two most important were the Fosse Way and the A5 Watling Street. The Fosse connects Exeter and Lincoln, entering the County at Stretton on the Fosse and travelling for 35 miles north-west to a junction with Watling Street at High Cross. Watling Street connected London with Wroxeter and it was also adopted as the 10th century boundary between Mercia and the Danelaw. Thus the 22 miles of its 27 miles route through the County, provides the straight line along the north-east corner of the county's boundary.

As to the rest of the pre-1888 historical county boundary line, the western boundary follows a natural ridgeway, rising from the River Avon at Evesham and continuing up onto the Birmingham plateau west of Alcester. The south-east boundary is even more prominent, as it is formed by the limestone escarpment of the Cotswold Hills, which give Warwickshire its highest elevation where it meets Oxfordshire. The rest of the county's boundaries follow the lines of Anglo Saxon and, in many cases, ecclesiastical landowner's estates, adjacent to the neighbouring counties of Staffordshire, Worcestershire and Gloucestershire.

Having established where Warwickshire is, the question I found most difficult to resolve was, when was it established? Prior to the Norman Conquest the

Anglo Saxon feudal tenant in chief of the area was Thorkel of Arden and it was probably his lands that formed the 'Shire' area that became Warwickshire.

Today the county covers an area of 885 square miles, somewhat less than the area it controlled in 1888. The inroads of City of Birmingham expansion (1931) and the establishment of Solihull and Coventry as unitary authorities (1974), took a boot shaped bite out of the old county area. The Warwickshire landscape therefore largely merges with the midlands countryside that surrounds it.

The north-west corner of the County, where the 'Way' starts, sits on the Birmingham Plateau. This is an area generally over 125m above sea level with the Lickey Hills to the west and a ridge rising 100m from our starting point, at Kingsbury, and dropping slightly as it curves around to the south. The higher ground effectively provides the rim to the plateau's saucer shape which the River Tame and its tributaries drain.

The County therefore straddles the line of England's north-south watershed. The River Tame drains the northern third of the county and becomes a tributary of the Trent, which discharges into the Humber estuary and the North Sea. The route to the sea for the rest of the County's water is the River Avon, which meanders its way west and south to join the River Severn at Tewksbury and then the Bristol Channel. The County also acts as the 'drain' to the sea for a much wider area, as all of the larger rivers rise outside our boundaries.

My landscape map shows the micro regions within the County and the largest is the Arden, which is where we start. This land sits between the rivers Tame and Avon and is largely a subtle landscape, gently rolling with the occasional hill. In the first part of the 'Way', as we climb the saucers rim, there are several vantage points that, on a clear day, give views westward to the summit of Birmingham City Centre.

Historically, back in Shakespeare's day, the region would have had a low population widely dispersed with its then Forest of Arden, other wooded areas, pasture and heathland. Today, as we shall see, there are still large areas of ancient woodland and in many smaller areas the historical landscape patterns still provide examples that Shakespeare would recognise.

The other areas on our route; the High Cross Plateau, Dunsmore, Feldon and Cotswold are described in the sections of the route that cross them. Warwickshire County Council has produced three detailed booklets *Warwickshire Landscape Guidelines* (available on line) that describe the distinctiveness that differentiates these different landscapes including the Mease Lowlands and the Avon Valley which we do not cross. The booklets note that by understanding these differences it is intended that the variety of the English Landscape can be maintained. I hope that by my layman's interpretation and description I draw the picture that will be recognised as you walk the 'Way'.

## The Centenary Way Route

The County Council's reasoning behind the launch of a Centenary Way was described as:

*'...a recreational footpath established by Warwickshire County Council to celebrate its 100th anniversary. It reflects the great variety of the county: its history, culture, landscape and nature. Following public footpaths, bridleways, canal towpaths and disused railways, it passes through some beautiful countryside and peaceful villages, by ancient woodland and winding streams: it reveals the immense changes that have taken place in the last century.'*

I walked the route of the 'Way' many years ago and like any other long distance footpath it provides both a walking challenge and the opportunity to experience and enjoy all of the facets described in the quote above. However in tackling this new guide on a circular walk basis, my experience and enjoyment was increased. The wider circles revealed an even richer picture of the County of Warwickshire.

I would guess that the original planning of the route involved the usual balance between the desired direction and an available off road route. In some places this has lead to unavoidable macadam. In planning my circles I faced the same dilemma and the selection of my route has lead to some longer circuits but even more enjoyment of landscape and places.

Our journey starts from Kingsbury Water Park, very much one of the jewels of the region. After the lakes it is a busier route to Shustoke and Furnace End but the back routes are through a quieter landscape of hedged fields, with a few small settlements. Leaving the 'vale' of the Tame we make our first climb from 95m to 167m at Birchley Heath following a narrow valley to reach the East Warwickshire Plateau and the area of Warwickshire's coalfield. The circuits to Bermuda Park include a diversion to Hayes Hill Country Park, old mining sites, villages and an urban section along a green corridor revealing the vast area of Nuneaton's bygone mineral extraction industry.

The walk to Coombe Abbey Country Park takes us half way around the Coventry bulge and follows the canal to Ansty. This section, despite the length of the canal walk, reveals the changing landscape on the edge of the High Cross Plateau and some fascinating history including a visit to Brinklow. On the walk from Coombe Abbey to Kenilworth we turn west along the bottom of the 'Coventry bite'. The sections between Wolston and Ryton on Dunsmore and Stareton into Kenilworth have no return routes. However between Ryton

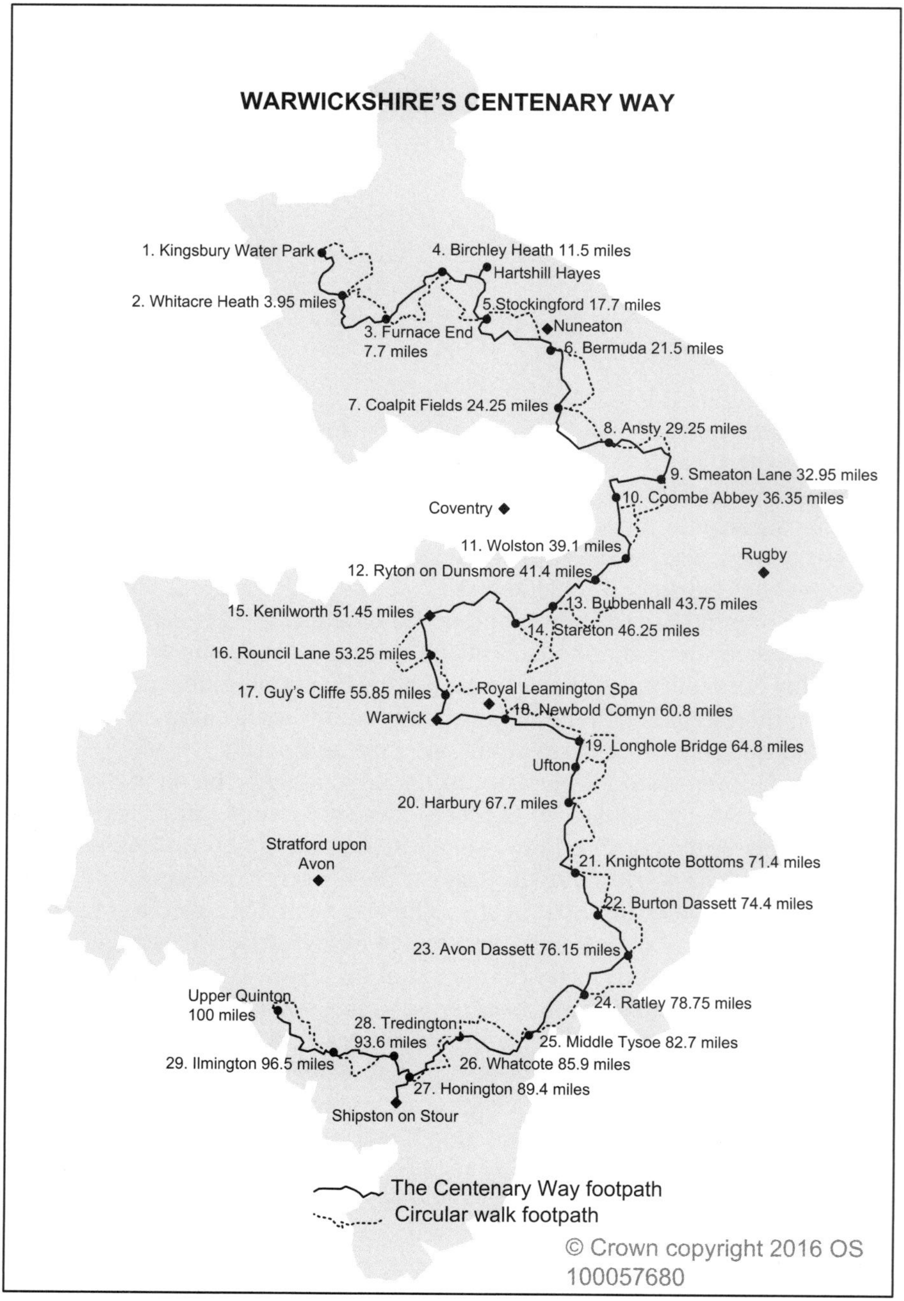
WARWICKSHIRE'S CENTENARY WAY
1. Kingsbury Water Park
2. Whitacre Heath 3.95 miles
3. Furnace End 7.7 miles
4. Birchley Heath 11.5 miles
Hartshill Hayes
5. Stockingford 17.7 miles
Nuneaton
6. Bermuda 21.5 miles
7. Coalpit Fields 24.25 miles
8. Ansty 29.25 miles
9. Smeaton Lane 32.95 miles
10. Coombe Abbey 36.35 miles
Coventry
11. Wolston 39.1 miles
Rugby
12. Ryton on Dunsmore 41.4 miles
13. Bubbenhall 43.75 miles
14. Stareton 46.25 miles
15. Kenilworth 51.45 miles
16. Rouncil Lane 53.25 miles
17. Guy's Cliffe 55.85 miles
Royal Leamington Spa
Warwick
18. Newbold Comyn 60.8 miles
19. Longhole Bridge 64.8 miles
Ufton
20. Harbury 67.7 miles
Stratford upon Avon
21. Knightcote Bottoms 71.4 miles
22. Burton Dassett 74.4 miles
23. Avon Dassett 76.15 miles
24. Ratley 78.75 miles
Upper Quinton 100 miles
28. Tredington 93.6 miles
25. Middle Tysoe 82.7 miles
29. Ilmington 96.5 miles
26. Whatcote 85.9 miles
27. Honington 89.4 miles
Shipston on Stour
The Centenary Way footpath
Circular walk footpath
© Crown copyright 2016 OS 100057680

and Stareton there are two long paths which reveal a much wider picture of the landscape and also visit another County Country Park at Ryton Pools.

The walk into Kenilworth passes the edge of Stoneleigh but you can take a detour through the centre to see more of its history. We pass through 'old' Kenilworth and leave there from the Castle where the circular path provides a 'camera' view point across the fields. The approach to Warwick provides no distant views and the slightly long approach through its suburb will be rewarded by the pleasure of the walk through the town. Leaving Warwick for Royal Leamington Spa; the walk follows a green waterside corridor alongside the River Avon, the Grand Union Canal and then the River Leam. You may wish to take a break and enjoy the pleasures of St Nicholas Park and Victoria Park together with the Pump Rooms and Jephson Gardens before reaching the wide spaces of Newbold Comyn.

The onward route takes us east along the Grand Union Canal to Longhole Bridge and then south into the 'big country' of the Feldon. Leaving the canal we follow the bridle way to Ufton which marks the skyline. From there the 'Way' continues south to Harbury and Knightcote Bottoms. The circular routes provide a choice of two or three loops of open country with, at the southern end, a visit to Bishops Itchington and its quarry. The onward route to Northend finishes with a climb to the summit of Avon Dassett Country Park but has unavoidable quiet macadam along its circular route. Continuing on a short leg to Avon Dassett the circular route takes in the very attractive village of Fenny Compton.

Leaving the Dassett Hills the 'Way' turns to follow the County's south-west border along a quiet lane across the M40 to the hamlet of Arlescote with its stunning Manor House. Our gentle stroll is now followed by an invigorating and undulating climb to Ratley. The circular route could have been the main route choice as you get to see the real charm of Ratley and Warmington.

We leave Ratley and take at first a zig-zag path along the scarp face of Edge Hill before following the top to eventually enjoy a paranomic vista at Sun Rising Hill. The village centre of Tysoe would always prove to be a satisfying destination for any walk. The onward route to Honington is across wide ranging countryside with, on the circular route, the opportunity to enjoy Oxhill which would otherwise escape the visitor's attention.

From Honington the 'Way' does not miss the opportunity to visit the attractive and historic town of Shipston on Stour in the southern tip of the County. You may make your own choice of route before continuing from Treddington for the last section along the northern edge of the Cotswolds. From here to Lower Quinton there is some unavoidable walking along usually quiet lanes. Ilmington provides yet another unique setting and the landscape across to Upper Quinton makes a fitting finish.

Throughout my descriptions I have indicate`d buildings and features that are 'listed' by Historic England. In Warwickshire there are a total of 6,026 listings but at many sites, particularly churches, there are separate listings for the building and specific external features. In the County there are 114 Grade I buildings of 'exceptional interest', and 373 Grade II* buildings 'that are important of more than special interest'. The Grade II listing is for buildings of 'special interest'. In some places in my descriptions I have abbreviated the listings to the reference (GI), (GII*) and (GII).

## How to use the Guide

For consistency each of the walks is described north to south along the 'Way' (in normal script) and the return route south to north back to the starting point (*in italic script*). If you decide only to walk the Centenary Way then you may split the 100 miles into section lengths of your choosing. However, as the route traverses largely rural areas and the circular walks are dependent upon the availability of connecting footpaths, car parking is not available at all my start finish points on the 'Way'. On the maps I have indicated the parking opportunities and in the narrative sections suggested the most practical start point. However on most walks there is a good degree of flexibility for you to start and finish where you choose, particularly if you are using a pub! Although I have indicated parking availability at pubs, with a (P), many of them are small and the courtesy of advising the Landlord of your intention is always appreciated.

The guide is split into chapters for each section of the walk. Each chapter first describes both the physical detail and also tells some of the underlying stories of the people and history. The route directions then wrap around the map, which I have re-drawn from the 1:25,000 OS Explorer Sheets.

The Centenary Way is way marked with logoed direction arrows, although in some areas they prove to be a little sparse. However all the routes are on and follow 'public rights of way' and way marking is fairly good along all of the paths. However the reality is, that in some places, there is some 'discretion' between the right of way and the path actually established on the ground.

In the guide I have taken a common-sense approach and shown the established route, between fixed points e.g. stiles and gates, etc. I have also made the warning note of 'crops' in a very few places where, notwithstanding, year on year crop rotation, there was potential for centre field path obstruction where the farmer had left it to the walker to re-establish the path across a field. At the end of the book I have added a public transport map. Clearly this information may change, but particularly if you are just walking the 'Way', it can provide some transport flexibility.

# CHAPTER 1

## Section 1: Kingsbury Water park to Whitacre Heath

We start along the Centenary Way at Kingsbury Water Park, which Warwickshire County Council describe as; 'Its premier waterside attraction and the jewel in the crown of Warwickshire's Country Parks'. Its total area is over 600 acres; with 15 lakes, plus walking and cycle routes, play areas and even a miniature railway. The park opened in 1975 and the historical name for this area was 'Bodymoor Heath', which probably gives a clearer indication of the terrain before the lakes arrived.

The lakes were formed by the extraction, which began in the 1930s, of the underlying periglacial gravel and sand beds, which had existed since the ice ages. The vast resource proved an irresistible source for material needed to produce concrete and mortar to meet the burgeoning needs of the Birmingham's exponential expansion, which had commenced in the 19th century. We circumnavigate the southern area of the park south from the Visitor Centre, then east along the old Kingsbury Road, reaching the old bridge over the River Tame. The bridge was constructed in 1783 and paid for by public subscription. The names of the benefactors are inscribed on the parapets between the middle piers.

The Tame starts from two springs in Oldbury and Willenhall, gathering the Rivers Rea, Cole and Blythe on its way to Kingsbury. From here it winds its way for another 17 miles to join the River Trent at the National Memorial Arboretum. The area drained by the Tame and its tributaries totals 1,490km$^2$ (575mile$^2$).

We now turn west through the Lea Marston Purification Lakes complex. By the 1950s the River Tame was more or less an open sewer. Even though enormous investment and changes in legislation had occurred by the 1970s the river was 'dead' and even as far as Nottingham its pollution affected the River Trent, as the information sign we pass explains. So the Environmental Agency converted the old gravel pits into balancing lakes. The river was diverted through the lake system enabling it to deposit its solid impurities on the lake bed, where they are removed by dredging. However our environmental controls are now so successful that the lakes may no longer be required and investigations are being undertaken to assess the new potential of this 370 acre area.

Perhaps we should congratulate ourselves on what we have achieved in the last 85 years or so. A material deposited over 20,000 years ago was removed to help construct a city, which in turn despoiled this landscape and the river. But now this landscape has been turned into a valuable community asset and the land intervention which indirectly caused the river pollution has played a major part in cleaning it. Today not only is there a multi use recreational area but the RSPB and Warwickshire Wildlife Trust Reserves north and south of the park provide the largest series of interconnected wetlands in the county. These now ensure that the Tame Valley's vital and diverse ecology provide wide ranging habitat for our birds, wild fowl, waders, fish, otters, plant and insect life.

A long path along the security fence around the southern lake leads to the edge of Lea Marston. The Birmingham Road crosses the Tame then the Birmingham-Derby railway which opened in 1839. We then pass the entrance to the Warwickshire Wildlife Trust Whitacre Heath Nature Reserve and continue to the village of Whitacre Heath. The return route shares the next section of the 'Way' for a few yards then carries straight on as the 'Way' turns right.

Turning from the road we start our first section across agricultural Warwickshire and cross the B4098. This road would have provided the original route for travellers between Tamworth and Coventry. As the path continues we climb and walk along the start of the East Warwickshire lip to the Birmingham Plateau. After Hurley at Camp Farm the path crosses a 'prairie field', which is certainly one of the biggest on the whole of the route. After the firing range the road crosses just a few hundred yards from Kingsbury Oil Terminal, the largest inland facility in the UK; watch out for road tankers! Entering Kingsbury through Kingsbury Meadow, the houses clustered around the church show its ancient rural importance. Although the village remained quite small, from the time of its Saxon origins, it grew in size when coal mining was established in the area and later as a dormitory for Birmingham.

Before descending to the Tame Valley we pass first the church of St Peter and St Paul (GII*). The building retains some of its 12th century origins and, except for some minor modern work, its structure was completed with work undertaken through the 13th, 14th and early 15th centuries. Then to the right are the remains of Kingsbury Hall a medieval enclosure castle and post medieval house. The name Kingsbury means a fortified place and the hall is probably on the site of the original defences. The massive curtain walls (GII) date from the 14th century and the house (GII*) dates from the late 15th century. The manor passed to John de Bracebridge from the King in 1208 and it remained in the family until the mid 16th century.

## Walk Directions

| | |
|---|---|
| Joining points | Water Park – pay and display: Whitacre Heath – kerbside parking: Kingsbury – car park |
| Pubs | Whitacre Heath – The Swan Inn (P) and Railway Inn (P): Kingsbury – the Royal Inn (P) |

1. Starting from the Visitor Information Centre entrance go to the entrance road and turn left to follow it past the first surfaced car park. Continue to turn left through a smaller car park and follow the path from it to turn right along the side of the lake. The path turns away from the lake to go around the fence of the sailing club and across the entrance road. Follow the path along the edge of the next pool, which is used by the model boating club. The path curves left around the end of the pool and, ignoring right turns, keep straight on; cross a bridge and join a road. Turn right along the road as it bends left and take the next path right between a fence and 'Causeway Pool'. Turn left along the pool edge and cross the 'old' Kingsbury Road.

2. From the road turn right along the path at the edge of 'Mill Pool' and continue until the path rejoins the road. Follow the road to the bridge over the River Tame and turn right along the river under the A4097. Pass the information board, describing Lea Marston Purification Lakes, and turn right. Follow the wide path around the western side of the lakes that then follows an arm of the river. Eventually the path curves away from the river and goes right of the end of the lake and turns to reach the road. Cross the road and take the footpath to the right of the gates and follow the left fence for about 1500 metres to reach the edge of the village of Lea Marston and the Birmingham Road. Turn left along the road, crossing the river and railway line, continuing for a further ¾ mile to reach Nether Whitacre at the junction with Station Road opposite the Swan Inn.

A. *The return route follows the Heart of England Way back to the start. From the Birmingham Road junction turn left then right along Middle Lane. Cross the railway bridge, continue past the 'Way's' turn off; to Bakehouse Lane and take the gate on the left opposite. Cross the field ¼ right to take the next gate and then cross the field ½ left to take the gate to the B4098. Cross the road with care to continue along Halloughton Lane, the road opposite.*

**Kingsbury Water Park to Whitacre Heath 3.95 miles**
**Circular walk total 8.4 miles**

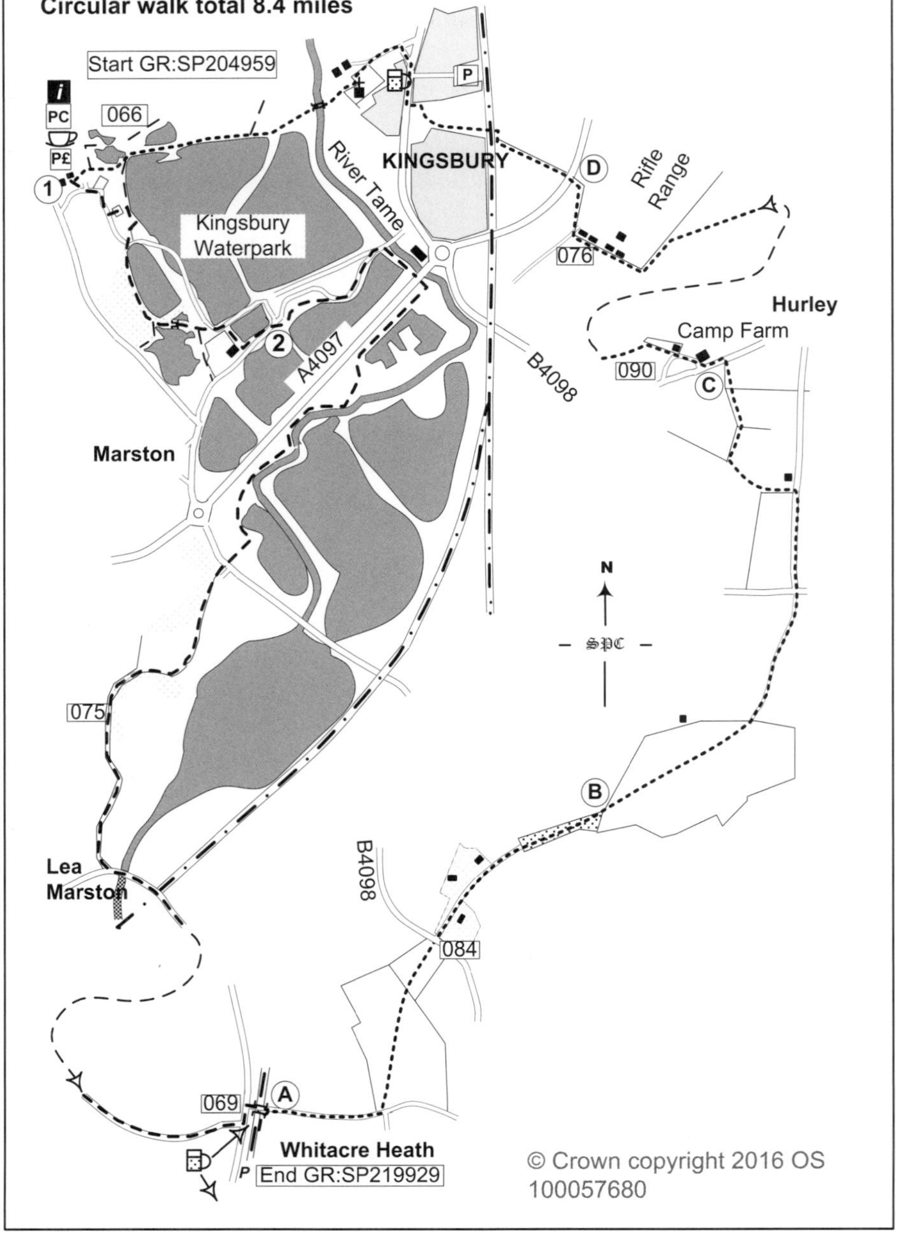

*Follow the lane downhill, keeping straight on as it swings left to a farm. Follow the bridle way and take the gate and continue through a narrow tree covered meadow to take a gate in the left corner. (Beware of placid highland beef.)*

B. *Turn right through the fence gap and cross the field ½ left to reach a hedge lined track. Follow the track to the road and cross straight over taking the lane signed for Hurley. Follow the lane and just before a house take the path left through the hedge gap. Follow the left hedge and from the corner cross ½ right to opposite field corner. Turn right to follow the left hedge through a hedge gap, then a bridge with stile, continuing to take the gate to the road.*

C. *Turn left along the road, pass a transport depot and take the right turn along a lane. As the lane bends left keep straight on, into a vast field, following the right hedge. From the corner way mark post turn ¾ right and aim for the distant green huts at the end of the firing range. Cross the field to a way mark post on the range perimeter and turn left. Follow the path around the range perimeter turning right over the entrance road to continue along the right hedge line turning left to the road.*

D. *This road serves the Kingsbury Oil Terminal and the petrol tankers travel at speed, cross with care. Take the track opposite, and keep straight ahead along the right hedge line to the railway. Turn right then left under the railway to enter Kingsbury Meadow. Follow the path which, as it approaches the road, turns right, crosses a bridge and follows a raised walk way. Take the gate to the road and turn right into the centre of Kingsbury. Pass the Royal Oak Inn, turn left and just after the bus stop shelter turn left along the 'private drive'. As the drive bends right, go left along the boundary fence of the church of St Michaels and All Angels. Take the gate into the churchyard and turn right to follow the path down several flights of steps, passing the remains of Kingsbury Hall. Follow the path across the River Tame and keeping to north edge of the lake continue to reach the Visitor Centre.*

## Section 2: Whitacre Heath to Furnace End

Leaving Whitacre Heath we cross a railway line, via a bridge constructed from local stone, and then turn right alongside it. You will be fortunate to witness a train along this line as it only provides access to Hams Hall or a convenient diversion when maintenance is carried out on the main line. The line, which

Railway bridge at Whitacre Heath

was opened in 1839, was built by the Birmingham Derby Junction Railway Company (BDJR) to, as its name suggest, join Birmingham and Derby. However the wider intention was to provide a service to London via the London Birmingham Railway.

But the BDJR were not the only company intent on maximising their return. The Midland Counties Railway (MCR) was constructing a line linking Derby, Nottingham and Rugby where it would also join the London-Birmingham Railway line and provide the through service to the capital. But all was not fair in the early days of railway construction. The MCR gained Parliamentary permission to construct a branch north of Nottingham, which would divert London passengers away from the BDJR route onto their own line. The BDJR were incensed and sought and obtained Parliamentary approval to extend their line to go straight through to join the London line at Hampton in Arden.

The BDJR opened their line to passengers in August 1839, ten months ahead of the MCR. The first train from Birmingham to London took seven hours for the 135 mile journey. For ten months they had the monopoly of Derby-London traffic. But with the opening of the MCR a shorter route, cutting about half an hour off the journey to London was available. A tariff war ensued. Writs were served by both sides and lost. Both the MCR and BDJR faced crippling losses which each were prepared to suffer, as long as the other side's was greater.

The outcome of this war was that the shareholders, many of whom had investments in all of the local railway companies, pressed for amalgamation. In May 1844 both the MCR and the BDJR were merged with the North Midland Railway to form the Midland Railway. The line between Whitacre and Hampton ceased effective operations in 1877, although to meet statutory requirements a daily single passenger train ran until 1917.

The presence of the railway lines feeding into Birmingham proved providential as the Warwickshire's coal seams were opened up to provide the fuel to industry and the expanding domestic demand. Then in 1928 the first of three power stations was constructed at Hams Hall, followed by a second in 1942 and a third in 1956. Until their closures between 1975 and 1992 the coal, feeding their steam driven turbines, all arrived by train.

The loop, built in 1909, between Water Orton and Kingsbury as well as providing a faster route for the passenger expresses avoiding the tight curve at Whitacre would also, no doubt, have provided a diversion around the many slow coal trains which went on to join a separate 'goods' line alongside the passenger traffic line at Water Orton.

Today the rail link at Hams Hall feeds a dedicated international freight terminal, handling over 100,000 sea freight containers annually. From the terminal, trains serve the docks at Southampton, Ipswich, Felixstowe, a similar terminal in Glasgow, as well as services via the Channel Tunnel. I think that we can accept that the original Victorian rail entrepreneurs could never have imagined that their desire to realise an immediate return on their capital through the short term London bonus, would have brought such a far reaching investment in the regions infrastructure, still paying back through its world wide connections today.

The path turns away from the railway line then rejoins it at its connection with the Nuneaton line opposite the site of where Whitacre Station stood. Up to only a short time ago you could cross the line here but the path now makes the much safer diversion over the bridge a few hundred yards east. On the other side of the tracks we cross the River Bourne and follow the path to Shustoke. The village sits astride the B4116 Coleshill Road with the Plough Inn at its centre

The village's most famous son was William Dugdale, born in 1605. He was the son of a Lancashire gentleman of modest means, who had settled in Shustoke having spent some years at Oxford as a tutor. Although William received a good education at King Henry VIII School in Coventry, he was only 17 years of age, when his father insisted he marry a Margaret Huntbach. Three years later his father died and William purchased Blythe Hall presumably now able to lead a gentlemen's life.

But by chance a few years later William met an antiquary called William Burton who aroused his interest in transcribing documents and collecting church notes. Through this work he met other antiquaries and began working with Sir Symon Archer on the history of Warwickshire. To widen his research he went to London and there he met and found the patronage of senior members of the College of Arms. He clearly impressed the College for in 1638, he was installed as a junior officer of the college and by 1639 promoted to the office of Rouge Croix Pursuivant of Arms in Ordinary. He continued his antiquary work but when civil war broke out in 1642 the King summoned him, with other heralds, to York. There he was deputed to go to Banbury and Warwick Castles to order their surrender. He then accompanied the King to Oxford where he was admitted to the University as MA and continued his antiquarian researches.

After the surrender of Oxford, in 1646, William returned to Blythe Hall and continued his antiquarian studies culminating in the publication of his own work *Antiquities of Warwickshire*, which was recognised as a model county history. He continued his work and upon the restoration of the monarchy William gained more promotion within the College of Arms. Finally in 1677 he was knighted, Garter Principal King of Arms. He died at his home Blythe Hall in 1686.

Turning off the main road between two Grade II listed buildings, even the gate piers of the left cottage should be noted as they have their own listing, the route continues past the Shustoke Reservoirs. The reservoirs, fed by the River Bourne, were built in the 1880s by Birmingham Corporation to meet its own drinking water needs. However Birmingham was already building a dam at the Elan Valley in Wales and as soon as that project came on line, in 1904, the water from Shustoke was diverted to meet Warwickshire's demands. The two reservoirs capacities are 92 thousand and 1.92 million cubic metres. Today under Severn Trent's management the large reservoir has a sailing club and the adjacent car park is a useful free facility.

Walking into Furnace End, its name originates from the furnaces operated by the Jennens family in the 1700s, we cross the River Bourne. On the right the large building is the Cottage Mill and then the Bulls Head, both Grade II listed dating from the 17th century.

From here we climb a little way up the lip of the Birmingham plateau and turn into a quiet lane. Following a footpath through the fields we enter a lane which provides a view across the plateau to the high ground of Sutton Coldfield. The lane continues through the hamlet of Botts Green, named after Robert Bott who lived here in 1708. As you reach the bottom of the hill, look out for an ornate black and white building on the right. Apparently, although the building has a date of 1593, the historians suggest it has an earlier origin and, although not visible from the road, it has one of the best local examples of timber-framing. Unfortunately the visible ornate black and white timbering is a false facade of 18th-century painted brickwork.

Another pleasant cross country section leads to Nether Whitacre and we walk around the church of St Giles (GII) which has 16th century origins, notably the tower, but was much rebuilt in 1870.

## Walk Directions

| | |
|---|---|
| Joining points | Whitacre Heath – kerbside parking: Shustoke Reservoir – free car park: Furnace End – no parking |
| Pubs | Whitacre Heath – The Swan Inn (P) and Railway Inn (P): Shustoke – the Plough Inn (P), Furnace End – the Bull Inn (P), Nether Whitacre – the Dog Inn (P) and the Gate Inn (P) |

1. From the Birmingham Road take Middle Lane, cross the railway bridge and, as the road levels out, turn right into the entrance to the bungalow. Turn right and follow the track towards the railway and turn left. Follow the track alongside the railway line, passing the footbridge over the line, and entering an open field. Turn left and follow the perimeter of the field, crossing a bridge and continuing ½ left to the corner of the field. Take the gate and turn right and follow the right hedge line which turns to follow the railway line climbing the bank to reach a lane.

2. Turn left then leave the road right to take the stile. Follow the right hedge line, passing the 'Colin Teall' interpretation board, to reach the main railway line at the old site of Whitacre Station, which closed in 1968. Take the gate and turn left and follow the path alongside the railway line and reach the bridge. Turn right over the bridge, take the gate and turn right to follow the hedge line around the field. The path turns left through the hedge and crosses a bridge over the River Bourne. Turn ½ left and follow the path, still showing signs of its original macadam surface from the days when it lead to the station. Take or go around the stile and continue to reach the B4114 Coleshill Road adjacent to the Severn Trent works entrance. Turn left along the road, passing the entrance to Shustoke Reservoirs car park, and opposite The Plough Inn, turn left along Bixhill Lane.

**Whitacre Heath to Furnace End 3.75 miles**
**Circular walk total 6.6 miles**

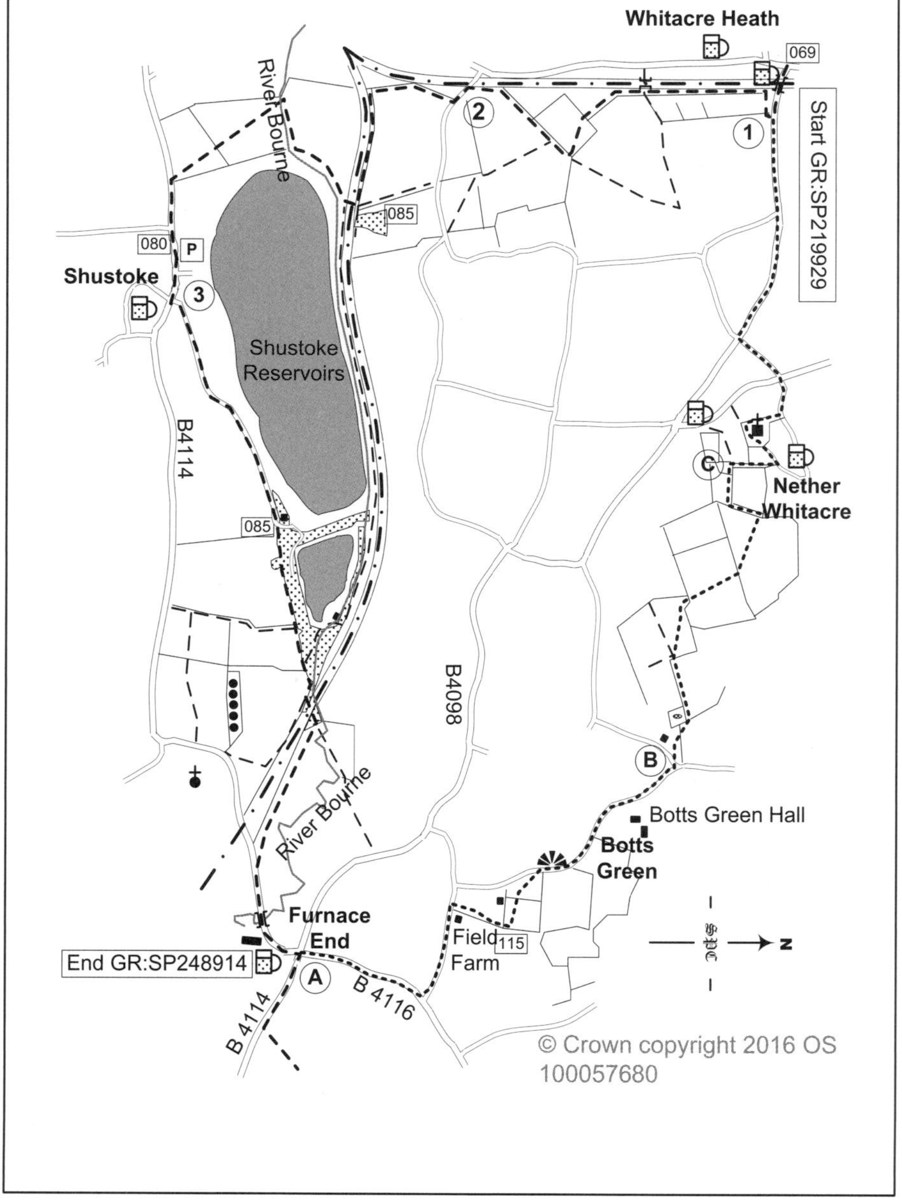

3. Follow the lane, with views over the reservoirs, to eventually pass a large house where the lane bends left. Turn right from the bend, leaving the lane to take the gate on the right. Turn left and follow the field edge, through the projecting finger of wood, continuing down the hill. Cross a bridge and continue down the hill to take a gate and turn right around the field at the side of the railway line. Go under the railway between the fences and take the gate and turn right through the trees to reach the open field. Turn right and follow the often 'sticky', field edge. Look for the gate right to the B4114 and turn left to pass The Bull Inn and reach the crossroads with the B4098 and the centre of Furnace End. Turn right to continue along the 'Way'.

A. *From the junction to return to the start of this section cross straight over and follow the B4116, Nuneaton Road. Follow the road to reach and turn left along Pound Lane. Continue and take the gate after the drive to Field Farm. Follow the right hedge and go around the end of a post and wire fence and turn left. Aim 30 metres right of the barn and take the gate, now bear right to the far corner and take the gate to the lane. Now look straight ahead - due west - and, on a clear day, see the distant view of Birmingham city centre 11½ miles away. Continue by turning right along the lane through the hamlet of Botts Green to reach a T-junction with Whitehouse Farm Lane.*

B. *Cross straight over and take the stile. Cross the field to pass the small building on the right and take the stile beyond on the right. Cross the corner of the field, ½ left, to take the stile and bridge. Follow the left fence and take the stile and steps. Cross the field ½ right to the bottom right corner, to take the bridge and stile. Now cross the field to the far side at the intersection of the overhead power line and take the stile. Cross the field ½ left and take the bridge. Turn left and follow the wide hedged path to the open field. Turn right along the right perimeter and take the stile at a fence and continue to the hedge and face two stiles. To detour to the Gate Inn, take the stile straight ahead and the path left across the field leads there.*

C. *To continue on the return route, take the stile right and the fenced path via a stile to the lane. Turn left for the church of St Giles, the Nether Whitacre Parish Church or turn right to take in the Dog Inn. Enter the churchyard and take the path to the right or go straight ahead to circle the church around to the right and follow the green path into Dog Lane. Turn left along the lane and cross the B4098 to continue down the hill of Deep Lane. Turn right along Middle Lane, for a little over ½ mile, to return to Whitacre Heath.*

## Section 3: Furnace End to Birchley Heath

So far we have walked through a landscape that has been sculpted by our ancestor's intervention. But this walk takes us through a rural landscape that our ancestor's would find little changed for the last two or three centuries. We follow the narrow valley of an unnamed stream, from the Birmingham Plateau up onto the East Warwickshire Plateau and climb 77m (253 feet). However, the intervention of a couple of 're-entrants', pushes the total height climbed to about 117m.

After leaving Furnace End, along the busy Nuneaton Road, we cross a couple of fields and the short steep climb along Sandy Lane provides an early 'tester'. Turning into the drive, towards Hoar Hall Farm, we commence our walk along the long narrow valley that leads us to Birchley Heath. Just before the farm, we leave the driveway and the route continues through meadows and arable fields. The ground is described as heavy clay and in wet conditions the virgin soil is certainly sticky and slippery. At about the half way point we reach the corner of Hoar Park Wood. Here, if you wish, the walk can be divided into two with a turn right down across the valley via the Hoar Hall Craft Centre.

Although Hoar Park Wood is not accessible to the public this ancient woodland is a Site of Special Scientific Interest (SSSI). It covers an area of 26.7 hectares and is described on the County's website, as having five different types of woodland which are 'nationally restricted in their distribution'. These different types of woodland are designated by the different combinations between the canopy trees and the variations in the understorey. The scientific explanation of the wood is fascinating and lengthy in the descriptions of the mix of arboriculture and plant species. The main tree varieties are sessile and pedunculate oak together with hazel, rowan, silver birch, holly and crab apple. There is also lily of the valley and common cow wheat, two plants that are rare in Warwickshire. It is probably unlikely that you may be walking late enough to see a bat but, a large tree at the centre of the wood is home to a large roost of Daubenton's bat (*Myotis daubentonii*). It seems that they characteristically fly and forage just above water, often using their large feet to trawl for insects from the waters surface. We apparently have an overall population of 95,000 over the whole of England.

On the final approach to Birchley Heath, Bentley Park and Monks Park Woods fill the view; their total area extends to 105 hectares. This area is also a Site of Special Scientific Interest because, so the County website informs us; 'of its range of sessile oak on the better drained soils, and alder, on the wetter soils'. This type of woodland is rare and Charnwood Forest, Chaddesley Woods and Wyre Forest have examples. However the County's arboriculturists in expressing their highly technical view of the woods before us state that;

'there is an unusual and widespread juxtaposition of sessile oak and alder and a wider ecological range of alder woodland than possibly in any other wood in Britain'.

If you wish to gain a closer look at the woods, a 650 metre diversion along the road north, to the corner of Ridge Lane, reaches the Hart pub. Otherwise, to return to Furnace End we follow Birchley Heath Road in the opposite direction. Leaving the road we set off back across a more open landscape of arable fields in a gradual downhill walk to Hoar Hall Craft Centre. The walk continues along a quiet lane, with open views, before turning back across the fields to cross the B4114, Nuneaton Road.

Monwode Lea Farm chimney

Just before reaching the road, by Monwode Lea Farm, the odd sight of a substantial isolated chimney appears. This Grade II listed structure, standing in the middle of the field, is all that remains of a 16th century house. No doubt it has been the subject of much conjecture as why the owner left it - but having been listed it is here to stay!

Monwode was the name of an ancient manor in 1365 but records of it disappear after 1481. Presumably this area has retained its attachment as, turning along the road we pass Monwode Lea Toll Gate cottage (GII), dated 1769. The cottage was built by the 'Ansley to Whitacre Turnpike Trust' to enable it to collect tolls from the users of the road.

The trust was established in 1762, by Act of Parliament, in a somewhat similar way to the later railway era development. A trust would be set up to 'adopt' and maintain an existing through-road that provided the link across the wider area of several parishes. By 1880 the turnpike system ended and roads became the responsibility of counties and boards. However in 1923 the Government realised that with the increases in road traffic, national routes should be identified numerically and be partly maintained centrally. The Nuneaton Road became designated the A47, part of the trunk road route between Birmingham, Leicester, Peterborough, Norwich and Great Yarmouth. The construction of the M6 and M69 created a by-pass as far as Nuneaton and in 1986 the road was downgraded to the B4114.

The last section, from the other side of the B4114 involves some long field crossings and a distant view of Over Whitacre Church as a sight line. As we come to the end of the walk we pass though the churchyard of St Leonard (GII*) where a church has stood since 1203 although this church was erected in 1766. I made a short diversion to the village hall (GII) which was originally built in Tudor Gothic style in 1840. A board displays all the local rights of way, giving me the impression that with Parish Council support, they remain unobstructed.

## Walk Directions

| | |
|---|---|
| Joining points | Furnace End – no parking: Birchley Heath – car park and kerbside parking: Hoar Park Craft Centre – car park: Over Whitacre Parish Hall – the car park appears to be walker friendly |
| Pubs | Furnace End – The Bulls Head (P): Ridge Lane – The Hart |

1. From the Furnace End crossroads turn right along the B4114 Nuneaton Road to take the gate on the left after about 275 metres. Follow the path between the fences and take the gate. Follow the right hedge and take the gate to the lane. Turn left along Sandy Lane and follow through the valley, almost to the junction with the B4116, to take the surfaced drive right. Follow the drive, past the cottages, to take the gate on the left at a post and rail fence, leaving the drive as it bends right.

2. Follow the left hedge to take a stile. Follow the hedge line through the next two fields via a stile then a double stile to enter a large open field. Turn left up the slope, following the hedge line, to the corner and turn slightly right to cross the field aiming for a lone tree at the end of a projecting hedge. Keep to the right of the hedge following it to a narrow band of trees, turn left and right through the hedge gap. Continue along the right hedge line to a marker post and stile, take the stile and turn left. (From the stile a path leads to Hoar Park Craft Centre, see directions paragraph (*i*) below).

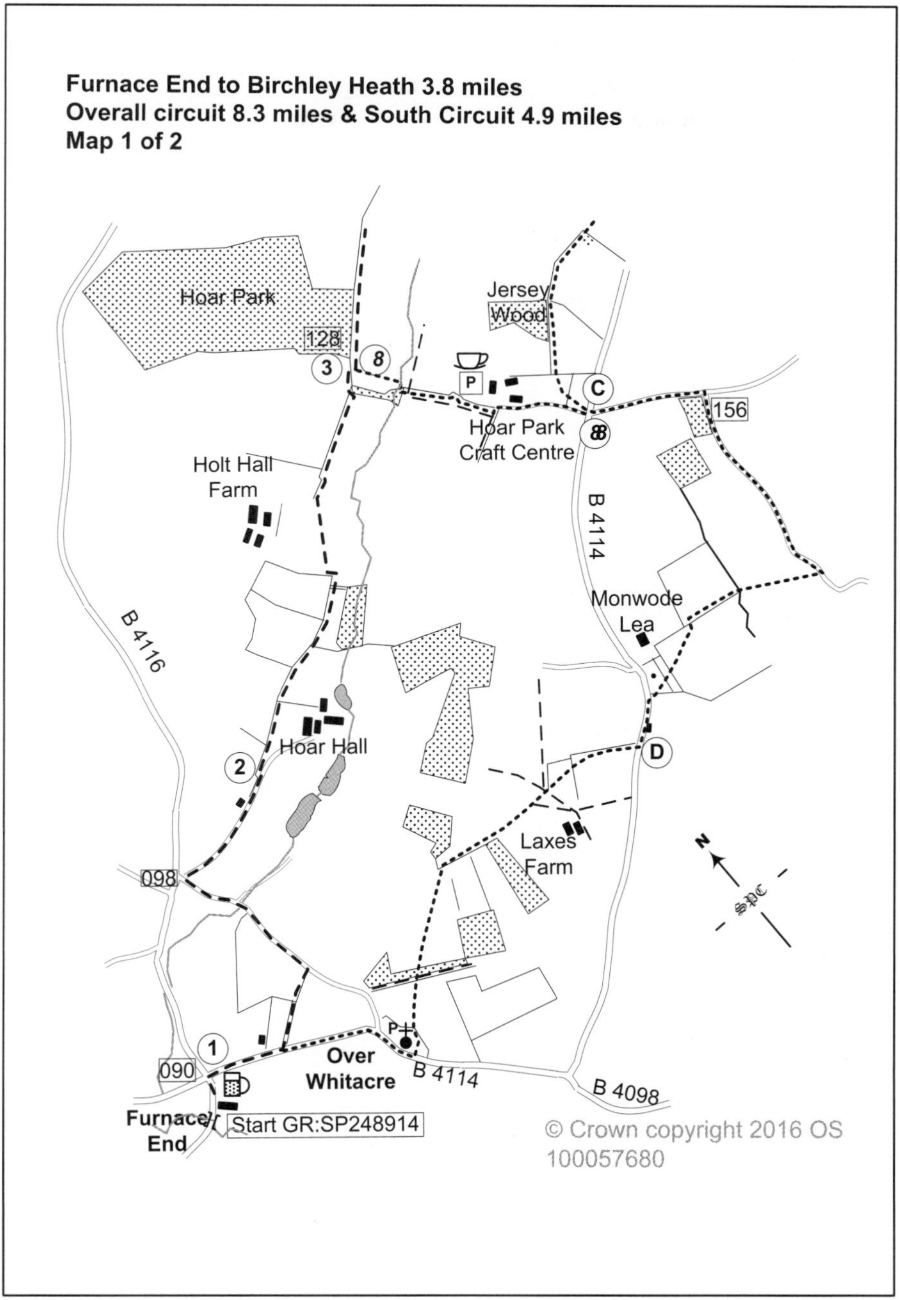

Furnace End to Birchley Heath 3.8 miles
Overall circuit 8.3 miles & South Circuit 4.9 miles
Map 1 of 2
Hoar Park
128
3
8
Jersey
Wood
P
C
156
Hoar Park
Craft Centre
8
Holt Hall
Farm
B 4114
Monwode
Lea
B 4116
Hoar Hall
2
D
Laxes
Farm
N
SPC
098
P
1
090
Over
Whitacre
B 4114
B 4098
Furnace
End
Start GR:SP248914

**Furnace End to Birchley Heath 3.8 miles**
**Overall circuit 8.3 miles & North Circuit 4.4 miles**
**Map 2 of 2**

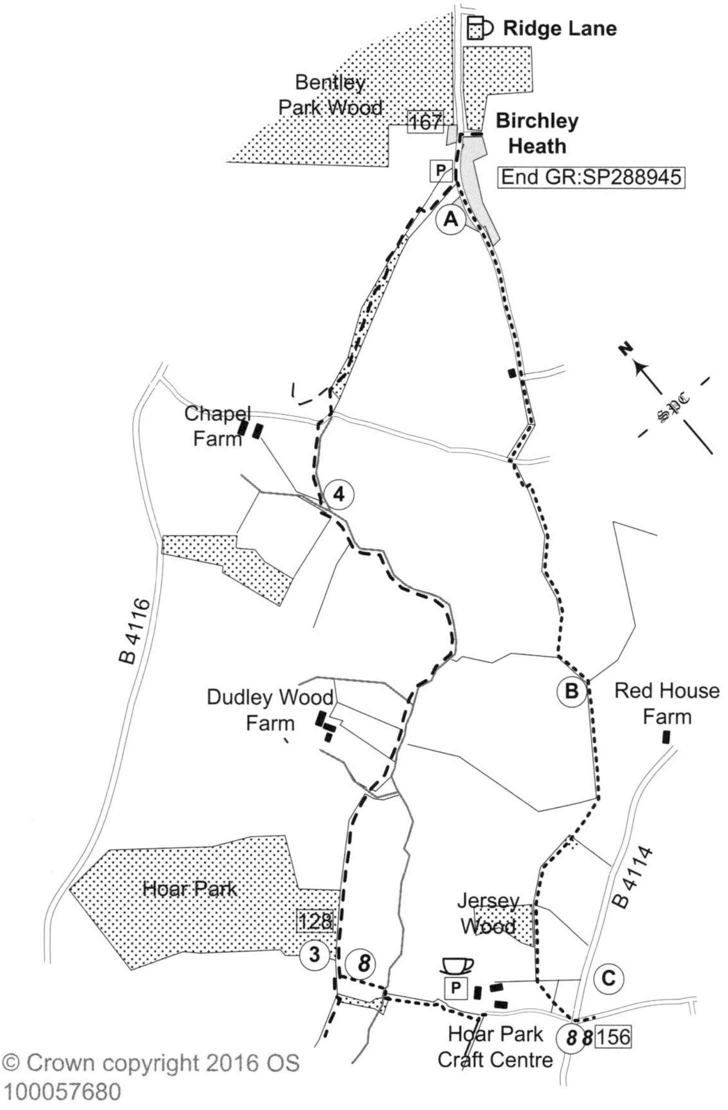

3. Continue along the left hedge line, after passing the woods of Hoar Park, reach the end of the field. Take the bridge and gate below Dudley Wood Farm. Follow the right tree line taking three gates then a bridge to enter a large field. Follow the right hedge line around the field as it climbs to go through a gap in a hedge projecting into the field, then through a gap into another field. Now look for and take a stile on the right and following the path through the trees to take the bridge and gate.

4. Follow the right hedge to take a gate and turn right along Green Lane. After 30 metres, as the lane bends right, take the track left. Leave the track, as it bends left and almost immediately turn right at a marker post into a narrow wood. Follow the path through the trees and then follow the hedge. At the gap in the hedge turn right and left through the play area and take the gate to Birchley Heath Road and turn left to continue on the 'Way'.

A. *From the playing field turn right along Birchley Heath Road until the road bends left and take the gate right. Follow the bridle way, take the gate and continue between the hedges to take a gate to the road. Cross the road left and right and take the gate. Follow the left hedge and turn left and right through the gap. Continue with the hedge line on the right for about 400m to its end and on the same line cross the field to the hedge opposite. Turn left and follow the hedge to the corner and take the gate.*

B. *Continue following the right hedge to reach a corner and cross the field ½ right to the right corner of the copse. Take the gate and follow the path through the trees and continue to follow the right hedge, passing Jersey Wood to take a gate at Hoar Park Craft Centre. Cross the field ½ left and take a gate continuing to the corner with the drive and a gate to the road. (If you wish to enjoy the Craft Centre facilities turn right down the drive or to take the opportunity to return to Birchley Heath see paragraph (ii) below).*

C. *Cross the B4114 and continue along Wood Lane opposite. Take the first right turn. Follow the lane as it eventually bends left to reach a marker post on the right. From the post, facing the field turn ½ right to cross the field aiming for a point in the hedge ahead where the hedge beyond intersects. Go through the gap in the hedge and take the bridge and the stile. Follow the left hedge and just before the end of the field take the gate left. Cross the field ½ right, take the stile and cross the 'chimney' field via a gate and then a gate to the road.*

D. *Turn left along the road, to pass Toll Gate cottage and then cross the road to take the stile. Follow the right hedge down the field to just before the corner turn ½ left to take a bridge at a marker post. Cross the field ½ left to the end of a hedge and the junction with a farm track. At this point there are two other 'rights of way' all making their way to the end of the wood straight ahead across the field. Follow the line of the end of the wood and continue along the hedge line to its end at a marker post. Turn left at the marker post and cross the field on a line to the church spire. A marker post on the tree line reveals the path through the trees to cross a bridge, then a stile to a track. Cross the track and take the gate and go slightly left of the church spire to take a gate. Enter the churchyard of St Leonards and exit to the B4114. Turn right along the road to return to Furnace End.*

*i From paragraph 2, from the stile go straight ahead down the hill across the field and cross the bridge over the brook. Turn right into the trees; follow the footpath, crossing the bridge over the ditch. Turn left, follow the footpath along the left hedge, cross the track and continue up the field. Join the track, turn left and right, adjacent the car park, and follow the entrance drive up the hill to the B4114 and follow the instructions at paragraph C.*

*ii From paragraph B, follow the drive to the car park and turn left along the track through the hedge. Turn right and go downhill between the track and the hedge. Continue to the brook in the trees, having crossed the track. Turn right, cross the bridge over the ditch and turn left to cross the bridge over the brook. Go straight ahead, up the hill across the field, to turn right at the marker post and follow the instructions at paragraph 3.*

# CHAPTER 2

## Section 4: Birchley Heath to Stockingford

The 'Way' through this section to Galley Common continues through a mixture of mostly rural setting that can still be traced on the late 19th century OS map. After passing Lady Wood Farm we turn left along Pipes Lane and under a partly demolished railway bridge which was at the end of the 'Stockingford Branch Railway'. The short walk, around the corner, takes us parallel with the line which we join where we leave the road. The line ran for 2½ miles south-east back to the Nuneaton-Birmingham main line and was constructed to serve Ansley Hall Colliery, which opened in 1874 and closed in 1959.

The site of the mine is shown on my map and would have covered an area of about ten hectares. The explanation for the length of line going north-west over the bridge was an intention to extend the branch to serve Baddesley Colliery. However it was never used, as that mine was connected to the main line at Kingsbury, a far simpler route given the elevational changes that would have been faced going north from here. As it was, although the construction of this line may have been simple, the drop from Ansley Hall to the connection with the main line at Stockingford was about 40 metres in 2⅓ miles, making it the steepest line in Warwickshire.

This did not prove too much of the problem in the early days but presented interesting challenges to the train drivers in its later years of operation. As the line itself was built to minimum standards, finding modern locomotives that could operate within the low axle limits of the bridges and have the braking capacity capable of holding twelve loaded wagons on the decline, was a problem. The crews apparently, became skilled at utilising the final rise, as the branch entered the Stockingford sidings, to ensure the trains stopped before the mainline.

Leaving the old line you can take the opportunity to climb a further 20 metres to Hartshill Hayes Country Park with its views north, over the River Anker to Leicestershire and the Mease Lowlands beyond. Returning to the 'Way', we shortly cross the line of the old railway and then turn right along the Coleshill Road through the western end of the village of Ansley Common. The village experienced its major growth in the mining era but now has a pleasant mixture of 19th, 20th and 21st century properties. Leaving the village we make another quiet rural crossing before reaching Galley Common at its western perimeter at Tunnel Road.

Having enjoyed the rural footpath we reach the edge of Nuneaton but this interruption to our countryside tranquillity would have been rather more brutal in 1894. It was in that year the Haunchwood 'Tunnel' colliery was opened, extending what was to become Nuneaton's south-western boundary. The new 'pit' was to tap into a seam of fine steam coal which was first worked, from its eastern end, in 1729.

This mine closed in the 1960s, when the corridor of coal and clay extraction finally ended. All that remains today, to remind future generations of the forgotten industrial history, is the large 'archaeological hump' lying alongside the railway line. The hump is the remains of the spoil heap of left from the mine workings.

Before we leave the railway line, a few historical notes, the first passenger services between Birmingham New Street Station and Nuneaton's newly built Abbey Street Station commenced in November 1864. As we have already seen the line became very important for moving coal and clay products both from this site and a number of others along the line. Today direct services operate to Stansted Airport passing Leicester, Cambridge and Ely on the way.

We walk alongside the railway and turn left over the tunnel entrance. The return route turns off right and the 'Way' continues alongside the railway then across the fields to Park Lane and the suburb of Stockingford.

From the top of the tunnel the footpath heads across to the village of Ansley which gives its name to the Parish which includes the villages of Birchley Heath, where we started, Ansley Common and Church End. Church End is the oldest part of the parish where the church of St Lawrence has 12th to 15th century origins.

The walk from Ansley crosses some large fields before turning back to the start along a quiet lane and then past Birchley Farm to head back up the field where we commenced walking at the start.

## Walk Directions

| | |
|---|---|
| Joining points | Birchley Heath – car park and kerbside parking: Hartshill Hayes Country Park – pay & display: Ansley Common, Galley Common, Ansley and at Stockingford – kerbside parking in adjacent roads |
| Pubs | Ansley – the Lord Nelson (P) and the Boot (P) |

1. From the gate to the play area turn left along Birchley Heath Road then right along The Rookery. Take the gate and follow the right perimeter around the field to take the gate and the plank bridge. Turn right take gated bridge and then follow the right hedge and at the approach to the barns take the gate and turn left between the buildings. Cross the drive, take the gate and follow the left perimeter. Continue to take the gate and bridge and cross the field to the road. Turn left through the remains of the old railway bridge and turn right along the lane. Continue to the bend in the road and take the right turn between the posts and follow the path around to the left.

2. Follow the footpath through the wide meadow, which becomes wooded as it sinks into the old railway cutting. After about 40 metres take the gate on the left down a small bank and follow the right hedge crossing two bridges and gates. At the hedge corner, cross the field to pick up the hedge opposite. Continue around the field bending right to reach a bridge and gate on the left. (*If you wish to visit Hartshill Hayes Country Park then continue at paragraph (i) below.*)

3. Continue around the field and take a gated bridge left and follow the left perimeter. Adjacent to the house take the gate left and cross the drive, take the next gate and join the drive going left. The right of way seems to leave and rejoin the drive, but it appears safe to follow the drive. Continue through across the line of the old railway, cross the road and reach the B4114, Coleshill Road. Turn right and cross over and continue to Limes Coppice and the North Arden Way information board. At the board turn left along the footpath and continue to reach and take the gate into the field.

4. The public right of way is ¼ left across the field but if it is not established, the 'adopted' line crosses to the corner of the wood and follows the edge of the wood straight ahead. From the south-east corner of the wood cross the field to the corner and follow the left hedge to take a gate. Join and follow the lane ignoring the first marker post to reach a large tree and a gate on the right. Take the gate cross the field ¾ left and take the gate. Cross the field joining the left hedge to take the gate on the left. Follow the right hedge to take the gate in the far hedge, and cross the drive. Keeping to the left cross the field and take the bridge and continue along the right hedge line and join a track. Take the gate on the right and turn left to take the gate to the road.

**Birchley Heath to Stockingford 5.4 miles or 6.2 miles via Hartshill Hayes CP. Return walk from point *8* 3.4 miles**
**Map 1 of 2**

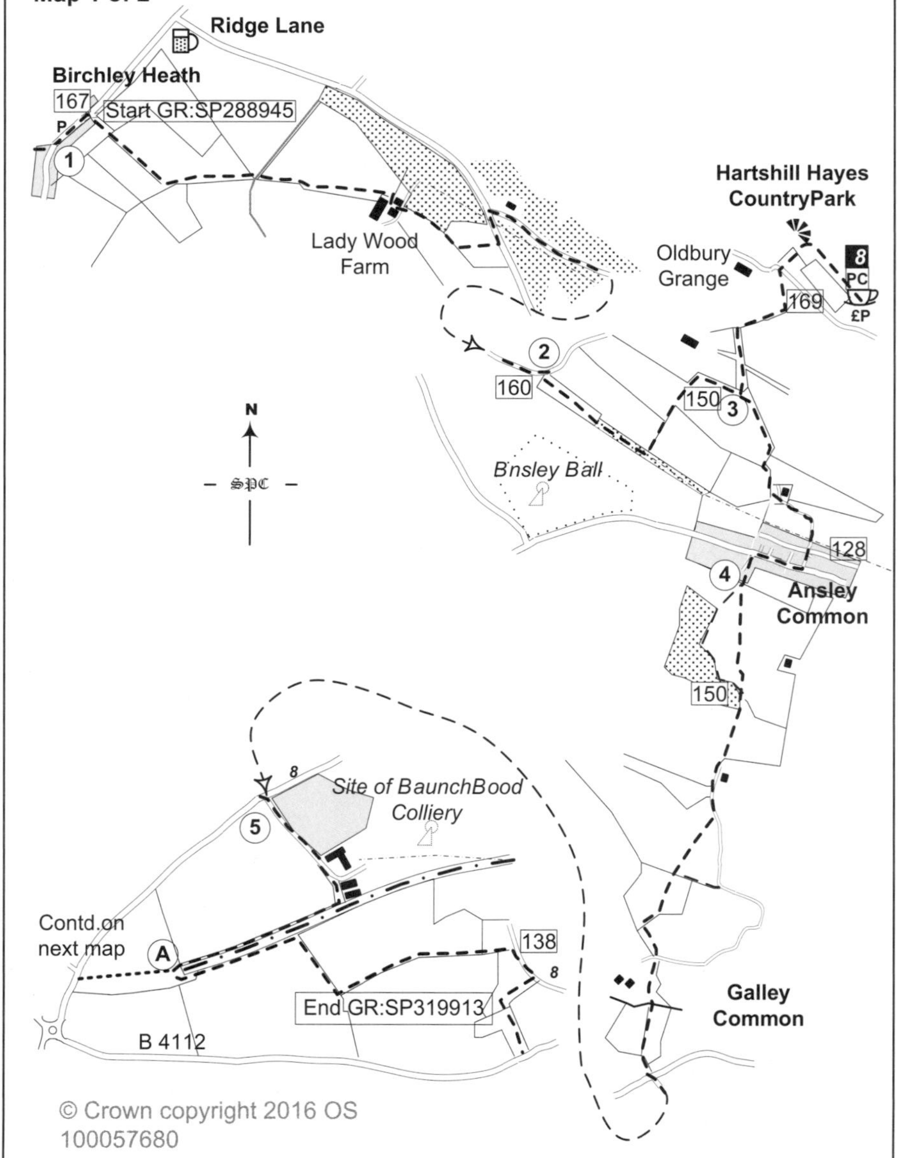

**Birchley Heath to Stockingford 5.4 miles or 6.2 miles via Hartshill Hayes CP. Return walk from point *8* 3.4 miles**
**Map 2 of 2**

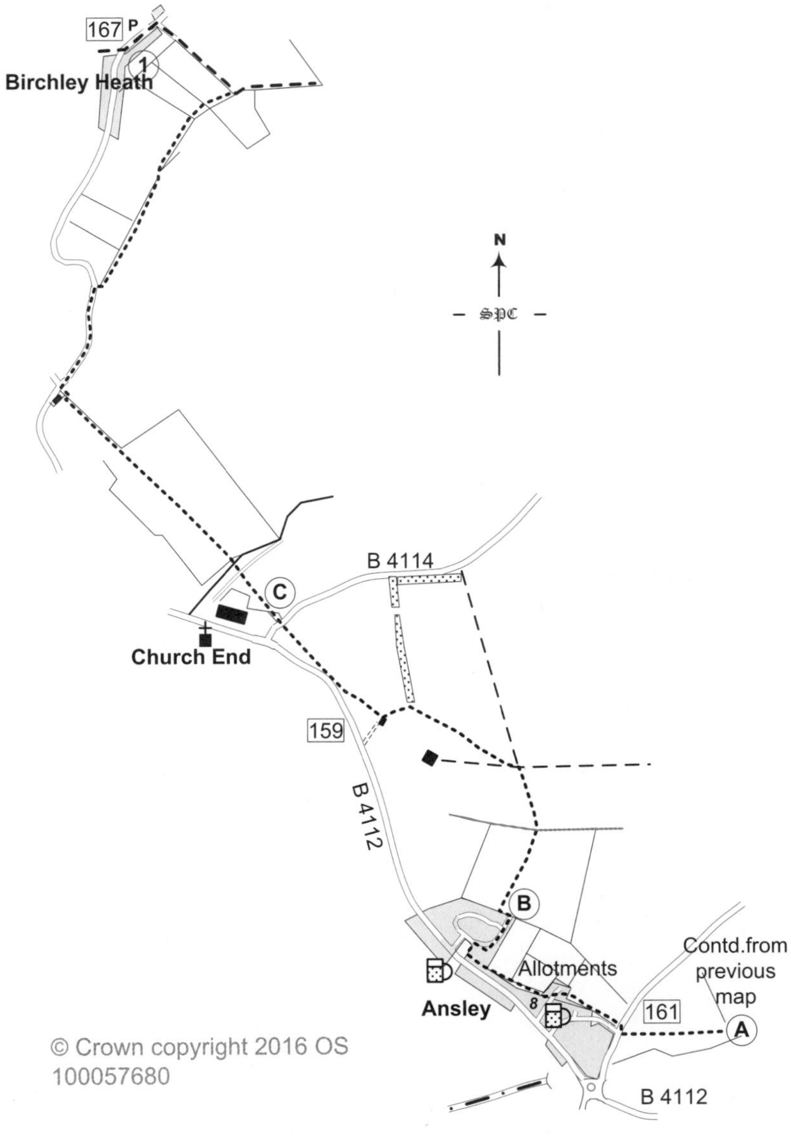

5. Cross straight over Tunnel Road and continue along Haunchwood Park Drive. As the road swings left take the footpath that continues straight ahead between the fences. Follow the footpath around the field to the right and continue alongside the deep railway cutting to reach, via a gate, an open field. To return to Birchley Heath go to paragraph *A*, but to continue the 'Way' swing around to the left over the tunnel below. Take another gate and continue at the edge of the field along the other side of the railway. At the corner of the field turn right to follow the left hedge and turn through the gap to the next field. Follow the right hedge to the end of the field and pass a redundant gate to go straight ahead to the road. Turn right along the road to continue the 'Way'.

*A. From the gate at the end of the railway cutting bear right and cross the field to the gate opposite the last house on the right in Tunnel Road. Cross the road and turn right crossing Nuthurst Crescent and take the gate on the left. Following the left fence line take the gate in front of the houses. Go between the houses and turn left and right to pick up a path at the side of the allotments. Follow the path to emerge into another estate. Turn right along Malthouse Close then right and left around St Lawrence Road continuing straight ahead to the end of the road. Turn left along the footpath behind the properties to reach and turn right into a field.*

*B. Cross the field, aiming for the right end of the trees. Cross the bridge and continue ¼ left across the field to reach a farm track and continue to the left to the end of the band of trees. Turn left and aim for the house and a marker post. The right of way turns right aiming for the bend in the road, however if the path is not established go to the road and turn right. At the bend in the road there is a gap in the hedge and a marker post. From the post cross the field through the hedge gap and cross the road. Take the hedge gap and follow the path between hedge and fence.*

*C. Take the gate and cross the field to the right of the fence corner and take the gates to cross the track. Continue to cross a bridge and take a gate. Cross the large, field aiming for the distant field corner and house. From the corner follow the field boundary to turn right through the hedge gap and left at the bungalow. Follow the left hedge and take the gate to the road. Turn right along the road and at the left bend turn right along the track. Follow the track until it bends right and turn left and right through the fence gap. Follow the right hedge keeping straight ahead through three gates to join the 'Way'. Turn left to return to The Rookery and Birchley Heath.*

i. *To visit Hartshill Hayes Country Park, take the bridge and gate left and follow the footpath uphill avoiding left and right turns. Continue to take a gate below Oldbury Grange and turn right. Follow the right perimeter to the summit and turn left across the field to take the gate to road. Cross the road and enter the park through the gates continuing forward to enjoy the distant view to south Leicestershire.*

ii. *If you wish to visit the Visitor Centre go right, around the reservoir fence.*

iii. *To return to the 'Way', go left around the reservoir and take the gate and cross the road. Take the gate opposite and go ½ left to the fence and follow it downhill to take the gate on the left. Follow the path downhill to reach two gates a few metres apart, take either to return to the open field and continue from paragraph 3 above.*

## Section 5: Stockingford to Bermuda Park

The first water course we cross, south of the B4112 and after traversing a few fields, is an un-named brook which feeds Seeswood Pool. The pool is part of the Arbury Estate which has been the home of the Newdegate family, since 1586. In the early 18th century coal was found on the estate and 3rd Baronet, Sir Richard was quick to realise its economic potential and begin to exploit it.

However it was his second son Sir Roger, who in 1764 constructed a canal system connected to Seeswood Pool to transport the coal from the pit heads. By 1795 there were two separate canal networks over 5½ miles long with over 15 locks. The main line commenced from a dam constructed at Seeswood Pool to raise the water level and connected to the Coventry Canal just above the Ashby junction. This system continued in use until about 1812 and now only a few remains of the watercourse are still visible within the estate.

However, the separate Griff Hollows Canal, commenced at a wharf where coal was loaded from a tramway connected to the collieries and then 'shipped' along a ¾ mile long 'arm' joining the Coventry Canal. This section remained in commercial use until the closure of the colliery in 1961. Evidence of this will be seen later along the 'Way'.

Leaving the road and following a field path we cross the main drive to Arbury Hall. The family still occupy the house and the head of the family, James Fitzroy, is the 4th Viscount of Daventry. However, more famously, Mary Ann Evans, better known as George Eliot, was born on the estate in 1819, where her father was the estate's agent.

I have to admit that I have not yet read any of her novels but I understand that both her fictional places and characters were based on her early

Warwickshire experiences. Certainly she would have lived at Arbury at a time when the estate's expanding income also enabled Sir Roger to enlarge and transform the original Elizabethan manor house, built in 1586, into a Gothic style Hall. The building is naturally Grade I listed, containing all the architectural features internally and externally demanded of the period and is open to the public during spring and summer bank holiday weekends.

The 'Way' continues through the southern tip of Nuneaton at Bermuda Park. This was also part of the Arbury Estate and the origins of the name 'Bermuda' rest with another member of the Newdegate family, Sir Edward (1825-1902). He was a second son and served in the Rifle Brigade retiring as a Lieutenant General and then being appointed Governor of Bermuda (1888-1892). The village was built at that time, to house the families of the miners working at the Griff Clara Colliery and the name celebrated Sir Edward's success and, whether irony was intended, bring a little sub tropical colour to industrial Warwickshire. As well as 90 houses, a working men's club and a mission hall were constructed. The village today is 'an area of restraint' and, despite the industrial, commercial and new housing that surrounds the village, it remains untouched by re-development.

Miner's Housing Bermuda Village

In planning to write this book I determined that, unless it was impractical, then each section should give the opportunity for a circular walk. I therefore make no apology for the urban nature of the return walk. However, as you will discover, the walk back to Stockingford soon joins a green corridor, which follows the old industrial artery of the earlier industrial age.

Looking back to 1884 the OS map shows no housing mass west of this line, except around the original village of Stockingford. The corridor follows the line of the railway line which branched off the main Nuneaton-Coventry line (shown on the map). However the greater area of the colliery and extraction workings extended over 2½ miles beyond both the Bermuda Park area in the south and the Nuneaton-Birmingham railway in the north.

We leave the industrial estate and enter Ensor's Pool, an abandoned old clay pit 220m long by 50m wide and 8m deep. Sadly, although still registered as a SSSI, its population of native *Austropotamobius pallipes*, which are white-clawed crayfish, probably no longer remain. Two surveys in 2014, conducted by Natural England, found no sign of the aquatic invertebrates, sadly the estimated 50,000 creatures, which are prone to a fungal disease, had died out.

In the 1930s this walk would have delivered a much different experience. Then, the Griff collieries produced 450,000 tons per year, had a fleet of 1,400 railway wagons and, by 1945, employed over 1,300 people. They had major customers in London and Birmingham as well as supplying the coal for Birmingham and Coventry's power stations. The earliest 'modern' pit shafts were sunk in the 1830s and the last pit closed in 1960. Although I found a lot of fascinating historical information on the brick and clay products industry, there is no statistical information. However from this area the production of bricks, including blue engineering, roof tiles, chimney pots and glazed drain pipes were produced and shipped widely. There were two main clay product companies, Stanley Brothers and Haunchwood, that as the clay deposits were worked out, finally closed in the late 1950s and in 1973 respectively.

Leaving the corridor we walk along St Pauls Road which was constructed to serve the first modern housing development, begun in 1923. The church of the same name was built in 1824, as a 'chapel of ease', by the 'noble people' of St Nicholas Church in Nuneaton town centre. Before the industrial revolution took hold Nuneaton was known for its ribbon making and hosiery. In 1819, as competition increased from abroad, the workers were told their wages would be reduced and they took to the streets. The worthies of the prosperous town centre felt that by building the strikers a church, the 'fear of god' could be put into the 'unruly masses'.

Leaving the church, a walk through the 60s and 70s estates takes us back down to the Nuneaton-Birmingham railway and through an underpass.

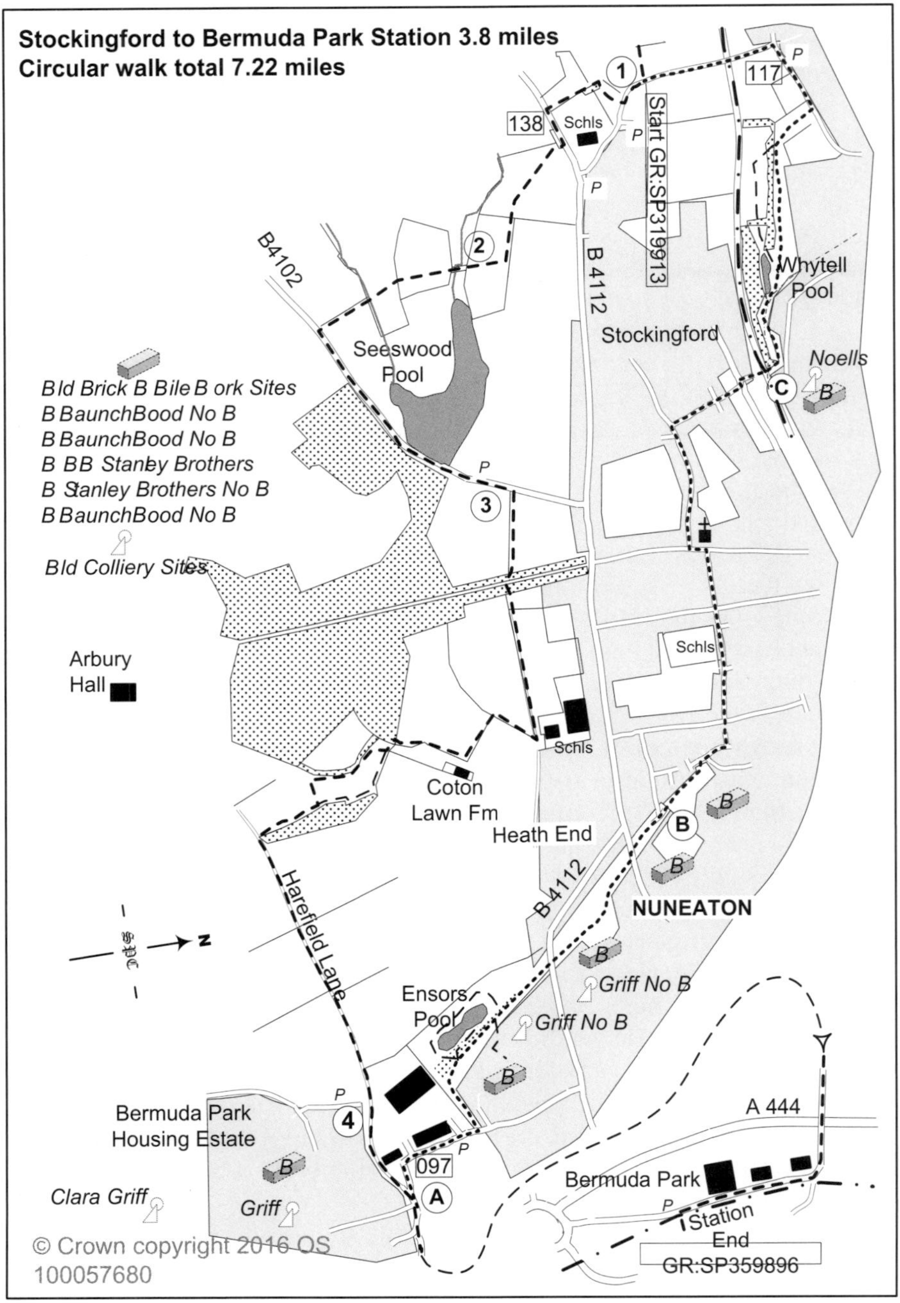
Stockingford to Bermuda Park Station 3.8 miles
Circular walk total 7.22 miles
1
138
Schls
P
Start GR:SP319913
117
B4102
2
B 4112
Whytell
Pool
Seeswood
Pool
Stockingford
Noells
B
C
Bld Brick B Bile B ork Sites
B BaunchBood No B
B BaunchBood No B
B BB Stanley Brothers
B Stanley Brothers No B
B BaunchBood No B
Bld Colliery Sites
3
Schls
Arbury
Hall
Schls
Coton
Lawn Fm
Heath End
B
B
B 4112
NUNEATON
Harefield Lane
N
B
Griff No B
Ensors
Pool
Griff No B
B
A 444
Bermuda Park
Housing Estate
4
097
Bermuda Park
B
A
Clara Griff
Griff
Station
End
GR:SP359896
© Crown copyright 2016 OS
100057680

Turning left into Whytell Pool, it is here that the Ansley Hall Colliery branch line entered the sidings shared with the Nuneaton Colliery and then at Stockingford Station (closed in 1968) joined the main line. The old line to Ansley Hall follows the footpath behind the houses along Beverley Avenue. After leaving this last urban wild life haven, our walk takes us back under the railway and climbs the hill back to the start.

## Walk Directions

| | |
|---|---|
| Joining points | Stockingford – kerbside parking in adjacent roads: Bermuda Park – kerbside car parking: Intermediate kerbside parking on the circular route |
| Pubs | None noted |

1. From Park Lane, just north of the school grounds, take the way marked footpath through the hedge. Cross the meadow aiming for the right end of the wooded area and turn left to follow the left fence line to the B4112, Ansley Road. Turn left along the road and opposite the end of the school building cross the road. Go down the bank through the hedge gap and take the gate. Cross the field ½ left to take the gate. Follow the left hedge to a marker post and turn right and cross the field.

2. Take the gate, continue between the fences to take gate and cross the next field and take the gate. Cross the field, take the steps, bridge and gate and continue with the right fence to reach and turn left along the road. Follow the road down and pass Seeswood Pool, and climbing the hill just after the last tree cross the road to take the gap at the side of a gate.

3. Follow the right hedge, cross the tree lined drive to Arbury Hall, continuing to reach a surfaced drive and turn right. Follow the drive around to the left to turn right along the edge of the field just before the entrance to Coton Lawn Farm. Follow the left hedge and continue through the corner of the wood into the next field. The Way follows the public right of way crossing the field and turning left along the field edge before turning back across the field and turning right to follow the left perimeter to Harefield Lane. However there is a well worn track that turns left and follows the left perimeter all the way to Harefield Lane. At Harefield Lane turn left and follow it for just over ½ mile.

4. Harefield Lane eventually reaches a modern housing development crossing the end of Mimosa Close. Continue straight ahead through the gate to reach the end of Harefield Lane and take the gate into Bermuda Road. Here the circular route turns left. To continue along the 'Way' pass the old mining houses of Bermuda Village on the right and continue left along Bridle Way. At Templar Drive take the footpath to the left which becomes a wide disused road bridging the A444 and terminates at the industrial estate of Bermuda Park. Continue straight into St Georges Way as it bends right and follow it to Bermuda Park Station. At the end of the station turn left under the railway and follow the footpath.

A. *From the end of Harefield Lane turn left along Bermuda Road following the road around to the right. Pass Tippers Builders Merchant and take the footpath left signed to Ensors Pool. Entering the nature reserve follow the footpath around to the right and keeping straight ahead join the surfaced path leading to the B4112. Cross the road, turning left then right into Lingmoor Park. Follow the footpath to cross the next road turning left and right to follow the footpath through the next park area. Continue to reach and walk along Cambridge Drive straight through to follow the footpath around the left edge of the park.*

B. *Follow the path into the top left corner and turn left between the houses and hedge to the road. Turn right and then left along Huntingdon Way. Take the first left and continue along the footpath through to Westbury Road. Cross over and continue straight ahead along St Pauls Road. Follow the road to reach the junction with Church Road and turn left then right along Wiclif Way. Continue and at the shops turn right along Wenlock Way to reach and cross over Kingswood Road. Turn left and right and follow the road, then footpath, through the subway under the railway.*

C. *Follow the path and turn left along Beverley Avenue and take the path left into Whytell Pool. Follow the path as it winds through the nature reserve turning right through a meadow area to reach Chesterton Drive. Turn left, passing the Equestrian Centre, and then left along Park Lane. Continue under the railway and up the hill passing the point where the 'Way' enters the lane from the north. Carry on for a further 180 metres to reach the start point.*

# CHAPTER 3

## Section 6: Bermuda Park to Coalpit Fields Road

We start from the Bermuda Park railway station, which was opened in 2015. The railway line first opened in 1850 but in 1857 the Spon End viaduct, just short of its terminus in Coventry, collapsed leaving only five of its twenty-eight arches standing. It was another three years before it re-opened in 1860. The line today, goes right through to Warwick but that line was built by another company to serve primarily the potential passenger demands of Kenilworth, Leamington and Warwick.

However the success of this line was generated by coal traffic, which could be moved to the south and west of England avoiding the bottleneck on the Birmingham-Euston line. Passenger services along the line were terminated in 1965 but a single carriage service was re-introduced in 1988 with the re-building of Bedworth Station. It has taken until 2015 to re-instate a fuller passenger service with the construction of this and the Ricoh Arena stations between Nuneaton and Coventry.

We commence our walk from the end of the station under the bridge, but first look the other way. The wide channel of water is the Griff Hollows Canal. The construction of the A444 dual carriageway terminated the canal and this channel remains as a long pool. We therefore now follow the path of the old canal arm to where it meets the Coventry Canal.

The Coventry Canal Company was formed in 1768 and James Brindley was appointed to build it. However his high standards came at a high cost and another engineer was appointed. Several other engineers worked on the construction by the time it was finally connected to the Trent & Mersey Canal at Fradley, just north of Lichfield. From its starting point in the centre of Coventry it is 38 miles long and has connections with the Birmingham & Fazeley, Oxford and Ashby canals.

The canal was an important route for goods between the north and London, as it avoided the lock flights in and out of Birmingham and cut 2-3 days off the journey. Locally, before the advent of the railways, the coal and clay products would have filled the barges. The southern Griff Mines Canal is shown on my map joining the main line on the elbow of the canal bend and marked by a wide band of trees.

Further along the Gilbert Bros Charity Dock was the loading point for coal from the Charity Colliery. The colliery was established in 1776, on land owned by the Reverend Nicholas Chamberlaine Charity, who let the mineral rights to operators who paid royalties to the Charity. This proved very lucrative and a school and almshouses were erected in the town. A second colliery, sunk in 1830, provided employment for silk weavers put out of work by the depression in the silk trade, The Nicholas Chamberlaine Trust continues today as a major benefactor to the town of Bedworth.

Just after the Charity wharf we reach the 30 mile long Ashby De la Zouch canal which opened in 1804. It was constructed to carry coal from the collieries in the Moira and Measham area. Unfortunately with the advent of the railways, it soon became economically unviable but, in 1846, the Midland Railway purchased it paying £110,000 for it, £74,000 less than it cost to build. In 1929 the northern end was closed due to mining subsidence and today the canal is run by the Ashby Canal Trust and 22 miles are navigable as far as Snarestone. They hope that with the subsidence largely finished, to eventually reinstate the whole of the canal and are seeking funding.

The return walk to 'Bermuda' starts from the bridge at Coalpit Fields Road. Just west of the bridge stood Newdigate Colliery, it ceased operating in 1982, the last pit to close.

Leaving the canal we join a wide 'black' track, leaving it to cross open countryside and the main railway line to London Euston. After crossing the railway we enter the village of Bulkington. Its name originates from the Saxon name Bochintone meaning 'the farmstead of Bulca's people'.

Although Bulkington has always been the biggest hamlet within the cluster of hamlets around it, the centre of the manor was established in Weston in Arden in 1285. The present Weston Hall Hotel (GII) is mid 16th century, substantially extended in 1892 and functions as a Best Western Hotel.

The village has a famous person, Richard Hayward, Sculptor (1725-1800). He was born and christened in Weston in Arden and in 1742 was apprenticed to Sir Henry Cheere, in London, for a full seven years at the 'customary' rate of £105. After gaining his freedom he played an active part in the affairs of the 'Masons Company' and in 1753 he went to work in Rome where he stayed for just a year. His abilities soon became wider known as it seems that whoever was in need of 'a lasting piece of fine marble statutory' engaged Richard. Westminster Abbey, the Duke of Marlborough and of course the Newdegates have examples of his work. But his most historical work is a piece undertaken in 1773 for a fee of £700. It is the oldest surviving public statue in the USA, the figure of the then, recently deceased Governor of Virginia, Lord Botetourt.

However, according to art historians, he reserved his finest works for his own family's 13th century church of St James (GII*), here in the village. His font consists of an ancient column for the base, which he brought from Rome, on which he has worked and inscribed. The bowl is white marble with 'delicate carvings depicting the baptism of Christ and of gifts being brought to the Virgin Mary. In 1781 Richard also produced a wall monument to his parents, who were great benefactors to the church, with 'Weeping Dacia' crying over a ruined landscape.

His own obituary described him as; 'a kind, intelligent, and warm friend, to many who will long deplore his loss', and added of his work that his

Richard Hayward wall monument

**Bermuda Railway Station to Coalpit Fields Road 3.25 miles**
**Circular walk total 9 miles**
**Map 1 of 2**

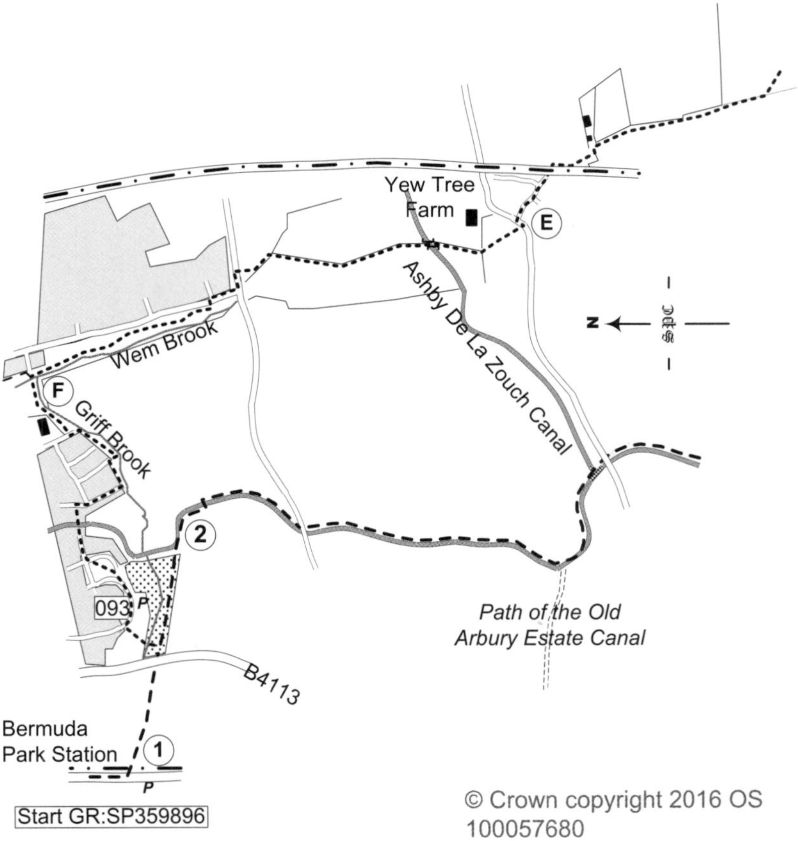

'performances in the line of his profession, dispersed throughout the kingdom, show him to have been an admirable master of the old school'. Modern scholarship has concurred with this judgement, seeing Richard; 'as a relic of the mason-sculptor tradition in an age when sculpture was increasingly seeking recognition as a polite art' and even suggesting that his techniques have had a possible influence on Thomas Banks.

Leaving Bulkington we follow a pleasant cross country route back under the railway and over the Ashby Canal to reach the south edge of Nuneaton. The path follows first Wem Brook and then Griff Brook before cutting across the corner of a mix of older and new infill housing. Then, via a footbridge across the canal, it is only a short distance back to the 'Way'.

## Walk Directions

| | |
|---|---|
| Joining points | Bermuda Park – kerbside parking: Coalpit Fields Road – car park and kerbside parking: Bulkington – kerbside parking and also available on the estate adjacent to the B4113 |
| Pubs | B4029 next to canal – the Navigation (P): Bulkington – the White Lion (P) |

1. Starting on the 'North Map', after the railway station take the underpass under the track. Follow the surfaced path, bear right under the B4113 and then pass a barrier into 'Griff Hollow' nature area. After a short distance, as the main surfaced path curves left, take the rising path right. Follow this path which eventually curves right to meet the Coventry Canal.

2. The 'Way' now turns right following a very narrow path along the edge of the canal. This path is partly boarded and can be a little wet, particularly at the start. After about ¼ mile the path reaches bridge no. 18. Cross the bridge and turn right to follow the canal for just over 1 mile to reach and cross the junction with the Ashby De La Zouch canal. Continuing on the 'South Map' follow the tow path for a little over 1½ miles to reach bridge no. 13 at Coalpit Fields Road.

*A. To return to Bermuda Park leave the towpath at the bridge and turn left along the wide, loosely surfaced, 'road'. (NB. this section, to point 'B', is the return route on the next circular walk.) Keep straight ahead between the*

## Bermuda Railway Station to Coalpit Fields Road 3.25 miles
## Circular walk total 9 miles
## Map 2 of 2

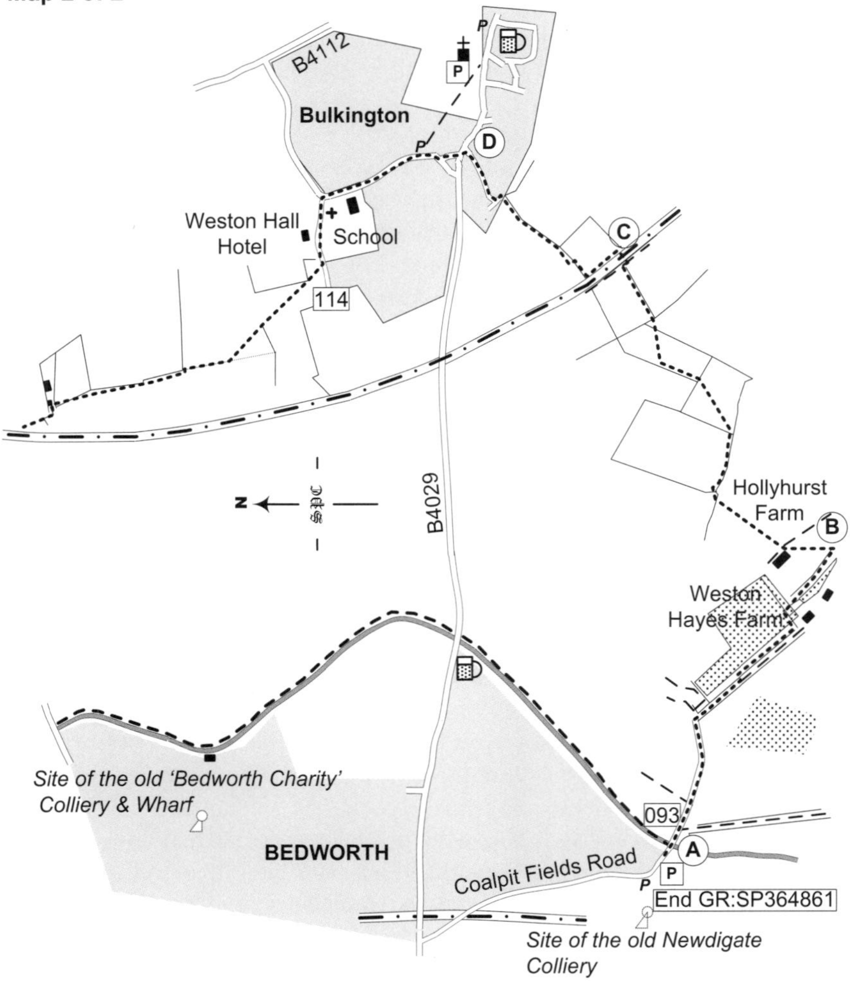

*stable enclosures and pass the gate to Minerals Lake. Continue to reach the junction of several tracks and turn right. Follow the twin concrete tracked drive way which leads to Weston Hayes Farm. Look for and take the stile on the left and turn right to continue towards the farm. At the approach to the farm buildings turn left, then right, to take or pass a redundant gate and take the next gate. Turn right and follow the fenced path to reach an open field and a marker post.*

B. *From the marker post, look over your left shoulder to see Hollyhurst Farm, cross the field aiming for the right side of the main house. Cross the entrance drive and, turning slightly left cross the field aiming for the yellow marker post and go to a hedge gap. Cross the bridge, take the gate and turn right to follow the hedge line. At the corner go through the gap, to the next field and continue along the right hedge line. From the corner of the next field turn ½ left and cross the field going through the wide hedge gap to follow the left hedge line. Reach a marker post and turn ¼ right to cross the field diagonally. Cross a bridge and continue to take another bridge. Now follow the right hedge line to reach a track. Turn right and left to follow the path under the railway line.*

C. *Turn left and follow the left perimeter turning right in the corner of the field. Continue up the field to go left and right through the hedge gap. Follow the hedge line, take the gate and follow the path between the houses at the edge of the village of Bulkington. Turn left along Leyland Road, then right along Benn Road. At the next intersection either cross the B4029 – Bedworth Road – and turn left then right into Weston Lane or turn right if you wish to visit Bulkington centre.*

D. *Follow Weston Lane, pass the school, and at the entrance to Weston Hall Hotel turn left along Mill Lane. Continue to the first open field on the right and take the gate. Cross the field ½ left to the field corner and bear left to the end of the hedge ahead. Now continue ¼ left to cross the field to turn right along a 'ditch' line and reach a hedge corner. Continue straight ahead with the hedge on the right. Continuing on the 'North map', take the gate and follow the surfaced 'road' alongside, then left under railway. Follow the road, ignoring the right and left turns, to reach Marston Lane. Turn left and take the stile on the right.*

E. *Cross the field to towards a gate and take the stile at the side. Follow the right hedge, take the stile and cross the Ashby De La Zouch canal and follow the track. Continue until the track bends left and turn right through the hedge to cross the bridge. Turn left, follow the hedge to cross the field corner to a gap in the hedge and reach the road. Cross the road and turn left then right along Marsh Lane. Continue to cross Northbourne Drive and then at the pedestrian refuge, cross Marsh Lane. Join the footpath straight ahead and turn right, following the winding route parallel to Marsh Lane. Opposite Sterling Way the path becomes surfaced and continues to emerge into the corner of an open 'park'.*

F. *Take the narrower path left over the Wem Brook bridge and continue past the school to the end of Raveloe Drive. Cross the hardstanding ½ left to follow a path alongside Griff Brook. Follow the path to reach a barrier and turn right into 'Red Deeps'. Now turn left to follow the footpath in front of the modern properties to emerge in Bradestone Road. Turn right continuing past the junction with 'Red Deeps' and in 50 metres take the footpath left between the houses. Cross the canal and follow Sorrell Road into the open green space ahead. Cross the green space ½ left and join Poyser Road. Follow the road around the bend continuing into Dorlecote Road. As the road straightens take the footpath left through the gates. Follow the footpath down the steps, cross the bridge over the brook and join the 'Way' turning right to return to the start.*

## Section 7: Coalpit Fields Road to Ansty

We start this section from a 'col', which my dictionary defines as being 'the lowest point between two mountain peaks'. Clearly with the adjacent contour peaks standing at a mere 110m above sea level it is stretching slightly, the actual physical interpretation of the terrain. Perhaps the alternative term of 'saddle' would be more appropriate as we cross England's north-south watershed line. So far, along the 'Way', all the watercourses have lead to the North Sea. We now enter the catchment area of the River Avon which will join the River Severn and discharge to the Atlantic.

Although the ground has been level, as the canal follows the contour, the adjacent ditches and streams have now turned to face south, but there is no mistaking our onward route. In just over a mile we reach Hawkesbury Junction where we turn left along the Oxford Canal. The junction of the two canals was the root of protracted disagreement between the two companies. The Coventry Canal Company's main aim was to get the canal open from Coventry to Bedworth and start making money by shipping the coal to the city, which they did in 1769.

The Oxford canal however, was not completed from Banbury to Coventry until 1777. The tale of its construction surrounds a lack of finance which both caused delays and attempted to minimise construction costs. This proved a false economy, as much of the original contour following route was straightened in the 1820s. The next section of the walk reveals an example, on the map at least, of the original cost avoiding route.

The Act of Parliament for the Oxford Canal contained clauses stipulating the rights to a toll sharing arrangement with the Coventry Canal, on goods that passed between the two canals. Various attempts were made to gain advantage and Brindley, Oxford's engineer, even attempted to move the junction further north so that the Coventry Canal would be robbed of the tolls on coal carried from Bedworth. The position of the junction was finally agreed at Longford that the two canals would run parallel for some distance.

This did not satisfy the Oxford Company as they would loose out on toll fees. They even tried to get new Acts of Parliament passed, which the Coventry Company defeated. Yet still the Oxford Company procrastinated and, although by now their canal was complete, they refused to make the connection at the junction. The Coventry Company therefore brought matters to a head and obtained a writ from the Court of King's Bench, which compelled the Oxford Canal Company to open the junction, which they did on 15 April 1777.

One last disappointment for the Oxford Company was that their water level was seven inches higher than the Coventry level and therefore, with every lock movement through the junction lock, they lost water. The 'Sutton Stop' junction was eventually moved to its present position at Hawkesbury in 1803.

The scenic junction has two cast iron bridges both dated 1837 and Grade II listed. The smaller, 'roving bridge', was cast as a single segmental arch and the larger in three arched sections. The plates on the bridges confirm that J Sinclair was the engineer when they were cast at the Britannia Foundry, Derby.

At busy times, it can be an interesting place to stand and perhaps enjoy refreshment at the mid 19th century Greyhound Inn (GII), while the boaters work out their strategy for making the u-turn between the canals, whilst avoiding each other. Just before the junction, is a disused Engine House (GII), built in 1821, which housed a Newcomen steam engine. The engine, which had already been in use for over a hundred years at the Griff Colliery, pumped water from the pits to feed the canal. By 1913 the shaft depths in the mine were beyond the power of the pump and it was decommissioned.

Leaving the junction behind, the canal sweeps around the old site of Coventry Power Station, the array of substation equipment on the opposite bank remains in evidence. As we walk alongside the M6 the area to the north

Sutton Stop canal footbridge bridge

is Sowe Common, from where the unseen River Sowe starts its winding course to join the Avon.

On journeys along the motorway I have always pondered the explanation for the position of the boat filled basin we next pass. This 'arm' under the M6, originally served the Wyken Colliery. Unfortunately by 1881 it was worked out, no doubt to the chagrin of the Oxford Canal Company. In 1958 the Coventry Canal Society, which was set up to protect canals from closure, discovered the old basin disused and overgrown, so they restored it and made it their headquarters.

The canal gets quieter as we leave the M6 behind, and we wind through fields before going under the M69 and reaching Ansty. Historically the medieval establishment of the Ansty parishes are described as the best example of an agrarian village community. My history source states that the settlement and late development of the area reflects the scattered medieval social structure of the time. Neither did their landlords, Coventry Priory and others, force especially 'irksome' manorial obligations upon their tenants. The Rose and Castle Pub is also close to the canal and the return walk starts opposite it, if you should feel 'obligated'.

After crossing the fields on the opposite bank of the canal and following the line of the M69, and its noise, for a short distance, we turn away to reach Barnacle, a name of Saxon origin derived from 'the hill slope marked by a barn'.

On the approach to the village we pass close to Barnacle Hall (16th century Grade II). At the time of the Civil War Captain Hickman, in the army of King Charles, had the tenure of the hall. A fact of which the Parliamentary forces were aware, so they plundered and burnt the house. Clearly the house survived and the Hickman's continued to live there into the 18th century.

From Barnacle the walk is cross-country passing through Hawkesbury Fishery to retrace the earlier route back to the canal.

## Walk Directions

| | |
|---|---|
| Joining points | Coalpit Fields Road – car park and kerbside parking: 'Sutton Stop', Hawkesbury – parking bays on the approach road: Ansty – kerbside parking in Grove Road |
| Pubs | Sutton Stop - the Greyhound Inn (P): Ansty – The Rose & Castle (P) |

1. Parking at the end of Coalpit Fields Road walk to the end of the road and cross the canal bridge to turn right along the canal tow path. The walk to Hawkesbury is just a mile to the junction with the Oxford Canal. The junction is very busy in the summer months but unfortunately there is no general parking here although the very popular Greyhound Inn does have a large car park. Leave the junction with the pub on your right to follow the Oxford Canal past the stop lock.

2. The Oxford Canal winds in series of sweeps before paralleling the M6 for just under ¾ mile and then turning away for a quiet rural section. The next traffic roar is from the M69 after walking under its viaduct we reach the village of Ansty. Turn right and climb the steps to the B4069 to return to the start of this section.

*A. Turn left over the canal for a short distance to just opposite the Rose and Castle Pub and take the gate on the left. Cross the field ½ left to reach and turn right along the canal through a series of stiles and gates to pass under the M69 again. Take the gate as you emerge from under the motorway and turn right. Follow the fenced path and take the next gate and continue straight ahead around the field turning away from the motorway to reach a gate just past the next corner of the field. Take the stile at the side of the gate and follow the right field edge and take the gate to the road.*

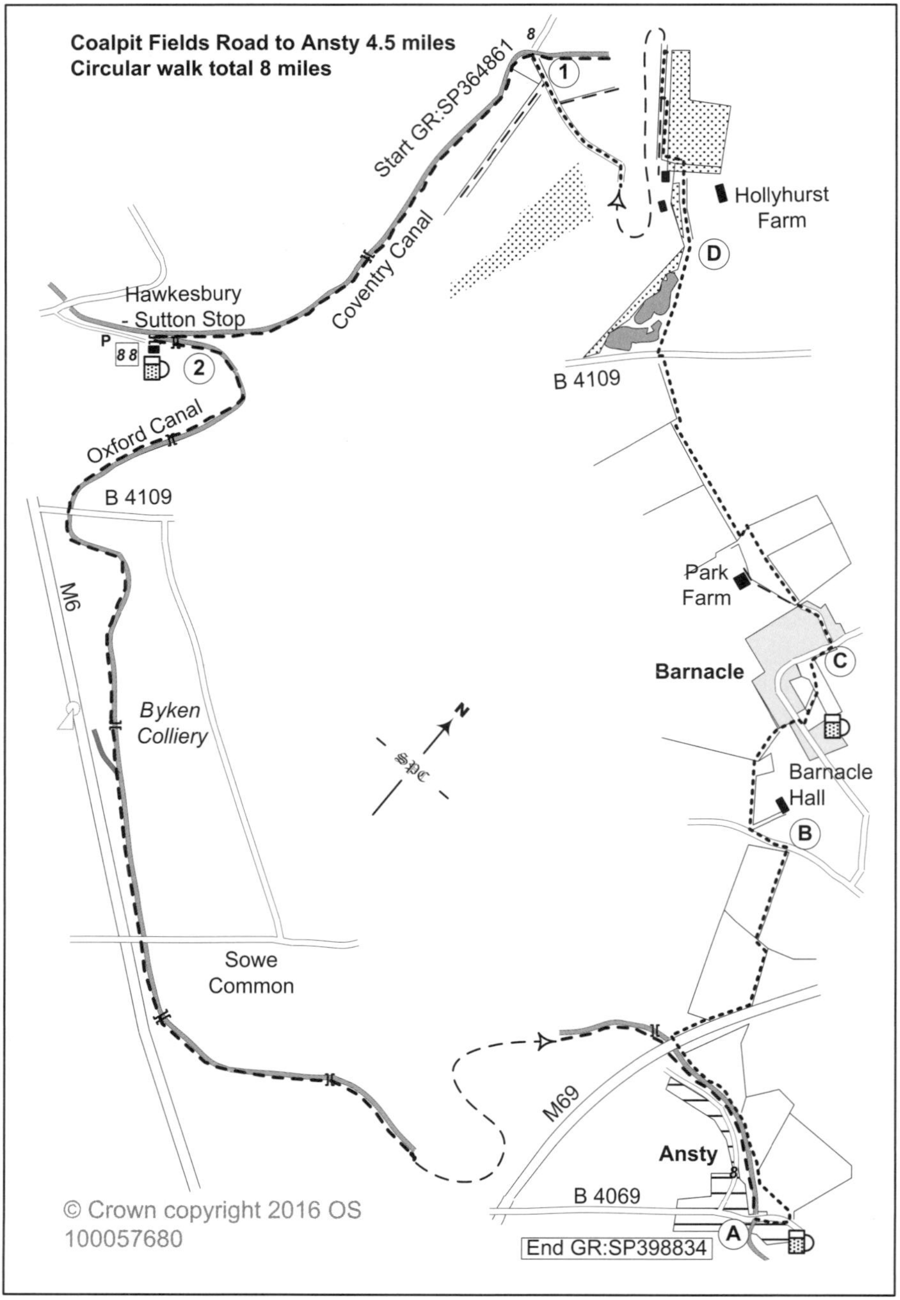
Coalpit Fields Road to Ansty 4.5 miles
Circular walk total 8 miles
Start GR:SP364861
1
Coventry Canal
Hollyhurst
Farm
D
Hawkesbury
- Sutton Stop
P
88
2
B 4109
Oxford Canal
B 4109
M6
Park
Farm
Barnacle
C
Byken
Colliery
N
Barnacle
Hall
B
Sowe
Common
M69
Ansty
B 4069
A
End GR:SP398834
© Crown copyright 2016 OS
100057680

B. *Turn left along the road and then turn right into the drive to Barnacle Hall to take the gate immediately on the left. Turn right to follow the field edge keeping straight ahead to take the gate. Turn right along the right edge continuing along a path to the road between the properties. Turn right and then left over the grass, turning left to follow the path continuing to take a gate. Continue along the mown path ½ left and then around to the right to take the gate to the road.*

C. *Turn left, cross straight over to follow Spring Road. Pass the impressive thatched School House Farm built in 1988 utilising materials from the original 17th century cottages. Continue along the road to the entrance to Park Farm and take the gate on the right. Follow the right hedge across the field crossing the bridge, turning left then right around the field to follow the left perimeter. Take the stile and cross the road turning left then right into Hollyhurst Lakes. Follow the wide stoned track passing the lakes and continuing with the hedge line to a marker post.*

D. *From the marker post turn left to retrace the steps, but in the opposite direction, taken on circular walk 6. Follow the path between the hedges. Take a gate on the left then a second gate (which was redundant) and follow the path around to the left then right. Follow the wide ride to a marker post. Take the stile on the left and turn right along the twin concrete track. At the junction with several tracks, turn left and follow the single surfaced track straight ahead to cross the canal and return to the start.*

## Section 8: Ansty to Smeaton Lane

From Ansty we continue along the Oxford Canal, which was first constructed to follow the 'contours' to avoid the excavation of cuttings, construction of embankments and installation of locks. But of course their change of policy only increased the cost and the time in completing the canal. As we approach the railway line the canal sits on a high embankment before entering a deep cutting. However the first 'cut', as shown on the walk map, turned left to follow the 90m contour in a 1.65 mile detour to avoid the ½ mile straight route with a 7 metre elevation change through the valley.

Leaving the canal we now enter the centre of Warwickshire's High Cross Plateau. The area is a narrow band stretching from Barnacle to Rugby and is the south-western termination of the Leicestershire Wolds. It is primarily an upland area at an elevation of over 100m. Turning away from the canal, along the farm road, I have marked a view point on the map. From here, the wide views in both directions illustrate the typical nature of the plateau's large scale open rolling vistas, with a feeling of space and emptiness.

This walk takes in two scheduled ancient monuments and the first is behind Mobbs Wood Farm. It is marked on the map adjacent '2' and is the site of the Cistercian grange of Upper Smite. Records reveal that originally the site had its own settlement of monks but they were transferred to Coombe Abbey in 1150. The monks then developed the area as a grange or farm. The reasoning behind scheduling sites like this, is that the Secretary of State considers them to be of national importance. Of all these sites, Historic England makes a widely encompassing generic statement of the wealth of historical information that would be revealed in the archaeological evidence that remains. This would tell the story of the lives and times of the people that inhabited the area and, as a 'Time Team' follower, each site, I am sure, would reveal fascinating information..

The onward path to Smeaton Lane now crosses the West Coast Mainline railway, which we have followed over the last two walks. This section of the mainline is the 50 mile Trent Valley line, linking Stafford, Lichfield, Tamworth, Nuneaton and Rugby. It was built by the London & Birmingham Railway Company and bypassed the two routes I described in the walk between Whitacre and Furnace End. However it seems that by 1845, when this line obtained Parliamentary Assent, investors were confident enough to place their money in a venture that would focus on passenger traffic, shortening the journey time between London and the north.

Reaching the M6 the return route swings off to the left and across the fields before following the pleasant Withybrook Lane for a little way. Leaving the lane we pass the second scheduled ancient monument. This is the deserted village of Hopsford which was recorded in the Domesday Book. However, although still occupied in 1631, it was already in decline. Although, like many other hamlets that have been scratched from physical presence, the earthworks, environmental and artefactual remains can still tell the story, should they ever be investigated.

From the lane our footpath slides down the plateau and turns to follow the original path of the contour-following-canal. The remainder of the walk crosses the canal and runs parallel with it to return through the fields to Ansty.

## Walk Directions

| | |
|---|---|
| Joining points | Ansty – kerbside parking in Grove Road: Final Canal Crossing – parking space in Colehurst Lane below the canal: Smeaton Lane – a wide verge |
| Pubs | Ansty – Rose and Castle (P) |

1. From Ansty continue under the B4065 along the Oxford Canal for approximately 1½ miles to reach the steps up to the high bridge which spans both the canal and the railway line. Climb the steps and cross the bridge and follow the wide concrete drive leading to Mobbs Wood Farm, with views right and left. Just before the farm complex, as the drive turns right, turn to the left to follow a footpath along the side of a fence on the right. Take the stile and cross the field slightly right to a stile just left of the wood of Scots pine. Take the stile and turn right through a gate to follow the wide ride to take the next gate. Follow the path between the fences and turn right through the hedge gap.

2. Follow the hedge into the corner and continue left around the field to go through the next hedge gap. Turn right and follow the edge of this field around the corner to reach the other end of the field and a hedge gap on the right. It is here that the return route goes left back across the centre of the field. However to continue along the 'Way' go through the gap on the right and follow the track, past the transmitters, to cross the M6. Now go straight ahead leaving the track to follow the left hedge line. Take the next gate on the left and turn right and continue in the same direction along the other side of the hedge. Take two further gates and cross the field slightly right to take a gate onto a driveway. Turn right crossing the railway and the canal. Continue along Colehurst Lane, where there is opportunity for car parking at the side of the road to reach Smeaton Lane.

*A. From Smeaton Lane retrace your steps along Colehurst Lane over the canal and railway to take the gate on the left and cross the field. Take the gate and follow the fenced path through the next gate to reach and turn through the gate on the left. Continue to cross the M6 and reach the gap in the hedge on the right as the track turns left.*

*B. Go through the gap and cross the field ½ left which eventually turns to the left to a marker post in a hedge gap. Go through the gap and turn right along the hedge line and through the hedge gap at the end of the field. Cross the next field ¾ left, then through the next hedge gap cross straight over the field to take a bridge. Follow the left hedge line through the next two fields to take a gate to the B4112 road.*

*C. Turn left along the road and then left at the bottom of the hill along the lane to Shilton. Follow the lane to reach Hopsford Spring Farm and, opposite it, turn left and go through the gap at the side of the gate. Enter the open*

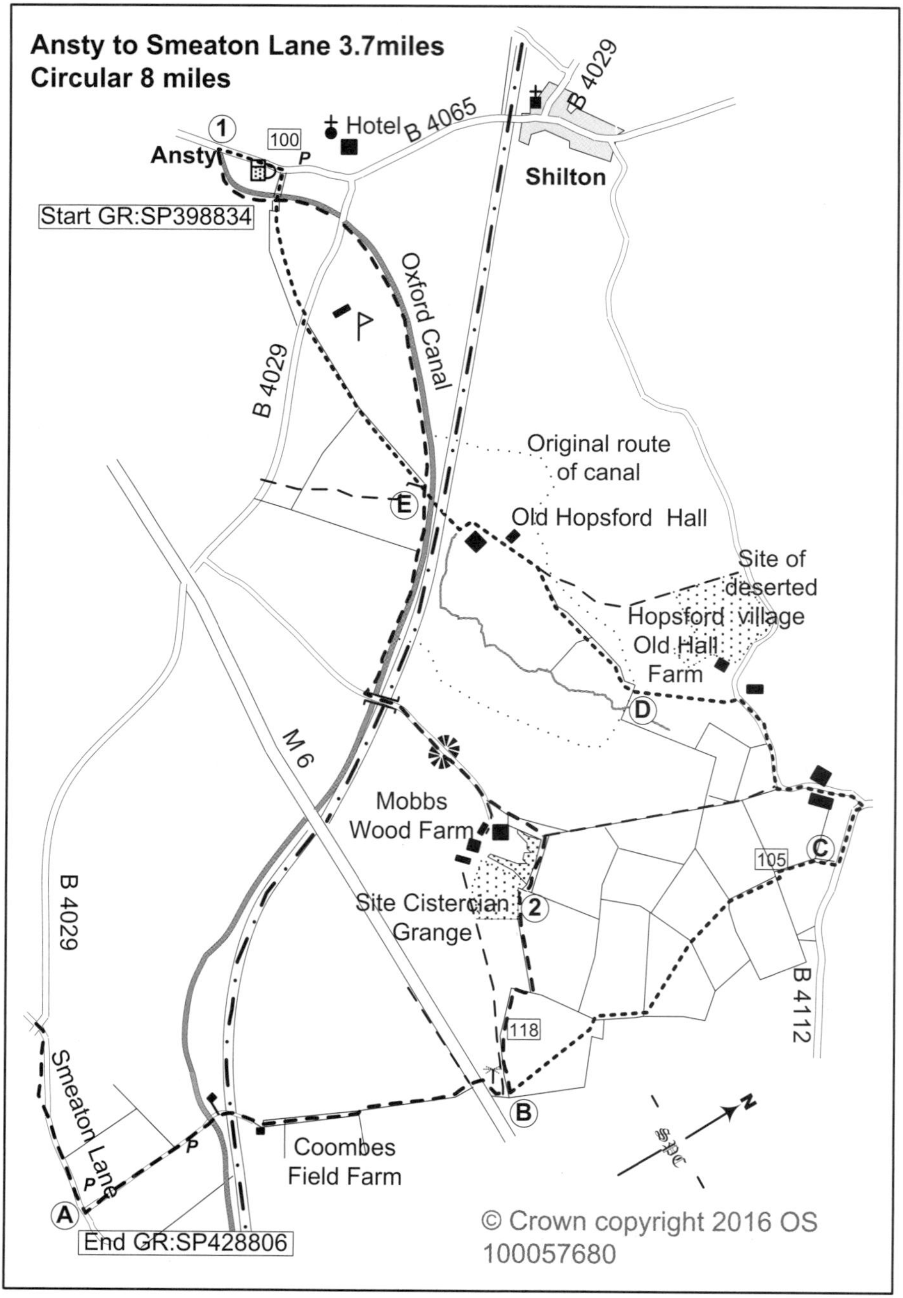

Ansty to Smeaton Lane 3.7miles
Circular 8 miles
1
100
Ansty
P
Hotel
B 4065
B 4029
Shilton
Start GR:SP398834
Oxford Canal
B 4029
Original route
of canal
E
Old Hopsford Hall
Site of
deserted
Hopsford village
Old Hall
Farm
D
M 6
Mobbs
Wood Farm
105
C
Site Cistercian
Grange
2
B 4029
B 4112
118
Smeaton Lane
B
P
P
Coombes
Field Farm
A
End GR:SP428806
N
© Crown copyright 2016 OS
100057680

*field and continue straight ahead across the field down the slope, aiming for a marker post partially obscured by trees, bending to the right through the hedge gap (noting the original course of the canal shown on the map).*

D. *Turn right and follow the hedge line continuing through the next hedge gap crossing the bridge. Continue along the right perimeter and join a track from the right. Follow the track past the barns, through the gate and continue under the railway viaduct and then through the tunnel under the canal.*

E. *At the bend in the track turn right across the field to join and follow the right hedge line. Take the next gate and continue to the road. Take the gate and cross the road right and left. Cross the field ½ right and take a gate continuing to cross the bridge over the canal. Take the gate and follow the path to join and turn left along the A4065 passing the Rose and Castle pub and return to the canal starting point.*

# CHAPTER 4

## Section 9: Smeaton Lane to Coombe Abbey

The walk to Coombe Abbey follows the road for some way, before we leave it to take the track to Hillfields Farm. As we walk along the track, to the right are the shapes of some large engine test buildings. These are in the south-west corner of the Rolls Royce's Ansty engine facility. Historically the site was inherited from Bristol Siddeley who merged with Rolls Royce in 1966. However the origins of this site, and the name, go back even further in Coventry's industrial history. In 1912 Siddeley-Deasy, a car manufacturer, was founded and in 1919 they merged with Armstrong Whitworth, becoming Armstrong Siddeley. That name is probably best known for its cars but in 1920 it started developing aircraft engines. Over the next few decades, by 1948, it was producing the Sapphire jet engine which competed with the Rolls Royce Avon. It is worth mentioning that our creator of the jet engine Sir Frank Whittle was born only five miles away in Coventry city centre.

The Ansty plant was built in 1935 and following the Rolls Royce branding became the headquarters of the Rolls Royce industrial and marine business. Through the years Ansty has been an important part of the Rolls Royce heritage. In 1968 the plant broke new ground in the development of first the Olympus and then the Tyne gas turbine engines for marine use. Both engines went into our own Royal Naval ships as well as other world fleets. Today the plant continues manufacturing the turbine blades and fan cases for the Trent family of civil aero engines.

I can admit in having some part in the history of the plant having managed a number of construction projects on the site, but my stories of those experiences are for a different book!

After passing between the buildings of Hillfield Farm we take a path across the fields into the very popular Coombe Abbey Country Park. The walk through the park takes us through natural woodland before the footpath circles the very attractive park and pools adjacent to the hotel.

'The Abbey of Cumbe', its original name, was founded by Cistercian monks in 1150. By 1291 the value of the Abbey and all its property, including lands in Norwich, was £140 per annum, making it by far the wealthiest house in the

County. However by 1322, despite the wealth of its holdings it was, 'burdened with debt, and 'reduced to much distress by defective rule'. Measures, it seems, given my interpretation of the complicated 14th century legal language, and the fact that the property was 'a house of royal foundation', enabled Abbott Richard to resort to a 21st century resolution and mortgage the property.

Ecclesiastical life at the Abbey continued, not entirely without impropriety it seems, until 1539, and the dissolution of the monasteries. The abbot, who had been parachuted into the post the year before, received a considerable pension of £80 per annum. The twelve monks that remained were less well rewarded, each receiving between £5 6s 8p and £8 per annum. Ownership of the abbey passed into private hands in 1581 and in 1622 the Craven family purchased it for £36,000. They retained possession for 300 years, extending and altering the buildings and in 1634 King Charles I granted a licence to enclose 650 acres of land to form a park. Between 1771 and 1777, the then sixth Lord Craven commissioned Lancelot (Capability) Brown to landscape areas of the parkland.

Since 1923, when the Craven family sold the property, the Abbey's ownership history has been chequered until Coventry City Council purchased part of the

Coombe Abbey Hotel

estate in 1958. Further purchases were made in 1964 and 1974 to secure the present park and the Abbey. The four star hotel was established in 1992 and has been extended a great deal since then and now has 119 bedrooms.

Leaving the park we walk for a distance along a busy road which in the summer, with the verges mown, is quite easy. From the road we follow a track and cross a mineral conveyor, which we turn alongside and follow. Sand and gravel extraction commenced in 1996 and the conveyor would have carried the material from the work face. The underlying strata is the same geology as at Kingsbury Water Park but overburdened with clay. In 2005 a further planning application was granted to extract the clay for use in roof tile production. The recommendation was given on the basis that sufficient clay would be left to seal the new lakes which will be part of the final landscape restoration. The original calculations were that the quarry would produce 3.5 million tonnes of material before expansion of the quarry would be required!

Leaving the quarry workings it is a short walk into Brinklow. The village main street has fourteen Grade II listed buildings plus the late 15th century Grade II* listed church of St John Baptist. At the side of the church, a path leads to the well preserved example of an early Norman timber motte and bailey castle, which is a scheduled ancient monument. It was built to command the line of the Fosse Way and is believed to have been built by William the Conqueror in 1069, to quell an uprising in the north. For some reason the main street is a ¼ mile west of where the Romans built the Fosse Way, but perhaps it was intended as Warwickshire's first motorway service area? After the Romans the 'service area' must have become so popular with the travelling public that the 'bypass' fell out of use. Historically Brinklow has always been a large village and no doubt its weekly market helped to support the six or seven ale houses recorded in 1676 and the 100 houses estimated in 1730. There are no records of when the market lapsed but today three pubs appear sufficient to serve the larger population and sate the thirst and hunger of the passing traveller.

From the village it is just over a mile across the fields before crossing Smite Brook via an attractive pack horse bridge and Smeaton Lane.

## Walk Directions

| | |
|---|---|
| Joining points | Final Canal Crossing – parking space in Colehurst Lane below the canal: Smeaton Lane – a wide verge: Coombe Abbey – pay & display: Brinklow – kerbside parking |
| Pubs | Brinklow – the Bulls Head, Raven and White Lion |

1. From the Grand Union canal bridge continue along the lane to the T-junction and turn right along Smeaton Lane. Follow the lane crossing the B4029 to continue along Peter Hall Lane. At the next intersection turn left and then right to take the gate and follow the track to Hillfields Farm. As you walk the track you will see the Rolls Royce Plant at Ansty on the right. The track continues between the barns at the farm and bends left. Continue up the slight incline through a gate to reach a gap in the hedge on the left and the well trodden path to the Country Park opposite a farm track.

2. Follow the path through a gap into the woods of the Park. Continue straight ahead over a bridge following the track on the left as it curves right to a Centenary Way marker post. Turn left along the path which becomes surfaced, cross the bridge over Smite Brook and pass the public conveniences on the left. Continue along the main path bending right following the line of the brook to cross the bridge over the lake with views to the impressive Coombe Abbey Hotel. Continue along the path to reach the Visitor Centre complex.

A. *From the Visitor Çentre follow the path left then turn right to the main entrance of the park. Turn left along the verge of the busy B4428 and continue past the junction with Combe Fields Road to reach the track on the right to Birchley Farm. Follow the track to cross the mineral conveyor at the corner of Birchley Wood and take the path left. Follow the path turning left and then right over the conveyor. The path continues between the hedge and the fence for about 1100 metres through the area of mineral extraction to reach the main access road. Turn left and right to cross the road and continue straight ahead to enter a field.*

B. *Cross the field ½ left, passing two islands of trees, and reach a track in the trees at the other side and turn right. Follow the track, past a bungalow, to reach the road. Cross the road and take the stile and follow the path along the edge of the field, to reach the road in Brinklow. Turn right then left into Broad Street, the main road through the village with plenty of opportunity for refreshment. Follow the road and turn left along Barr Lane passing between the Health Centre and the recreation area. Continue along the track to reach and take the gate on the left. Cross the field ½ left to reach and take a gate and turn right to follow the field edge. Follow the right field edge through three further gates. Now turn right along a bridle way to reach Smeaton Lane via the bridge over Smite Brook. Turn left and then after short distance turn right along Colehurst Lane to reach the starting point.*

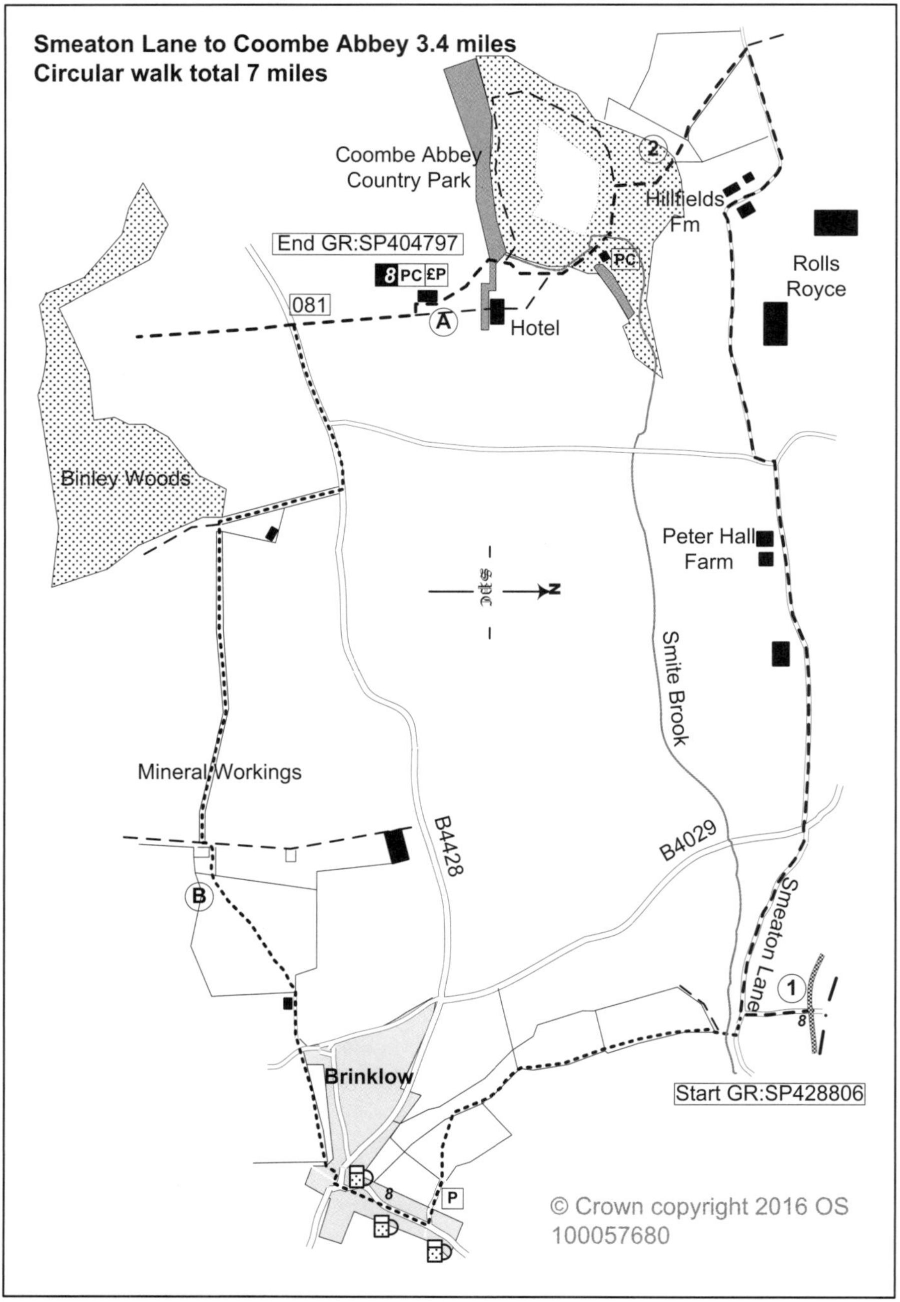
Smeaton Lane to Coombe Abbey 3.4 miles
Circular walk total 7 miles
Coombe Abbey
Country Park
2
Hillfields
Fm
End GR:SP404797
8 PC £P
PC
Rolls
Royce
081
A
Hotel
Binley Woods
Peter Hall
Farm
N
Smite Brook
Mineral Workings
B4428
B4029
B
Smeaton Lane
1
8
Brinklow
Start GR:SP428806
P
8
© Crown copyright 2016 OS
100057680

## Section 10: Coombe Abbey to Wolston

From the area of Coombe Abbey we have crossed the border line from the High Cross Plateau into the area of Dunsmore which is summarised as characterised by low glacial plateau, with sandy soils, being well-wooded, and having remnant heathland vegetation. The aerial picture today of the area is of a planned landscape of large fields and small villages. This wedge of the county between Rugby, Coventry and Leamington Spa also, as we shall see, has large stretches of woodland.

The human influence on the land has been evident since the time of pre-historic man. No doubt then and through the centuries the Rivers Leam and Avon have been the first attraction for both habitation and farming. The pattern of farming seems to have been established from Saxon times as also were the parish boundaries. All the parishes extend from the higher heathland down to the rivers so that each community had areas of meadow, arable and pasture. We shall see, as we continue our journey, that the area has never the less proven to be a suitable home for the arable prairie landscape. However, mature hedgerows sprinkled with ancient oaks remain, and in the uncultivated areas a wide variety of flora and fauna are abundant.

Leaving Coombe Abbey we see the first example of this area of the Dunsmore's visually most predominant feature as Birchley and New Close Wood fill the view. These are examples of the ancient woodland that this area of the County has in the largest concentration. On the footpaths we follow from here to Stareton, we will pass or walk through not only these woods but the woods of Bubbenhall, Ryton, Wappenbury and Princethorpe, Waverley, Weston and Cubbington. The total area covered by them all is, by my rough calculation, 5.2 $km^2$.

Leaving the wood we walk along the entrance drive to Brandon Stadium, the home of the Coventry Bees Speedway team and the venue for stock car racing. Walking into Brandon Village there are several Grade II listed buildings including the red telephone box and 'Woodcroft' the house opposite. Also listed in Main Street we pass the originally 17th/18th century built white thatched cottage.

Continuing, leaving Brandon, we pass under the railway viaduct (GII), built around 1835, and then cross the River Avon, for the first time, via the 18th century Wolston Bridge (GII). Looking over to the right, the raised banks of the earthworks mark the site of the 12th century Brandon Castle. The original owner of the castle was Geoffrey de Clinton but it passed to Nicholas de Verdon who improved its defences. Perhaps he had ideas above his station, because in 1266 the castle was captured and destroyed by the garrison of Kenilworth Castle and it was not restored.

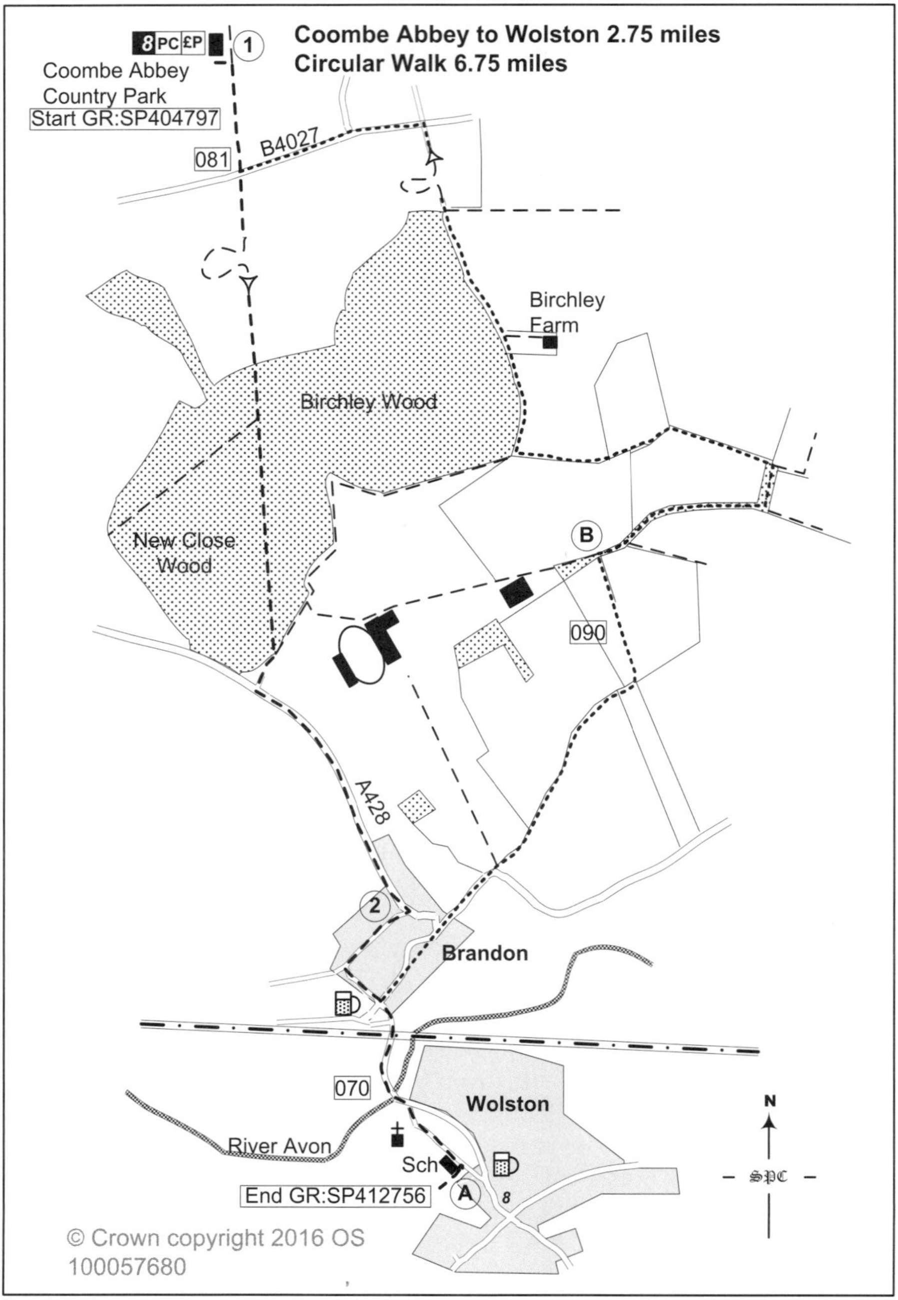
Coombe Abbey to Wolston 2.75 miles
Circular Walk 6.75 miles
8 PC £P
1
Coombe Abbey
Country Park
Start GR:SP404797
081
B4027
Birchley
Farm
Birchley Wood
New Close
Wood
B
090
A428
2
Brandon
070
Wolston
River Avon
Sch
A
8
End GR:SP412756
N
SPC
© Crown copyright 2016 OS
100057680

The Grade I listed church of St Margaret was established on the site in the 12th century with a low tower, of which the lower structure is original. The tower was altered in later years and in the 17th century was raised to form the bell tower. The reset of the church is mostly modern. If you walk into the centre of the village along Main Street just before the crossroads there is a fine Grade II listed 18th century red brick house typical of the period.

The return walk retraces our steps over the river and under the railway, to rejoin the A428 for a short length and take another pleasant cross-country route, to follow the B4027 back to the Abbey.

## Walk Directions

| | |
|---|---|
| Joining points | Coombe Abbey – pay & display: Wolston – kerbside |
| Pubs | Brandon – the Royal Oak (P): Wolston – the Rose & Crown |

1. Start from the Coombe Abbey Visitor Centre walking down the main drive to reach and cross straight over the B4027. Take the gate and follow the track leading to the combined mass of Birchley and New Close Woods. Take the gate into the woods and follow the main track straight ahead. At the southern edge of the wood take the gate and turn right along the drive to reach and turn left along the A428. Follow the road into Brandon and turn right into Main Street.

2. Follow the road around to the left, crossing Brandon Lane, to continue past the Royal Oak car park. Continue under the railway bridge to take the footbridge over the River Avon. Turn left and right along the road, over a farm drive, to take the gate on the right. Follow the path past St Margaret's Church and continue to the school. To continue along the 'Way', immediately after the school entrance take the footpath right between the school and the houses. If you wish to visit Wolston, continue along the path.

A. *Our return route to Coombe Abbey retraces our steps to the corner of the Royal Oak car park. Turn right along Avondale Road to the junction with the A428. Continue straight ahead, taking care as there is no footpath. At the right bend cross and leave the road to continue straight ahead along the farm track. Follow the track for just over ½ mile to reach and take a gate where the track diminishes to a path. Follow the path turning left through a gate to follow the field edge then hedge on the right, to a band of trees.*

*B. Enter the trees and turn right along a footpath, through the trees, first bending left then curving right. At a field corner follow the path turning left and continuing through the trees. At the next junction, turn left over a bridge onto a footpath, then follow the right hedge to a corner. Turn right through the second gap and turn left to follow the left hedge line towards Birchley Woods. Continue to take a stile and reach the corner of the field at the woods. Turn right and follow the edge of the field, along the tree line and join the surfaced track leading from Birchley Farm. Follow the track over the mineral conveyor to reach and turn left along the grass verge of the B4027. Pass the junction with Coombe Abbey Fields Road and turn right along the drive to the Visitor Centre.*

## Section 11: Wolston to Ryton on Dunsmore

This is the first section of the Centenary Way with no alternative public footpath right of way and therefore no circular walk. When I walked the route I also discovered that gravel extraction had commenced, although the public footpath was not affected. The explanation is that on 6th February 2014 Smiths Concrete was granted planning permission, at Wolston Home Farm, over an area of 84.7ha to extract an estimated 900,000 tonnes of sand and gravel. Work commenced in spring 2015 and is expected to take 6 years.

Meanwhile, to those of us who like 'boys toys', there may be some interesting large machines at work to generate additional entertainment as we cross the area. The right of way will be maintained, although there will be occasions when the path will be diverted, to ensure safe passage at all times. After reinstatement has been completed there will be a new permissive path following the river between Wolston and the sewage works and also new pools and tree planting.

The normal path across Wolston Home Farm would touch the bank of the River Avon approximately 28 miles from its source at Naseby, in Northamptonshire. Already it has passed through two reservoirs. The first, virtually at its source, feeds the Grand Union Canal and at just a few miles further along at Stanford, a 500 million gallon reservoir, provides drinking water to Rugby and the surrounding area.

Although the river at this point is small, it has already been joined by the River Swift close to Rugby and between here and where we leave it, at

Warwick, it will be joined by the tributaries of the Rivers Sowe and Leam. During its total length of 85 miles it will have been joined by many other rivers and streams to drain an area totalling 1,032 $miles^2$.

We cross the A45 dual carriageway, which has always been a main highway across the heath connecting Coventry to London via Watling Street. Before the true motorway age it was also the main route from Birmingham to London even being improved with a short section becoming the M45. Turning off the road into Ryton on Dunsmore, in recent historical times many workers just referred to their work place as ‘Ryton’.

For over 50 years all West Midlands police officers started their training at the Police Training Centre on the outskirts of the village before commencing their probationary period on the beat. Since 2011 it has become the College of Policing which is to become established as a statutory body, independent of government.

The other cadre of workers worked at the car factory. The original factory complex was built in 1939 by the Rootes Group to manufacture aircraft engines to support war production. After the war Humber car production was transferred from another plant and then, between 1952 and 1962, the main cars produced were various models of Hillman Minx and Hunter. By 1969 the total Hunter production was 150,000 and in that year the Avenger was launched.

Like other UK car producers in the 1970s Chrysler hit financial difficulties and in 1978 sold out to PSA Peugeot Citroen. At first the old Talbot name was revived and the first model was the Horizon. However from the 1980s the brand name became Peugeot and the models produced were the 306, 309, 405 and finally, when production ceased in 2006, the 206. Today the 57ha site has been redeveloped as an industrial, commercial and logistics park.

## Walk Directions

| | |
|---|---|
| Joining points | Wolston & Ryton & Dunsmore – kerbside parking |
| Pubs | Wolston – the Rose & Crown(P): Ryton & Dunsmore – the Blacksmiths Arms (P) |

**This section of the walk crosses an area of sand and gravel extraction which commenced in 2015 and will continue until around 2020, when the area will be reinstated. At all times the footpaths will remain open and protected from the working areas although there will be signed temporary diversion routes throughout the project.**

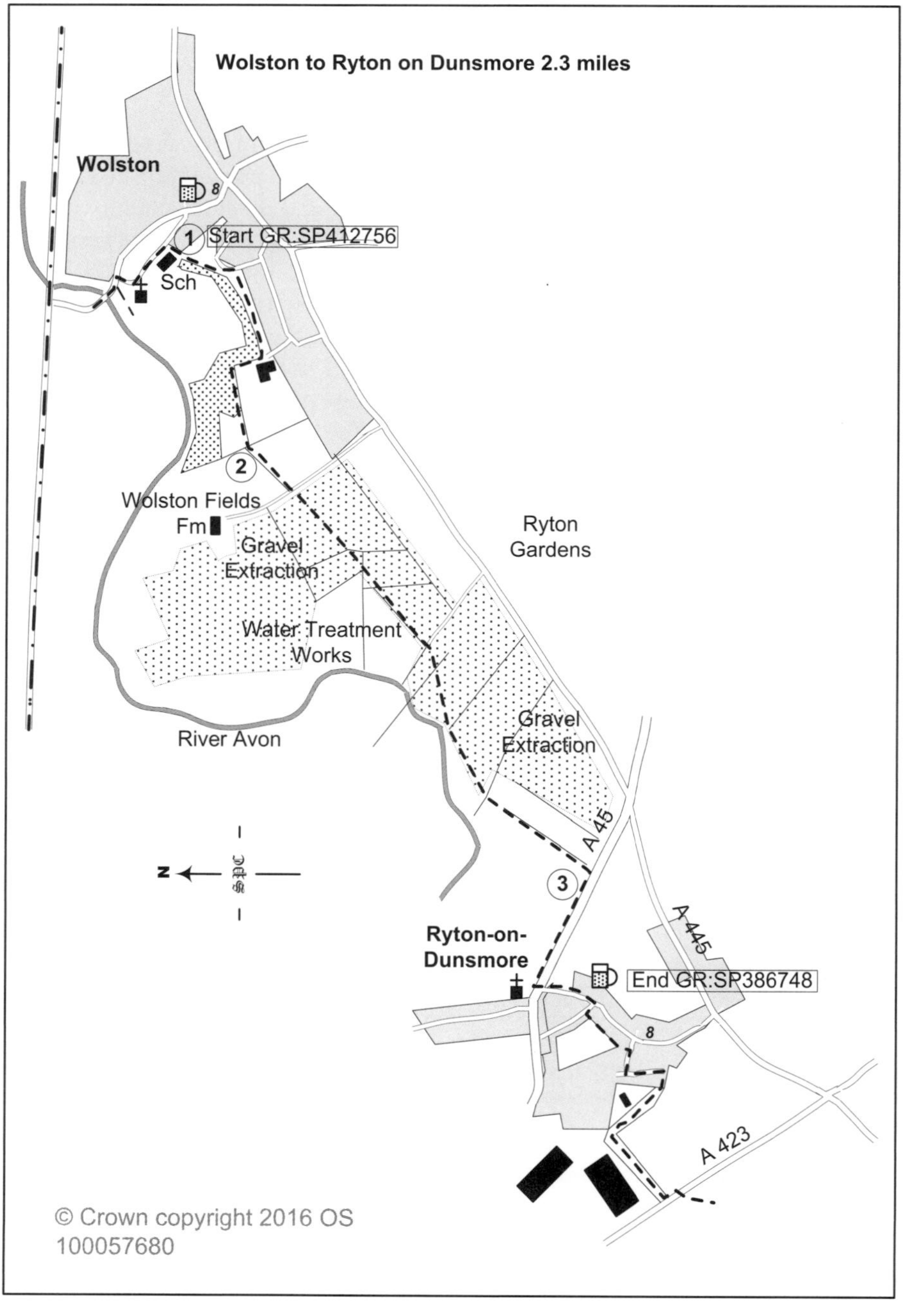
Wolston to Ryton on Dunsmore 2.3 miles
Wolston
8
1
Start GR:SP412756
Sch
2
Wolston Fields Fm
Gravel Extraction
Water Treatment Works
River Avon
Ryton Gardens
Gravel Extraction
A 45
N
3
A 445
Ryton-on-Dunsmore
End GR:SP386748
8
A 423
© Crown copyright 2016 OS 100057680

1. Taking the path along the side of the School which leads to Paddocks Close. Follow the footpath around the bend in the road and turn right before house no. 117 and go between the garages. Continue along the footpath, cross the end of the next road and take the footpath down the side of house no. 33. Approach the Community Centre and turn right to go around it and take gate and follow the fence on the left. At the next corner the right of way continues between the fence and the edge of the wood. If this path is overgrown then follow the path inside the edge of the wood, as I did, to reach the first cultivated field.

2. Keep straight ahead, following the fence on the right, to cross the paved drive left and right, serving Wolston Fields Farm. The gravel and sand extraction area commences here but continue straight ahead across the field through three hedge gaps. Now follow the left hedge line to approach the fence to the Water Treatment Works and continue between fence and hedge to reach the access road. Leave the road at the edge of the field and cross the field ½ right to reach the River Avon and continue left to cross the bridge over the ditch. Now cross the field ½ right to cross a bridge at the next field edge. Cross the field straight ahead to continue along the right side of the hedge ahead. Follow the hedge, then grass bank, to reach the A45, take the gate and the steps and turn right.

3. Continue along the footpath to reach and take the pedestrian underpass under the A45, which leads into High Street and the Blacksmiths Arms pub.

# CHAPTER 5

## Section 12: Ryton on Dunsmore to Bubbenhall

Our walk to Bubbenhall is fairly short and, after leaving the housing area, follows a fence alongside the south tip of the 'newly' developed park that replaced the Ryton car plant. After crossing the A423 Southam Road the path turns to follow a bridle way that leads into the north corner of Bubbenhall.

Walking along 'Lower End', amongst the modern buildings, looking to the left, is the 18th century Abbey's House together with the 17th century Yewtree Farmhouse, the Malt Shovel and the 'Cottage' all of which are Grade II listed. Bubbenhall has existed since before the first records were made of it in 1086. The parish web site's brief historical records seem to confirm that it has enjoyed the same quiet existence that we see today. However, in the deeper national historical records of the 14th century, with the birth of Joan Gatesby on 23rd March 1352, Bubbenhall has played its part in the national dramas of that time.

Prior to her birth, the manor of Bubbenhall was owned by the FitzWyth family and Joan's mother Agnes was the daughter of Robert FitzWyth, the last in the male line. In 1361 he assigned the Manor to Agnes's husband, whose heir was Joan. However by the time of Robert's death, his first wife had died and he had married again and lived in Aspley Guise with his second wife, who had survived him.

Meanwhile, Joan Gatesby had continued her life, becoming the heir herself to the manor and marrying John Beauchamp of Holt Esquire. However, their full entitlement to the Manor of Bubbenhall was put in question when Joan's grandfather's second wife, also named Joan, sued for one third of the manor as dower.

The Beauchamp rebuttal was simple, that no dower was due as Joan; "On the Tuesday after Michaelmas 1362, abandoned her husband and went to live in adultery with Roger de Careswelle in the hospital of St. Thomas at Southwark". The claimant responded that; "Roger de Careswelle came to Aspley Guise, with armed force, wounded her husband mortally, beat her, and carried her off to Southwark. But, she had escaped and returned within four days to find her husband dead. She had then 'appealed' Roger and his cohorts and they had been outlawed". The court accepted her story and she was awarded her dower and in 1375 a settlement was made.

Despite this loss to Joan and her husband's estate, it was perhaps of little concern, for the Beauchamps were now moving in royal circles. John had established himself in the court circles of Edward III and then Richard II. Richard II thought so highly of John that he acted as godfather to their son. One must assume that John was more than happy to be on Richard's inner circle, despite the King's fluctuating relationships with parliament and his powerful Lords determination to diminish the royal power. Unfortunately for John his continuing promotion at the court was to bring about both his, and the King's downfall. In January 1387 King Richard, against parliamentary opposition, made John the new Steward of the Household and then later, in October, granted him the title Lord Beauchamp, Baron of Kidderminster.

This was too much for the five leading Lords, who included the Earl of Warwick, whom some said was jealous of his cousin John. They formed a council known as the 'Lords Appellants' and presided over the 'Merciless Parliament'. They seized control of England by banishing the King's circle of cronies including John. On the 12th May 1388, Lord John Beauchamp, having been impeached by Parliament and condemned by the Lords for treason, was beheaded at the Tower of London. For Joan, her son inherited the title, becoming the 2nd Baron and not all of their lands were forfeited so, we must assume, that at least she ended her days in comfort.

At the end of Bubbenhall's main street, leaving the 'Way', we shortly enter the County's Ryton Pools Country Park. The park opened in 1996 and was reclaimed from land that ha been used for landfill, following the extraction of sand and gravel. The park is very popular with families, particularly in the summer and at weekends providing a great outdoor experience. The path we take skirts the west side of the park and leaves by the side of Ryton Wood.

The wood is managed by the Warwickshire Wildlife Trust and has been granted SSSI status. Parts of the wood have been confirmed as 11th century and that it has been wooded since the end of the last ice age. There are also large ditches which indicate the woods historical man made medieval boundaries. The wood is truly worth taking a detour, particularly at quiet times to enjoy its wide variety of trees, plants, insects and birds.

The way forward is at first along the surfaced Paget's Lane leading to Shrub Lodge. Here we join the ancient bridleway of Nunwood Lane, which winds around the perimeter of Wappenbury Wood. The wood is another area of ancient woodland managed by Warwickshire Wildlife Trust and is

St Giles Church Bubbenhall

accessible to the public except on Wednesday and Saturdays. Leaving the pleasant woodland area, we turn along the very quiet Burnthurst Lane and cross the Oxford Road. From here we walk two short sections of a lane with a connecting footpath to then follow a long footpath through the fields to the A45 and Ryton on Dunsmore.

## Walk Directions

| | |
|---|---|
| Joining points | Ryton on Dunsmore – kerbside parking: Bubbenhall – kerbside parking & lay-by on the A445: Ryton Pools – pay and display |
| Pubs | Ryton the Blacksmiths Arms (P): Bubbenhall the Malt Shovel (P) and Three Horse Shoes (P) |

1. From the Blacksmith's Arms Pub, continue along High Street and turn right into Featherston Crescent then left into the park. Follow the footpath through the park keeping left to reach 'Warren Field'. Turn right then left at the T-junction and continue to the end of Warren Close. Now turn right by no. 24 and follow the footpath through the fenced area turning left after 200 metres and continuing to reach and cross the A423. Turn left for a few yards and take the stile into the field and cross ½ left to the far corner. Take the gate and follow the fenced path turning left to take the gate. Turn right and follow the hedge on the right around to the right and take the stile. Continue for a further 300 metres, turn left and follow the track alongside the hedge on the right. This track continues to Bubbenhall and joins 'Lower End'. Continue along 'Lower End', passing the Malt Shovel Pub to reach Spring Hill and turn right to continue along the 'Way'.

A. *To return to Ryton on Dunsmore turn left, passing the Three Horseshoes Pub and continue to reach and turn left along the A445. Continue along the footpath until reaching a pedestrian barrier. Cross the road and turn left to follow the footpath on the other side. The footpath leads into Ryton Pools Country Park. Follow the path to the Visitor Centre and take the 'red' way marked path to Pagets Pool. Follow the path across the park and take a gate on the right signed 'Wappenbury Wood'. Take the path, passing the pool, to take the gate into Paget's Lane and turn left to pass Shrub Lodge.*

B. *Follow the track to Wappenbury Wood and continue along the main track, curving left then right through the open wood. Exit the wood and follow the hedged/fenced track turning to the left at 'Shady Acres'. Continue to reach the junction with Burnthurst Lane and turn left along the lane. Follow the lane to reach and cross the A423 into Finacre Lane. Continue along the lane until reaching a way mark post at the half way point of the third field on the left. Cross the field to take a stile. Now go right of the barns, pass the duck pond, to pick up a track which continues through the 'farm yard' area and turns left to continue to the lane.*

C. *Turn right along the lane and, at the junction with Plott Lane, turn left to take the gate on the right (before the gated entrance). Cross the field to the far corner and cross through the hedge line, enjoying the views to Coventry, to turn left and follow the left hedge. Continue along the hedge line, taking seven stiles, to reach the A45. Turn left along the A45 continuing along the left footpath and crossing the A445 road. After the A445 crossing continue for about 370 metres and, at the way mark post, turn left and follow the*

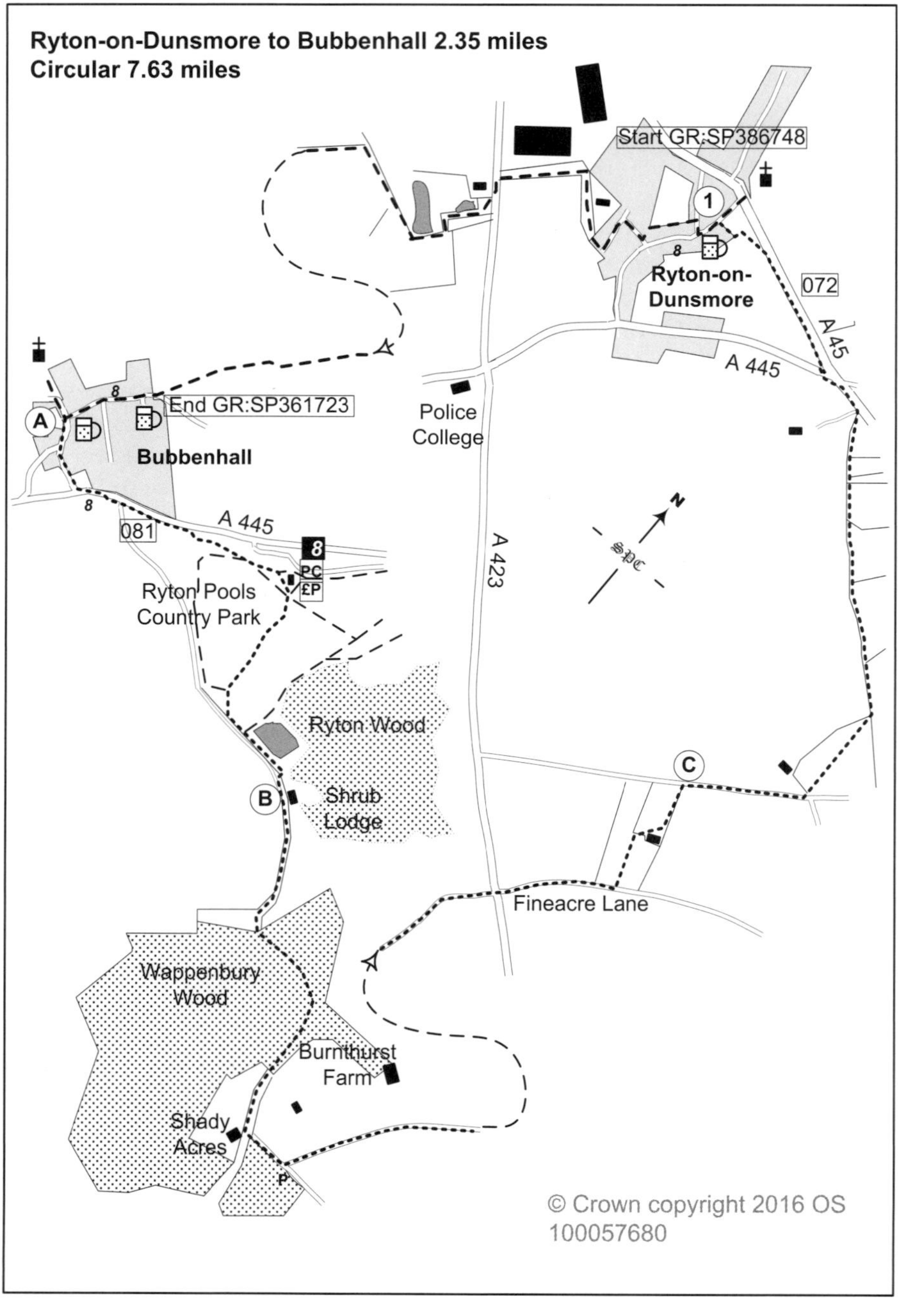
Ryton-on-Dunsmore to Bubbenhall 2.35 miles
Circular 7.63 miles
Start GR:SP386748
1
8
Ryton-on-
Dunsmore
072
A 45
A 445
Police
College
A
8
End GR:SP361723
Bubbenhall
8
081
A 445
8
PC
£P
Ryton Pools
Country Park
N
SPC
A 423
Ryton Wood
B
Shrub
Lodge
C
Fineacre Lane
Wappenbury
Wood
Burnthurst
Farm
Shady
Acres
P
© Crown copyright 2016 OS
100057680

*path behind the houses which enters High Street. Turn left to continue to the Blacksmith's Arms.*

## Section 13: Bubbenhall to Stareton

The 'Way' turns right from Lower End and along Spring Hill, passing the impressive Manor House on the corner. It seems that this building was subject to major rebuilding in 1966 and during high winds the original timber framework was blown down. No doubt the external features are in keeping with its original historical appearance.

As we bear right into Church Road, the Church of St Giles (GII) appears at the end of the lane. The church was built late in the 13th century when it consisted of the chancel and the nave. However it appears that the 12th century font is evidence of an earlier church. The tower was added in two stages in the early and late years of the 14th century. The south entrance door, inside the modern porch, has a richly moulded and detailed pointed arch.

From the churchyard the path crosses a field next to the Avon and continues a short distance along the lane before taking a cross-country path to join Stoneleigh Road. The continuing road route to Stareton follows the perimeter of Stoneleigh Park, first passing the Grade II listed early 19th century Tantara Lodge. This was the London Drive entrance to the estate, now a private house.

Turning towards Stareton we pass the Abbey Business Park, but look through the trees and spot the nissen huts, that betray the sites origins. During the Second World War it was the home of the US Army's 307th Station Hospital, where injured personnel were brought for rehabilitation. A little further on, as the road drops into a dip, look to the right to spot a cottage set back from the road. This is Beehive Cottage built at the same time as Tantara Lodge as another gate house.

Climbing the rise into Stareton there is a mixture of cottages, houses and farm buildings that reflect the rural history of this hamlet over the last 500 years. Like Bubbenhall it would have been a settlement perfectly placed next to the river in its landscape.

The return walk to Bubbenhall is almost entirely off road and, at 6.2 miles, is the longest we undertake. We start by leaving the road and following a bridleway which is also a 'County Road' and therefore open to all traffic. You may therefore, apart from a tractor, find a 4-wheel drive vehicle or off-road motor cyclist sharing the track.

It is at this point that the HS2 railway line appears. After crossing the A445 the route follows field paths and then turns south towards North Cubbington Wood. At the corner of the wood we join not only the public footpath but a

A cottage at Stareton

permissive path. This is part of a DEFRA conservation scheme to provide wider grassland margins around arable fields and create habitat for insects, small mammals and birds.

If you take a detour into the village of Cubbington, within a few yards down the hill are, opposite each other, the Grade I listed church of St Marys and the Kings Head pub. The church has a register of all its vicars dating back to 1346 and at its southwest corner is the old 18th century manor house. The earliest part of the church, constructed in red sandstone is 12th century including the tower.

Continuing across the fields the footpath takes us through Cubbington Woods which at its south-east corner is a massive wild pear tree that was voted the National Champion Tree in 2015. However, its continuing life will be shortened, as it stands on the line of HS2.

We join the road for a short distance at the edge of Weston under Wetherley, passing Grade I listed St Michael's church. This building has the same 12th century early history as the others in the area but, was mostly rebuilt early in the 13th century and the tower added a century later. From the road we continue north following a long uphill path that runs parallel with Weston and Waverley Woods.

We only follow Weston Lane for a short distance as a new permissive path, at the side of the Bubbenhall Quarry access road, provides a more pleasant route. The provision of this path would have been part of the planning permission conditions for granting the sand and gravel extraction. If you notice that the incoming vehicles are loaded it is because they are bringing the excavated material from Wolston Fields Farm for processing here.

After crossing the A445 it is just a further 10 minute walk back to Bubbenhall.

| | |
|---|---|
| Joining points | Bubbenhall – kerbside parking & lay-by on the A445: Stareton – a 'casual' lay-by just before the village: Cubbington & Western under Wetherley – kerbside parking |
| Pubs | Bubbenhall the Malt Shovel (P) and Three Horse Shoes (P). Cubbington – the Kings Head |

## Walking Directions

1. Turn right along Stoneleigh Road and then turn right along Church Road to the church of St Giles. Take the gate and follow the path left of the church to leave by another gate into an open field. Cross the field to take a stile and follow the path to the road. Turn left up the hill and then turn right along the drive to Quarry Field House. After a few yards bear left and follow the footpath and take the stile into a field. The right-of-way goes left through a gate then right to another gate and back into this field, although an unobstructed path continues down the field to take a gate directly to the road.

2. Cross the road, take the gate and cross the field ½ right, via two gates, to the far corner and take the gate. Continue with the hedge on the right and take the gate, then the gate on the right. Turn left along the hedge line at first, then cross the field to marker post and turn right. Follow the ditch/hedge via a gated bridge to cross another bridge and reach the road. Turn left along the road to reach a junction at Tantara Lodge and turn left. Continue to the next junction and turn right. Continue to Stareton, passing

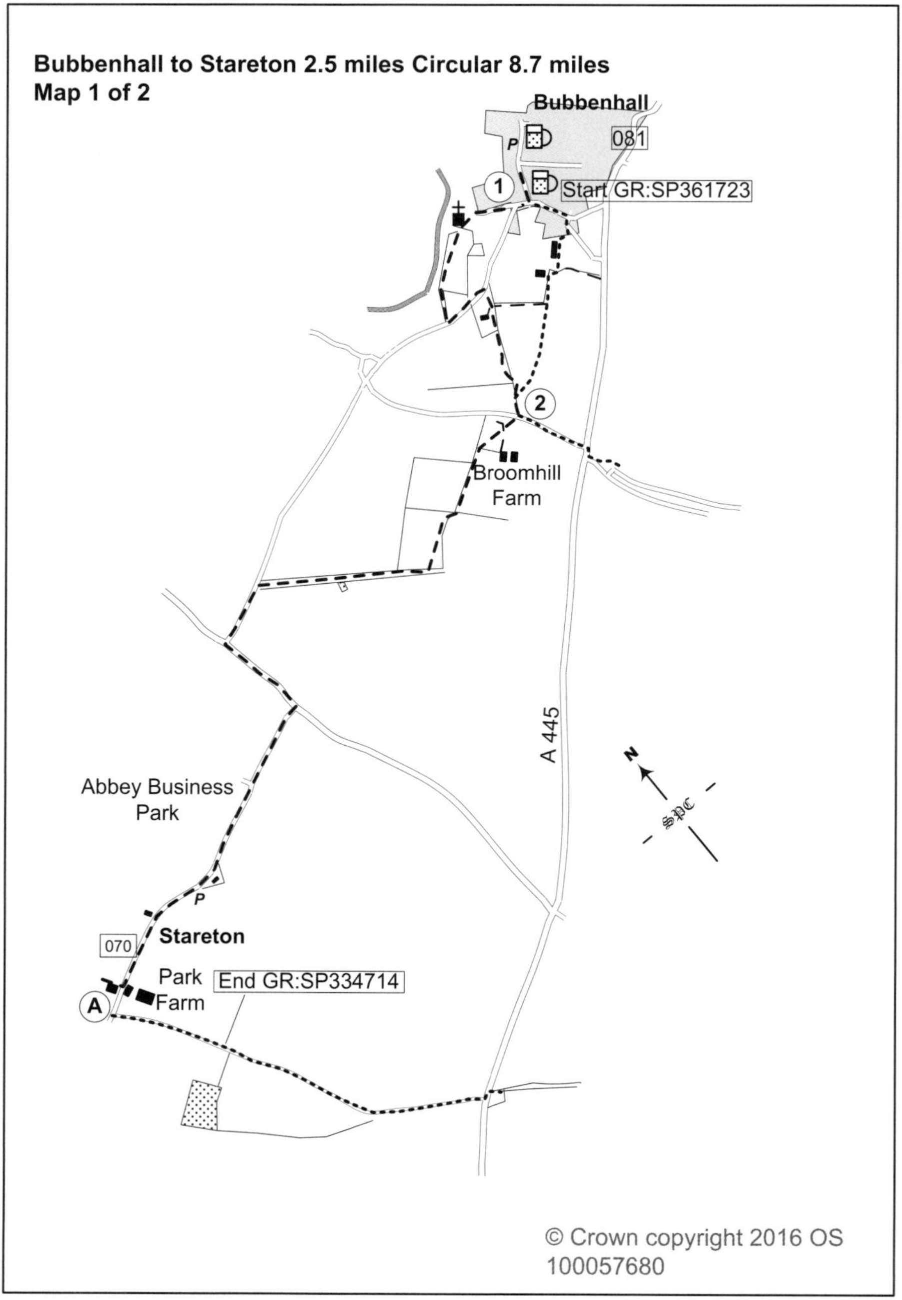
Bubbenhall to Stareton 2.5 miles Circular 8.7 miles
Map 1 of 2
Bubbenhall
P
081
1
Start GR:SP361723
2
Broomhill
Farm
A 445
N
SPC
Abbey Business
Park
P
Stareton
070
Park
Farm
End GR:SP334714
A
© Crown copyright 2016 OS
100057680

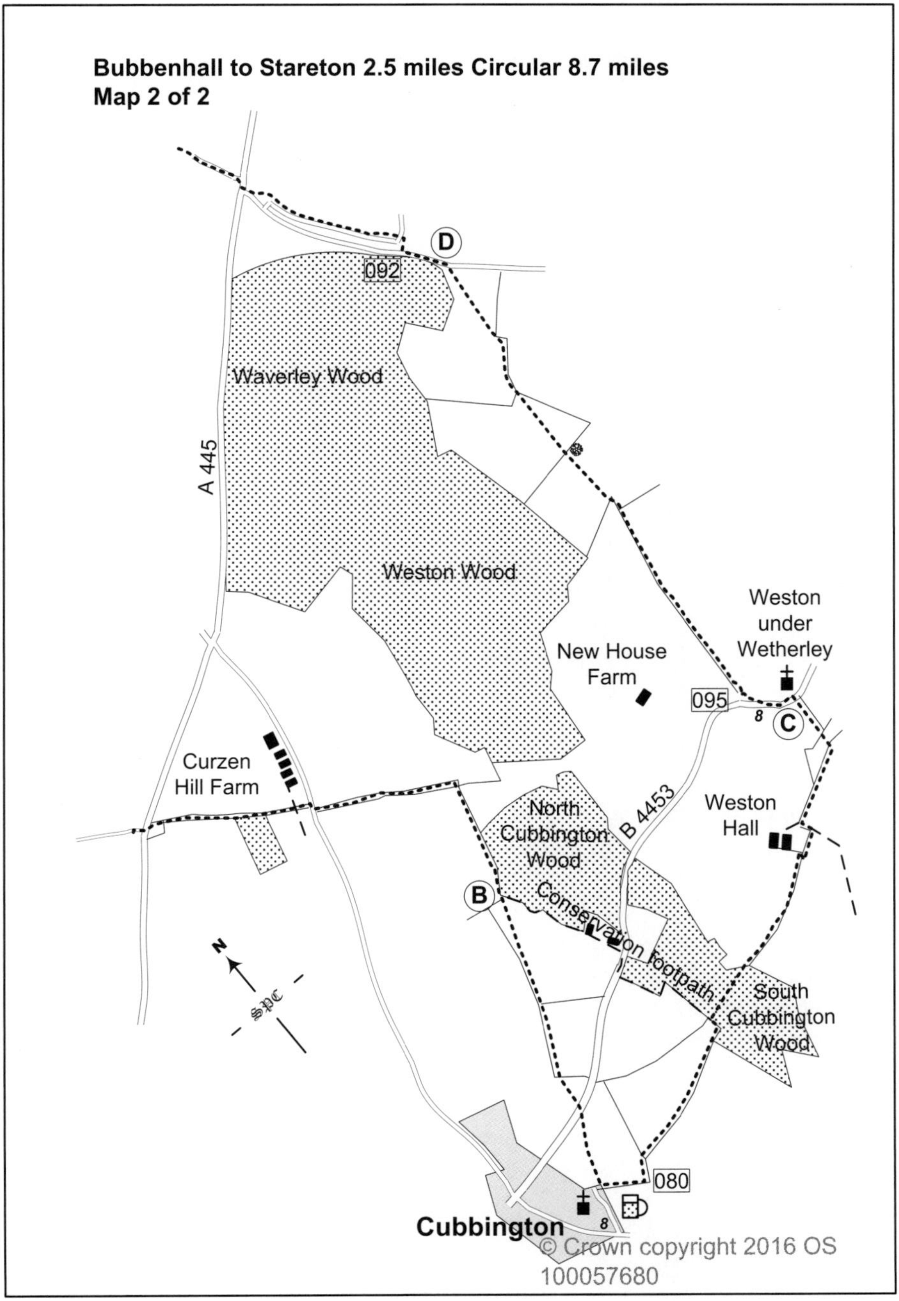

Bubbenhall to Stareton 2.5 miles Circular 8.7 miles
Map 2 of 2
D
092
Waverley Wood
A 445
Weston Wood
Weston
under
Wetherley
New House
Farm
095
8
C
Curzen
Hill Farm
Weston
Hall
North
Cubbington
Wood
B 4453
B
Conservation footpath
South
Cubbington
Wood
N
SPC
080
Cubbington
8

Abbey Business Park, and a small parking lay by on the left. Opposite Park Farm take the footpath on the right next to the post box.

A. *To return to Bubbenhall continue for 130 metres and take the track on the left. Follow the County Road for just over ¾ mile to reach A445. Cross the road left then turn right into the driveway of the house. Keep to the left fence and take the stile and continue straight ahead along the fenced path via a stile then two gates to reach the road. Take the gates either side of the road and continue straight ahead. Follow the fenced path to the end and turn right over the bridge. Follow the edge of the field alongside the wood through the next hedge gap and cross the field ½ right to reach and follow the right hand field edge through the next hedge gap. Continue along the next field edge to the end of the field and go through the hedge gap, cross the field ½ left and cross the road. Cross the field ½ right aiming to the left of the houses and continue to the corner of the field to turn left or alternatively you may wish to make an attractive diversion to the church of St Mary opposite the Kings Head pub.*

B. *Continuing in the field, follow the hedge line around the field taking the first gap through the hedge on the right and over a bridge. Continue with the right hedge line of the next field following left to turn right through South Cubbington Wood. Leave the wood and follow the right hedge line ignoring the conservation walk on the right and at the end of the field cross a bridge. Turn right and left and follow the left hedge line to reach and turn left along the track then right to follow a path along the next left hedge line. As the edge of the field curves right take the bridge/gate on the left and follow the fenced path via another gate to reach the road opposite the church of St Michael at Western under Wetherley.*

C. *Turn left along the road and take the lay by on the right to take the path around the left side of the double gates into the field. Follow the left hedge line through two gaps in cross hedges. At a point where 'new' tree planting has been undertaken the path goes left and right through a hedge gap and crosses the field through a hedge gap continuing into the corner of the next field. Take the gate and follow the path with left hedge line almost to the next corner. The path now strikes ½ left across the field to the far corner and via a gate reaches the road.*

D. *Turn left along the road for 200 metres and take the stile in the fence on the right. Cross the quarry access road and take the stile in the hedge. Turn left and follow the path parallel with the road to eventually return back to the public road. Turn right then right at the junction to cross over the A445 and turn left along the minor road which leads to the Centenary Way crossover point at '2' above. Take the gate on the right and follow the right hedge and take the gate on the right. Although the right of way crosses the field I was advised that crops normally block the field. The normal route is to turn left and follow the field perimeter to reach the stile.Now take the stile and go straight ahead between the barns and turn right then left along the road to Spring Hill.*

## Section 14: Stareton to Kenilworth

Turning off the lane in Stareton we enter the estate of Stoneleigh Abbey. The path drops down and we cross the River Avon, via a stone bridge, and enter the area of the deer park. The park extends back to Tantara Lodge and includes a golf course and the business park. The site of the Abbey is in the western half of the estate, the other side of the Coventry Road.

However the original Abbey site was at Radmore, on Cannock Chase in Staffordshire, where two devout hermits, Clement and Hervey, scratched a living. They must have attracted a following because King Stephen granted to them, and their companions, land for tillage and pasturing their cattle. Seemingly their determination to pursue a monastic existence was often disturbed by foresters and they appealed to Empress Matilda to help them. Her solution was to suggest that if they adopted the faith of the Cistercian order, 'for which she had much affection', then their site could become an Abbey.

Contentment unfortunately did not last, because of the continued 'troublesome and burdensome foresters' and the Abbot petitioned Henry II to transfer them to his manor in Stoneleigh. This was granted and the foundation of the church was laid on 13th April 1155. The order remained until the dissolution, in 1539, when the last Abbot, the twenty-second to serve, retired on an annual, but more miserly pension than the Coombe Abbey Abbot, of £23.

The Abbey was immediately granted to Charles Brandon, Duke of Suffolk and then in 1561, it passed, into the ownership of Sir Thomas Leigh, Lord Mayor of London. The Leigh family quickly brought about major changes, as they developed the estate into a thriving agricultural community. Forty-five houses were built for the workers and their families and also the almshouses, which still stand beside Stoneleigh's village green. They also continued to help the local people by ensuring that provision was made for their education with the building of a school and a library.

In the early part of the 18th century the Grade I listed West Wing range of state apartments, four stories high, were built to designs by the Warwick Architect, Francis Smith. Later the separate Grade II* listed conservatory, stables and riding school were built. Public access to the Abbey is accessed from the B4115 and is open to the public and is undoubtedly worth a visit.

The path continues up the hill and crosses the Coventry Road and continues down into the valley to cross the River Stowe next to the attractive Park Lodge Cottage (GII). To the right across the meadow is the Grade I listed, 12th century church of St Mary the Virgin. As with all the other local churches the red stone parts speak of its Norman origins. The village itself is very much worth a short diversion, having thirty-four separately 'listed' buildings, although no pub. Lord Leigh closed it at the end of the 19th century, when a party of Coventry cyclists, who had stopped for refreshment, whistled and called after his daughter.

From the village the path joins the Coventry Road and then crosses the A46. The 'Way' leaves the road and follows a field path, which crosses the route of

Park Lodge Cottage Stoneleigh

HS2, before threading its way through Kenilworth Golf Course. Kenilworth, it seems, takes it name from the Saxon word Chineworde, which in itself has many derivatives, but refers to Cynehild's farm a common name but less usually, a female.

After leaving the golf course we soon regain a 'soft' path following Finham Brook through Ladyes Hill. We cross under the Coventry and Royal Leamington Spa railway line and continue into the oldest part of the town.

Walking from the junction of Manor Road and New Street to the traffic lights, there are seventeen listed 18th/19th century Georgian buildings. Continuing along High Street the 'parade' of similar buildings is more or less continuous along both sides of the street. Leaving High Street, we take the path around the Grade I listed St Nicholas Church and into Abbey Fields. This park effectively splits the town in two, from its original settlement here and the modern expansion to the south, that accelerated with the arrival of the railway.

The church sits at the north side of the Abbey ruins and dates from the middle of the 14th century. The Augustinian monastery was founded as a priory in about 1124 on the northern part of land granted by Henry I to Geoffrey de Clinton, his chamberlain and treasurer. As you will see, all that remains above ground is the 14th century Gatehouse. The explanation for the dereliction of the buildings is that they were 'robbed out' for use in the castle. However there are displays explaining the layout of all the buildings.

Leaving the park, the 'parade' of attractive listed buildings continues with 17th century cottages on the left and more 'listed' Georgian properties on the right. Around the green, opposite the Castle, there are a group of late 16th century timber framed cottages. Crossing the road the 'Way' follows a narrow path around the southern walls of the Castle, to arrive at Mortimer's Tower on the dam. The dam was the first structure, along with the keep, to be constructed by Geoffrey de Clinton. However, given the castle's military importance, in 1173, King Henry II garrisoned it against his rebellious sons and acquired it outright in the 1180s; compensating Geoffrey de Clinton with property in Buckinghamshire. By the early 13th century King John was building curtain walls and improving the dam to strengthen its defence. However within a few years Henry III passed the castle to his brother in law, Simon de Montfort and the baronial wars ensued and Simon died at the Battle of Evesham in 1265. The war continued and Simon de Montfort junior defied the King and retired back to the castle which resisted a siege for six months. In December 1266 they surrendered and were allowed to leave with their lives spared.

Disagreements continued between the crown and nobility until in 1371 John of Gaunt, fourth son of Edward III, became the owner and started converting it from a feudal stronghold into a palace. On his death, in 1399, his son seized the throne and became King Henry IV. The castle remained of strategic importance even acting as a fortress during the Wars of the Roses.

In 1553 John Dudley was granted Kenilworth by Edward VI, but relationships clearly foundered as he was soon executed. However in 1563 Elizabeth I granted Kenilworth to her own favourite, Robert, John Dudley's son. Robert undertook much work, by way of embellishments to the castle and wholesale remodelling of the landscape.

After Dudley's death, in 1588 Kenilworth was sequestered by the crown. But by 1642, in the opening month of the civil war, the castle was taken by the Parliamentarian army. In 1649, not wishing to maintain the garrison, it was made 'untenable' and the dereliction we see today was undertaken so that the defences were breached. Leicester's Gatehouse remained as it was converted to a house but whatever else had value was robbed out.

The rescue of the castle started in 1937, when the car manufacturer, Sir John Siddeley, bought the castle and put it in the hands of the Ministry of Works, together with substantial funding for repairs. It opened to the public in 1958 and work has continued notably with the recreation of the Elizabethan garden in 2009.

## Walk Directions

| | |
|---|---|
| Joining points | Stareton – only the 'casual' lay by is available: Stoneleigh Road – lay by: Kenilworth – pay and display car parking in Abbey Fields and at the Castle |
| Pubs | Kenilworth the walk passes, in order, the Royal Oak, Virgins & Castle, Claverdon Arms and Queen & Castle |

1. Follow the path from the post box, alongside Stareton Cottage and take the gate through the woods dropping downhill and crossing the open area slightly right to cross the two bridges of the River Avon. From the bridge enter the open meadow and continue uphill ½ left to reach and go through the band of trees alongside the road. Take the gate and turn right to the end of the parking area and cross the road to take the gate opposite. Follow the path through the band of trees and continue to reach the fenced pond and bear right following the left edge of the trees. The path continues picking up a fence on the right, then through a gate downhill to reach and cross the River Sowe. Follow the lane through the junction to keep straight

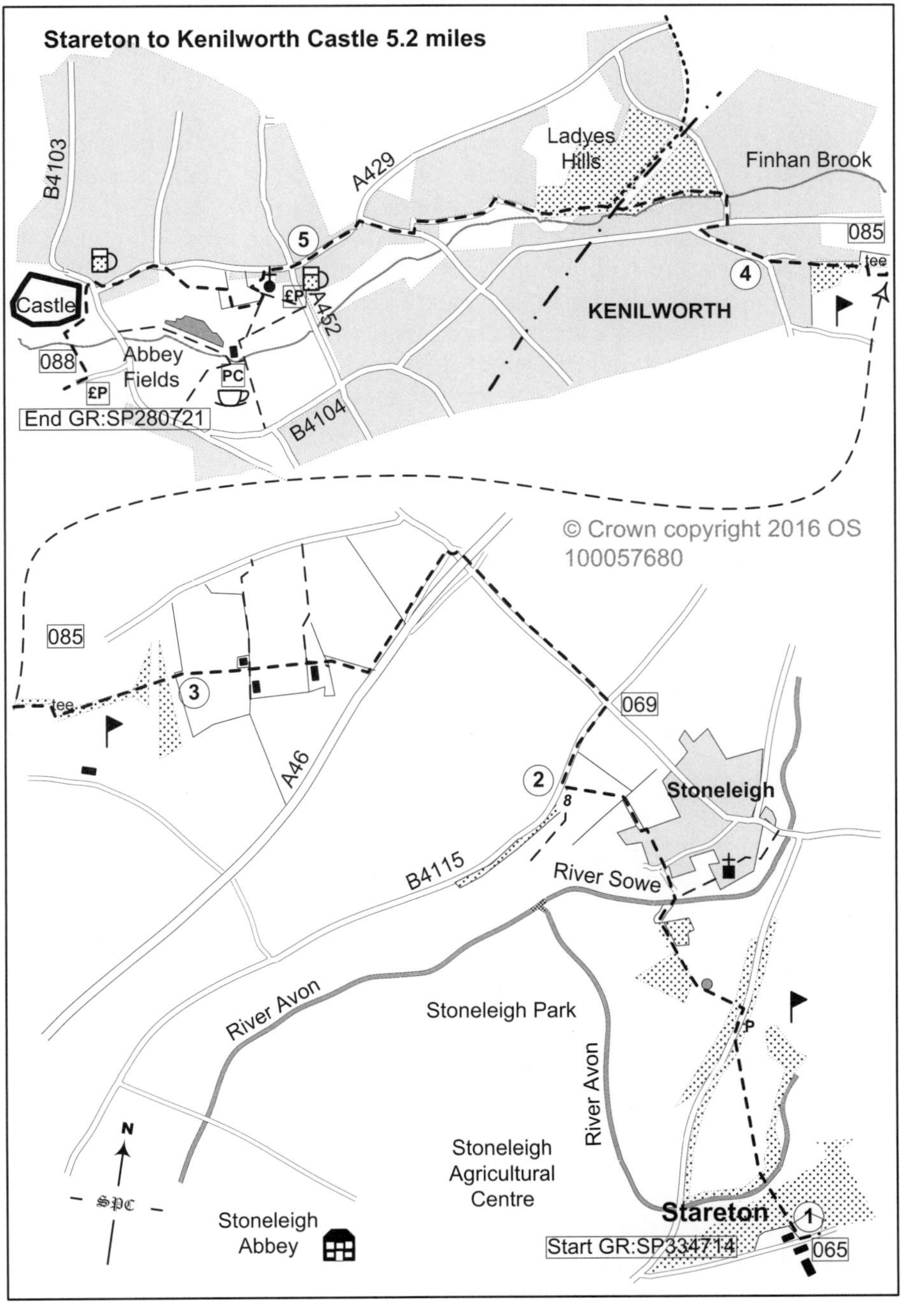
Stareton to Kenilworth Castle 5.2 miles
B4103
Ladyes Hills
Finhan Brook
A429
5
085
4
tee
KENILWORTH
Castle
£P
A452
088
Abbey Fields
PC
£P
End GR:SP280721
B4104
© Crown copyright 2016 OS 100057680
085
3
tee
069
A46
2
Stoneleigh
8
B4115
River Sowe
River Avon
Stoneleigh Park
P
River Avon
Stoneleigh Agricultural Centre
N
SPC
Stoneleigh Abbey
Stareton
1
Start GR:SP334714
065

ahead and take the footpath alongside Holly House. At the end of the path take the gate and continue between the fences across the field to take a gate. Cross the meadow ½ left and take the gate to the road.

2. Turn right along the road to reach the junction with the Stoneleigh Road and turn left. If you walk along the right verge you will find a narrow path where the grass is worn down to the original macadam surface! Continue to cross the slip road from the A46 north and then cross over the road and cross the slip road from the A46 south. You will see a flight of steps descending the embankment to a gate. Take the gate and turn left to follow the hedge line to take a gate. Continue along the hedge line to take the next gate and turn right to follow the fence line. The path enters the drive way adjacent the houses, keep straight ahead to leave the drive via a gate. Cross the field to the left of a house, cross another drive and keep straight ahead across the field to take a gate into the golf course.

3. Take note of the warning signs and follow the way mark posts, cross two fairways and the separating band of trees. Now keep to the same line to follow the left side of the next fairway keeping in the tree line. The way marked path now goes to the left of the 13th tee area and turns right in front of it to pass behind a green. Continue to the edge of the fairway and turn left and follow the line of the trees to exit the course via a gate. Follow the footpath, behind the largely unseen houses, to reach Knowle Hill.

4. Turn right down Knowle Hill and turn right and then left into Common Lane. Cross the bridge over Finham Brook and take the gate on the left to follow the path through Kenilworth Common and Ladyes Hills. Continue under Milbrook Grange railway viaduct, where the path becomes surfaced. Keep straight ahead ignoring paths right and left to join and continue along Lower Ladyes Hill. At the end of this road turn left and then right to continue along Manor Road. At the junction with the New Street (A429) turn left and continue to the 'old' centre of Kenilworth, at the traffic lights.

5. At the junction cross straight over and continue along High Street for about 75 metres and turn left down a drive way to St Nicholas Church. Follow the drive way around the church and turn right to follow the cemetery wall. Keep the wall on your right to the 'barn' and now turn right along the surfaced path, turning left at the next path. Follow the path to the top of Abbey Fields and reach High Street. Turn left along High Street to the junction with the B4103 and cross over to the take the pedestrian

gate adjacent the parking area. Follow the path around the castle walls and climb the steps onto the entrance causeway and turn left to the entrance kiosk and car park.

# CHAPTER 6

## Section 15: Kenilworth to Rouncil Lane

Leaving the Castle the 'Way' follows a bridleway which, except for a short section around Oaks Farm, remains in good walking condition throughout the year. The path is fairly straight, flat and for most of the distance follows the field edge, to reach Rouncil Lane. It seems that originally the lane was called 'Roundshill', perhaps shortened from 'round the hill', which in turn perhaps a cartographer misinterpreted in translating the description given to him in local dialect.

The Ordnance Survey map, unusually, records the name together with the identification 'Park Pale'. The latter term identifies the fence which surrounded the boundary of Wedgnock Park. History attributes the beginning of the Park to Henry de Beaumont, the first Constable of Warwick Castle, who was created Earl of Warwick by William II. Initially the area was quite small and consisted of agricultural land but over the centuries more land was acquired including woodland and a deer park. But it is not until 1253 that history records the Park by name and a little later when it was described as enclosed.

By 1845, purchases, settlements and acquisition had increased the park to a total area of 1146ha; stretching, in a rough diamond shape, roughly 4 miles north to south and 1¾ miles wide. However over the next hundred years the park was gradually sold off, but still remains an area of largely typical rural south Warwickshire landscape.

The 'Way' turns left along the lane and the return route makes a right and left to continue along the bridleway leading along a concrete drive to Goodrest Farm. After about 340 metres, looking to the right, a field appears with concrete emplacements spread across it. A sign on the gate into the field may also carry an explanation. The structures are the remains of the site of the 1940 Bannerhill Second World War anti-aircraft battery. Four of the original 3.7 anti-aircraft gun placements remain, plus a single, partly sunken, control room. This site was one of ten sites that defended Coventry as part of its anti-aircraft defences. Rather controversially, at the time, the site was operated by men and women. Young Auxiliary Territorial Service girls were recruited and trained in spotting, predicting and aiming while the regular soldiers operated the guns. Each gun was capable of firing 20 rounds per minute and the shells could reach up to 30,000 feet.

In 1944 with air attacks no longer active the camp was converted to house about 80 prisoners of war. Local recollection was that security was rather relaxed and prisoners did useful work on the farms and in the local community.

Continuing along the drive, we turn right as the drive continues left to the Grade II 18th century Goodrest Farmhouse. Behind the present building there originally stood a moated house built by Thomas Beauchamp, the 13th Earl of Warwick in 1374. The original Grade II* bridge dated 1441 still stands. The original building was a hunting lodge and may also have provided a resting place on journeys between the two castles.

The bridleway, from Goodrest Farm to Wedgnock Lane, marked the 1550 boundary of Wedgnock Park, although by 1845 it had extended a further 2 miles northwards. The land gradually rises as we reach and turn right along Wedgnock Lane another bridleway which also provides access to the several cottages and farms along it. Our route follows the lane for just over ½ mile before turning right to follow field paths which lead and cross Inchford Brook via a substantial bridge.

We follow and then cross the brook to return to Rouncil Lane. From the lane, after leaving the farm drive and crossing the field, there are two paths. I have chosen the slight climb up the hill. It is the more pleasant route and has the advantage of providing a distant vista of Kenilworth Castle before dropping down the hill and returning to it.

Kenilworth Castle

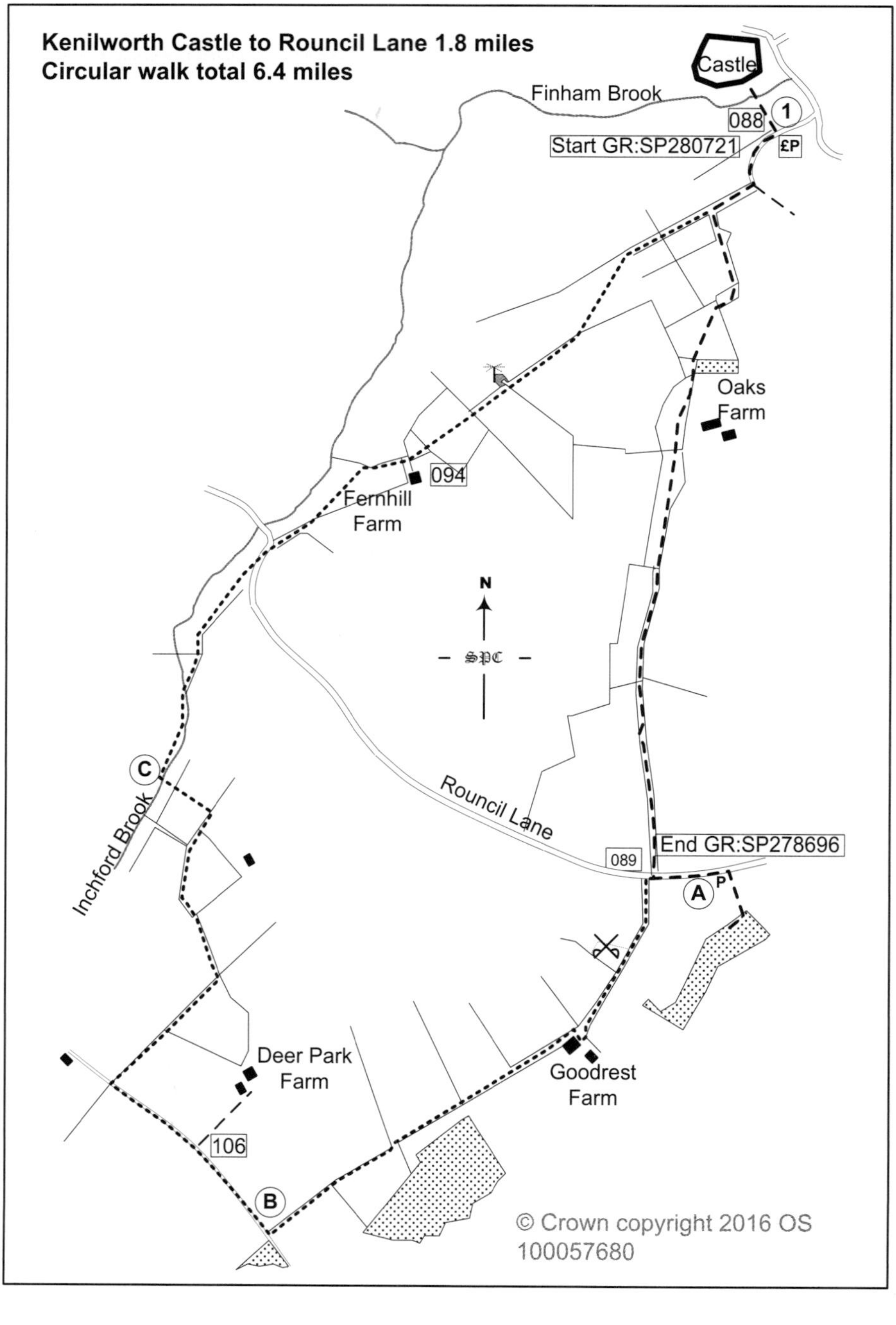

Kenilworth Castle to Rouncil Lane 1.8 miles
Circular walk total 6.4 miles
Castle
Finham Brook
088
1
Start GR:SP280721
£P
Oaks
Farm
094
Fernhill
Farm
N
SPC
Rouncil Lane
End GR:SP278696
089
A
P
C
Inchford Brook
Deer Park
Farm
Goodrest
Farm
106
B
© Crown copyright 2016 OS
100057680

## Walk Directions

| Joining points | Kenilworth – Abbey Fields & Castle pay & display: Rouncil Lane – a large 'casual' lay by |
|---|---|
| Pubs | None on the circuit |

1. With the Castle car park on the left continue along the lane and turn first left. Cross the cattle grid and turn right then left between the fences and continue to take the gate in the corner of the field. Turn right and follow the path, ignoring the gate on the left, to take the gate at the end of the path. Turn ½ left, to cross the field to take the gate and then cross the bridge. Go straight ahead, through three narrow fields taking gates, and then enter a large field and continue along the left hedge line to take a gate into Rouncil Lane. At the lane the 'Way' turns left 200 metres to a lay by and the return to Kenilworth goes right.

A. *Starting from the lay by return along the lane past the gate taken from the field and turn left along the surfaced drive to Goodrest Farm, passing the site of Bannerhill Heavy Anti Aircraft battery. Continue to turn right from the farm drive along side the barns at Goodrest Farm. Take the gate and turn left to follow the bridle way. Continue through three fields taking the gates then, turn left and right, to continue in the same direction to reach a private lane and turn right.*

B. *Follow the lane up a gentle incline to the summit, where the surface changes. Continue down to the bottom of the hill and turn right through a gap in the hedge to take a bridleway. Continue with the hedge on your left through a gate to reach a track and turn left along it to reach two gates on the right. Take the second gate and follow the left hedge line downhill around the field. Ignore the gates on the left to reach the far corner of the field and take the gate. Continue along the left hedge to reach and turn left through a gate on the left. Cross the field, take the next gate then cross the bridge and turn right.*

C. *Follow Inchford Brook and then after 300 metres take a gate and cross the bridge. Follow the path left through a largely overgrown area and take a gate into a field. Continue between the fences to take a gate to Rouncil Lane. Follow the lane left for a short distance and turn right along the drive to Fernhill Farm. After 150 metres, take the gate on the left and cross the field ½ right. At the hedge, ignore the gate and turn right to follow the left hedge up the hill. At the corner take the gate and follow the track through three gates gradually enjoying distant views of the castle. Continue past a transmitter mast, adjacent a pond, and take a gate on the left and cross the field ½ right. Follow the path between the fences through two gates to rejoin the 'Way' and turn left and right back to Kenilworth Castle.*

## Section 16: Rouncil Lane to Guy's Cliffe

Leaving Rouncil Lane we enter the north-west corner of the Warwickshire Golf Course complex; which covers nearly 190ha of land, next to the eastern side of the historical Wedgnock Park. We follow the 'Way' through the woods and around the 9th green of the 'King's Course' and cross Tuttle Brook.

As we leave the wood we enter the area of an Ancient Monument. Historic England's description is: 'Wedgnock Park pale, dam, two watermill sites, bridge and hollow way'. Having rounded the bushes and entered the open meadow, straight ahead is a low bank which forms the dam. To the right is Cuttle Brook and the bridge which carried the hollow way. The full description of the monument, although lengthy, is not helpful in visualising or understanding how the mills operated. As we have discovered with other monuments the site is important because of its archaeological and historical context in the locality. Helpfully, it also states; 'that by 1086 there were over 5,600 corn mills in England'; but no indication is given of when this site was operational.

It is believed that the bridge and hollow way predate the pale which was in place by 1550. The 'pale' is described as a fenced, bank beside a ditch. Although the original 'fence' has gone, evidence of the bank and ditch remain, as we can see as we follow the line along the golf course perimeter. Ahead of us are the woods of Larch Covert which the 'Way' follows via a narrow path at their eastern edge.

At the side of the path are several short concrete posts stencilled MOD which marked the perimeter of the Warwickshire Regiment's '1,000 yard' firing range on the other side of the woods. The range has existed since 1901 but, with the closure of the Regiment's HQ at Budbrooke in 1960, the range was purchased and operated privately. Today you may still hear firing but the area it also a multi discipline outdoor adventure centre.

Continuing along the 'pale' line, the path, which can be rather 'muddy', enters the area of an old quarry. The quarry was briefly reopened in 2012 to provide stone for the repair of the 'the Court House', Warwick Town Council's Grade I listed headquarters. However, quite a large quantity of material was quarried to ensure that the masons would have stock available for any other work to buildings built of the same stone.

Leaving the quarry the 'Way' follows a track and then a footpath alongside the outside of the 'pale', to the corner of the field. As we turn away we enter a large arable area where the old 'pale' line can be seen continuing away to the right. As we cross the area of crops on the right is the Grade II* 17th century Woodloes Farmhouse. We reach Woodloes Lane, just below the house and turn left to follow the lane over the A46 and down the hill. However before reaching the Coventry Road. just after the pair of white cottages. look to the left to see the perimeter wall of the Guy's Cliffe walled garden. A 'Friends Organisation' has been formed to undertake the project to reinstate this garden which would have provided the produce for Guy's Cliffe House.

As we return to Rouncil Lane, along the Coventry Road, we pass the entrance to Guys Cliffe House, which is reviewed in the next section. Next we pass the Saxon Mill pub where a mill first operated on the site in the 12th century, when its name was Gibbeclive. The present building's origins are of the mill constructed in 1822 which remained working until 1938.

After crossing under the A46 we regain the stub of the Kenilworth Road and stand at the bottom of Blacklow Hill. When the A46 was constructed, in 1970, archaeological excavations were conducted and evidence found of human habitation over a period of 20,000 years. The earliest finds were the largest group of Mesolithic flint implements ever collected in the Midlands, as well as Romano British pottery and Saxon burials which contained a sword.

There is also, though not accessible, a memorial dated 1812 to Piers Gaveston, who was executed on the hill in 1312. As with our earlier character, John Beauchamp, finding the favour of the King could prove fatal. Gaveston, was perhaps not so deserving of our sympathy, he revelled in his position as a favourite of Edward I and encouraged Edward II 'in his despotic activities'. Gaveston even taunted the barons of England with nicknames, referring to the Earl of Warwick as the 'Black Dog of Arden'. His end came when, having been brought back from exile by the King, he was captured by the Earl of Pembroke. Despite guarantees of his safety, he fell into the hands of Lancaster and Warwick and after the pretence of a trial he was taken to Blacklow Hill and executed.

We re-enter the golf course and join the perimeter road, before following the footpath into some impressive woods. The County describe the area as: ... 'a small Victorian wooded garden featuring some magnificent mature conifers and some fine broadleaves'. We may wander around the area and perhaps count the 38 broadleaf specimens, but it is the 24 conifers, including various varieties of Sequoia, which are the most impressive. The garden was part of the Wootton Court estate, which extended to 21ha and was the home of the Wright family for two generations until 1952. The house, which is now privately owned apartments, was built in 1860.

The path continues across a wide meadow and then through a field to the churchyard of All Saints Church (GII). The present church was built in 1799, having only a few details of the old Saxon/Norman building. Most of Leek Wotton's houses are 18th century with some Grade II listed. The diversion shown on my map reveals some interesting architecture, but also the village pub, the Anchor Inn. The last stretch of the walk passes the Warwickshire Police Headquarters, which for many years has been for sale. The present grade II listed house was built in 1861 by Henry Christopher Wise, whose family wealth was inherited from his great-great-grandfather who had amassed his fortune as gardener to Queen Anne and retired to Warwick. The property passed through the extended family until in 1948 it was sold to Warwickshire County Council and became the police headquarters.

## Walk Directions

| | |
|---|---|
| Joining points | Rouncil Lane – a large 'casual' lay by: Guy's Cliff – lay by on the A429, by the Saxon Mill pub: Wootton Court – 'dog walkers' car park |
| Pubs | Guy's Cliffe – the Saxon Mill (P): Leek Wootton – the Anchor Inn (P) |

1. From the lay-by, in Rouncil Lane, take the gate and cross the field to take the gate into the environs of the Warwickshire Golf Course. Turn right and follow the path through the perimeter of the woods. The path continues around the right side of a 'green' and right over a bridge. Continue along the path, as it winds through the woods, to take a gate. Turn left and right into a field and follow the left hedge around the field, ignoring the gate into the golf course. Continue to the corner and take the gate and follow the left perimeter, passing a pond and then an old fence line. The path continues through an uncultivated area, which can be very wet and may require a circuitous route to avoid the worst watery conditions. Pass another gate into the golf course and continue into the corner of the field to take a gate into the woods.

2. Follow the well marked path through the woods adjacent to the old Warwickshire Regiment Firing Range. The path gradually falls and goes through the small quarry, used for the repairs at the 'Old Court House', adjacent to two flights of steps. As the path leaves the wood turn right along a track to the bottom of the hill. As the track curves away left

**Rouncil Lane to Guy's Cliffe 2.6 miles**
**Circular Walk Total 5.6 miles**

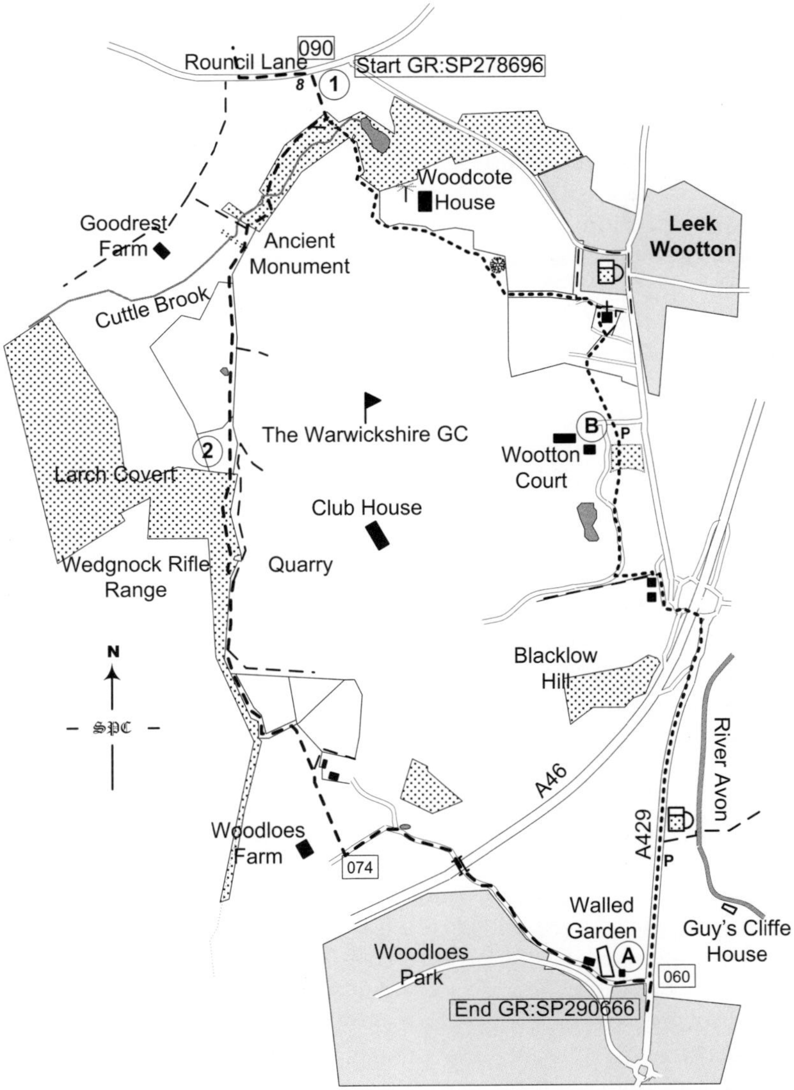

continue straight ahead along a path leading through a hedge gap. Follow the path, between the fence and hedge, around the paddocks to reach a gate. Take the gate and continue straight ahead through the field, passing the houses of Middle Woodloes, to reach Woodloes Lane. Turn left along the lane, ignoring the left turn, and climb the incline to cross over the A46, and continue downhill to reach the A429 Coventry Road.

A. *To return to Rouncil Lane turn left along the Coventry Road to the A46 junction. Follow the footpath around to the left under the flyover. Cross over the slip road and take the steep footpath straight ahead. Turn right at the top and after the second house take turn left along the drive and immediately take the gate on the right. Follow the left fence and at the approach to the golf course road turn right and follow the road. As the road bends left keep straight ahead through the trees and bear left to pass through the tunnel of grape vines to reach the car park.*

B. *Cross the car park and the entrance road through the fence gaps. Climb the hill ¼ left to take a gate then another, cross the drive and take the gate on the right. Keep to the left 'hedge' line to take a gate and cross another drive and take the steps and the gate into the churchyard. If you wish to see more of the Leek Wootton and the pub then follow the dashed line on the map otherwise, exit the churchyard to the right of the church. Turn left and take the footpath to the right of the brick wall. Follow the path through two gates to re-enter the golf course and turn right. The path follows the perimeter of the golf course re-entering the wooded area at the north end of the complex. Follow the path, keeping to the right as it climbs the hill, exit the wood and cross the field back to Rouncil Lane.*

## Section 17: Guy's Cliffe to Newbold Comyn

I live in Woodloes Park and regularly walk the 1¼ miles to the centre of Warwick. The last stretch climbs the hill that lead Æthelflaed, Lady of the Mercians, to build a fortress here in AD 914, and establish Warwick in our recorded history. Æthelflaed was the daughter of King Alfred of Wessex and, at 16 years of age, was married to the much older Æthelred, the ruler of Mercia. Given Æthelflaed's high birth, her husband appears to have been happy to share with her both the government of Mercia and control of its armies.

The fortress at Warwick was one of a network of ten 'burhs' that provided places of refuge for the local communities, control of communication routes and a military base. From the bases the Mercian army could campaign against 'the Danelaw', the lands controlled by the Danish Vikings in the South Midlands and East Anglia. By late 917 the Vikings were either conquered or had surrendered, but Æthelflaed died in June 918 before she could receive their pledges of allegiance.

During the 10th century it is probable, with the establishment of the burh, that Warwick acquired some administrative importance with the shire centred on the town. But it is the physical setting of Warwick and its strategic geographical position near the centre of England that ensured its continuing military importance.

By 1066, with England conquered by the Normans, one of William the Conqueror's first steps was to instruct Thorkell of Arden to improve the defences of the old burh with a ditch and a gate. Thorkell, the Sheriff of Warwickshire, had turned traitor against King Harold, and was one of only two Saxon men permitted by William to retain their status and lands. Two years, later in 1068, the benefit of the established Saxon fort was fully realised. With an uprising in the north, Warwick became the site of one of the chain of motte and bailey castles built to enforce and maintain power over the country.

Warwick Castle Guy's Tower

The death of the 'Conqueror', in 1088, brought his son William II to the throne and the inevitable adjustments to the chain of power. In Warwick he installed Henry de Newburgh as Constable of the Castle and granted him the title, Earl of Warwick. Perhaps the traitor Thorkell deserved no sympathy for even his lands were lost to the new earl, who even adopted the Saxon's emblem of the 'bear and ragged staff', which is retained by the County today.

Over the following 790 years the castle passed through the hands of eight families giving rise to twenty-seven Earls and seven Barons. During those many centuries the title holders and their families have played an extensive part in our history. The castle buildings suffered only a little war damage, as its owners expanded the buildings to provide, at first, more impressive defensive features and then, in later centuries, extensive family apartments. Even Capability Brown has left his imprint on the landscape. The castle was sold in 1978 and today, in the hands of Merlin Entertainments, it still keeps Warwick on the map.

Having climbed the hill we enter Northgate Street, according to the architectural historian Alex Clifton-Taylor, 'the most handsome Georgian street in the Midlands'. On the 5th September 1694, at this point, the Great Fire of Warwick burnt itself out, having devastated the town destroying 157 houses. The magnificent range of buildings on the right are the Grade I listed Old Shire Hall and the Law Courts. Although the original building was not badly damaged by the fire a decision was made to replace it. The gentleman architect Sanderson Miller was engaged, he also designed Hagley Hall, and the present building was completed in 1754.

Since all of the buildings destroyed by the fire were timber framed, it was decided that the new buildings should be non-combustible. The houses were also to conform to a new Act of Parliament setting a standard of design and construction 'for more regular and uniform rebuilding of houses demolished by fire'. The terrace of houses along the left side of the street, were built to the new standards and records remain of the original owners and history of the properties. In the 1930s the whole terrace was purchased by the County Council to house the education department. In 2015/2016 the terrace, now in private hands, was converted back to provide 21th century living space without compromising its Grade II listed significance.

At the end of the street, in the Old Square is the Grade I listed Collegiate Church of St Mary which was founded on this site in 1123. Although destroyed by fire and rebuilt, the crypt remains from the original Norman building as well as the 15th century Beauchamp Chapel. Its history and architecture mirror, celebrate and record the events of the town, county and its regiment.

Continuing along Church Street; both sides are lined with Grade II listed properties; we reach the historical main crossroads of the town. Here it was decided that the four corner houses should be built on a more grandiose scale. On three corners are the larger stuccoed houses and on the fourth, the Court House, the original the home of Warwick Corporation, and the Magistrates Court.

The site had been acquired in 1554 and, although the building escaped the Great Fire, the Corporation determined that they should have a new Headquarters. The architect Francis Smith, a Borough Alderman who had overseen much of the town's reconstruction, was engaged. Building commenced in 1720 and his brief was to construct a building that enhanced the Town and the status of the Corporation.

Warwick Town Council remains as custodians of the Court House, which is Grade I listed, and undertook a £1m refurbishment project, supported by the Heritage Lottery Fund, in 2014. Today the building houses the Warwickshire Yeomanry Regimental Museum and the Visitor Information Centre. Pop in and discover more of the history of the building and the town.

Leaving the Court House along Castle Street, ahead is the late 15th century Okens House. This is a first example of the timber framed buildings which would have filled the streets of the town before the fire. If you have no other opportunity to spend more time in Warwick take a diversion along Mill Street, all the listed properties on both sides of the street form a grade II* listed group.

After leaving the town centre, starting at St Nicholas Park, the 'Way' follows a 3¾ mile green corridor to join the Grand Union canal. We walk beside the River Avon in this popular park which provides entertainment for both participants and the perambulating observer. Leaving the park the path continues alongside the river and goes under the Birmingham and London Marylebone railway line. It opened in 1850 and was operated by the Great Western Railway and originally terminated at Paddington. Next, as we walk behind the Tesco's store there are some significant old concrete wharf walls. These are all that remain of the coal fired Avonside Power Station, that operated here between 1920 and 1973, and was served by a branch from the main railway line.

Our Avon riverside excursion concludes, after passing under the Grand Union Canal aqueduct. A staircase provides a short but steep climb to the tow path. This section of the canal was opened in 1799 by the Warwick to Napton Canal Company, but more of its history is covered in the next section. The view from the aqueduct does not quite reveal the Avon's confluence with the River Leam, which we will shortly be following. The River Leam rises at Hellidon Hill, just over the border in Northamptonshire. The county boundary actually follows the rivers course for a short distance before the Leam turns west to complete its 19 mile journey to the Avon.

Crossing Princes Way the path takes us under the viaduct carrying the Coventry to Leamington Spa railway line which was opened by the London and North Western Railway in December 1844 but terminated a little north of here at Milverton. The line was intended to provide passenger services from Coventry to Kenilworth, Warwick and Leamington. The Milverton Station, a mile from both Warwick and Leamington town centres was to serve both. Its geographical conundrum lead to its name changing eight times, all different permutations of Milverton, Warwick and Leamington. In March 1851 this line was extended as a branch from Milverton to Rugby via Leamington Spa where a new station was built. The line ran parallel to the GWR London line, which had its own separate station opened in 1852.

Passenger services to Rugby ceased in 1959 and the line closed completely in 1965. In 1977 the line was reopened for passenger services linking the north east, Leamington and the south coast via the GWR line.

Meanwhile passenger services between Birmingham, via Leamington, to London ceased in May 1969. Only a few trains a day ran between Leamington and Birmingham until, in 1996, Chiltern Railways won the franchise to re-introduce a Birmingham to London service. The final contribution to the re-introduction of local passenger services will be the opening of a new Kenilworth Station, by the end of 2017.

The 'Way' now enters Victoria Park, the start of the Grade II listed Gardens and Pleasure Grounds which stretch along the River Leam to the edge of Newbold Comyn. After passing the children's play area we reach the Royal Leamington Spa Bowling Club. The impressive greens have public access and every August host the Bowls England National Championships. After we cross the river we enter the Pump Room Gardens complete with its bandstand and the Grade II listed Royal Pump Rooms.

Royal Leamington Spa sprang to prominence because of its saline springs. Although the springs had existed for centuries it was the realisation by the landowners that their health giving qualities could generate a business opportunity. In 1784 Abbott's Original Baths were opened and others followed. In 1801 the parish of Leamington Priors had a population of 310 people, living mostly south of the river, but by 1828 the population had exploded to over 5,000 people and the growing town had expanded northwards.

The Pump Rooms, and Assembly Rooms opened in 1814, were the start of the regency style development north of the river. The visit by Queen Victoria in 1830 could only have helped to promote the towns place in the social calendar and her granting of the title 'Royal', in 1838, must have sealed it. Certainly its

The Royal Pump Rooms

popularity as a place to not only visit but live is confirmed by the 1851 census figure of 15,724. Before we cross 'The Parade', the main street through the town centre, a visit to the Pump Rooms can provide refreshment as well as an insight into the visual history of the Spa in the museum and art gallery.

Across from the Pump Rooms are Jephson Gardens which, when they were opened in 1846, were named in honour of Dr Henry Jephson for his services to the town. He came to the town at the age of 20, in 1818, to work for Charles Chambers, who was Surgeon Extraordinary to the Duke of Clarence. Jephson completed his studies and eventually became a partner in the practice as a surgeon apothecary. His success possibly out-shone his mentor, for the local chamber of business acknowledged his ability to attract the 'sick and opulent from all parts of the Kingdom'.

Undoubtedly Jephson became a very wealthy man, but he devoted much of his time to philanthropic causes in support of the town and its people. His hard work did not reward him physically for by the age of 50, he was blind. In retirement he lived, until his death at the age of 79, in the care of his family.

The next part of the green corridor is Newbold Comyn. This was farmland in the ownership of the Willes' family for over 400 years until they sold it to Leamington Corporation in the 1960s. From the Leisure Centre we climb to the top of the Campion Hills, with views across the town and then follow an urban route and finally field paths to return to Guy's Cliffe. A footpath behind the houses leads us down into Lillington and then its old village centre.

The area around the Grade II* listed church of St Mary Magdalene provides a small oasis of a bygone day. Unfortunately the church's 14th and 15th century origins have been overtaken by the 19th century alterations. On the opposite corner to the church stands the Manor House, dated around 1700, the building and its railings, gates and piers are Grade II listed. The 1894 OS map reveals that the area around the church, still stood alone outside the creeping urban area. The first housing lined the west side of Lillington Road and both sides of Kenilworth Road but with no development between. The map also shows a tree lined Northumberland Avenue still awaiting its housing development.

From Northumberland Avenue we cross the fields to reach the picturesque hamlet of Old Milverton, which has also largely escaped the passage of time. The church of St James (GII), despite its pleasant setting, was rebuilt in 1880 and funded by Lord Charles and Lady Anne Bertie-Percy. The last stage on the walk follows a path down to the River Avon, with a view of the sad remains of Guy's Cliffe House.

The history of Guy's Cliffe is very much tied to Warwick Castle and their support, over the centuries, of the site as a home for religious hermits. However, after the dissolution of the monasteries, the site was sold and in 1547 a

Derelict Guy's Cliffe House

substantial mansion was built. Ownership passed through various hands until, in 1750, it was purchased by the Bertie-Percy family. They had land in Leamington Spa which they sold or developed during the town's boom years, generating new wealth to support their aspirations at Guy's Cliffe. But their financial success was not sustained and Guy's Cliffe was vacated in 1939. Its sad decline commenced, despite several attempts by property companies to realise its commercial potential. In 1992 a major fire occurred during the filming of a TV episode of *Sherlock Holmes*, leaving the desolate ruin that we can see today. The property is owned by Guy's Cliffe Masonic Properties who occupy a small area, still intact. Hopes remain that the rest of the property can be rescued.

The final step of this history filled walk re-crosses the River Avon weir at the picturesque Saxon Mill.

## Walking Directions

| | |
|---|---|
| Joining points | Guy's Cliff – lay–by on the A429, by the Saxon Mill pub: Newbold Common – free car park: Warwick – Cape Road free car park outside business hours: all town centre street and car parks are pay & display |
| Pubs | Guy's Cliffe – the Saxon Mill: Newbold Comyn – the Newbold Comyn Arms: Town Centres have many pubs |

1. From Woodloes Lane turn right along the Coventry Road for about ⅔ of a mile, crossing the roundabout, the Grand Union Canal and the junction with Guys Cross Park Road. Continue to reach house no. 29 and take the footpath between the properties on the right to reach Lakin Road. Turn left, opposite the Wild Boar pub, and then right along Woodcote Road to reach the rear entrance of the railway station. Now turn right to take the footpath alongside the railway embankment and continue to reach and turn left through the 'tunnel' under the railway. Follow this path up the hill, alongside Priory Park, to reach Cape Road adjacent a large car park available only outside business hours.

2. Cross the road and turn left to reach the junction with the A445. Cross this busy road via the pedestrian refuge and turn right and left into Northgate Street. Continue along the street passing the old County Court Buildings and then under the tower of St Mary's Church. Joining Church Street continue down the hill to cross over Jury Street into Castle Street, passing the Old Court House, headquarters of Warwick Town Council.

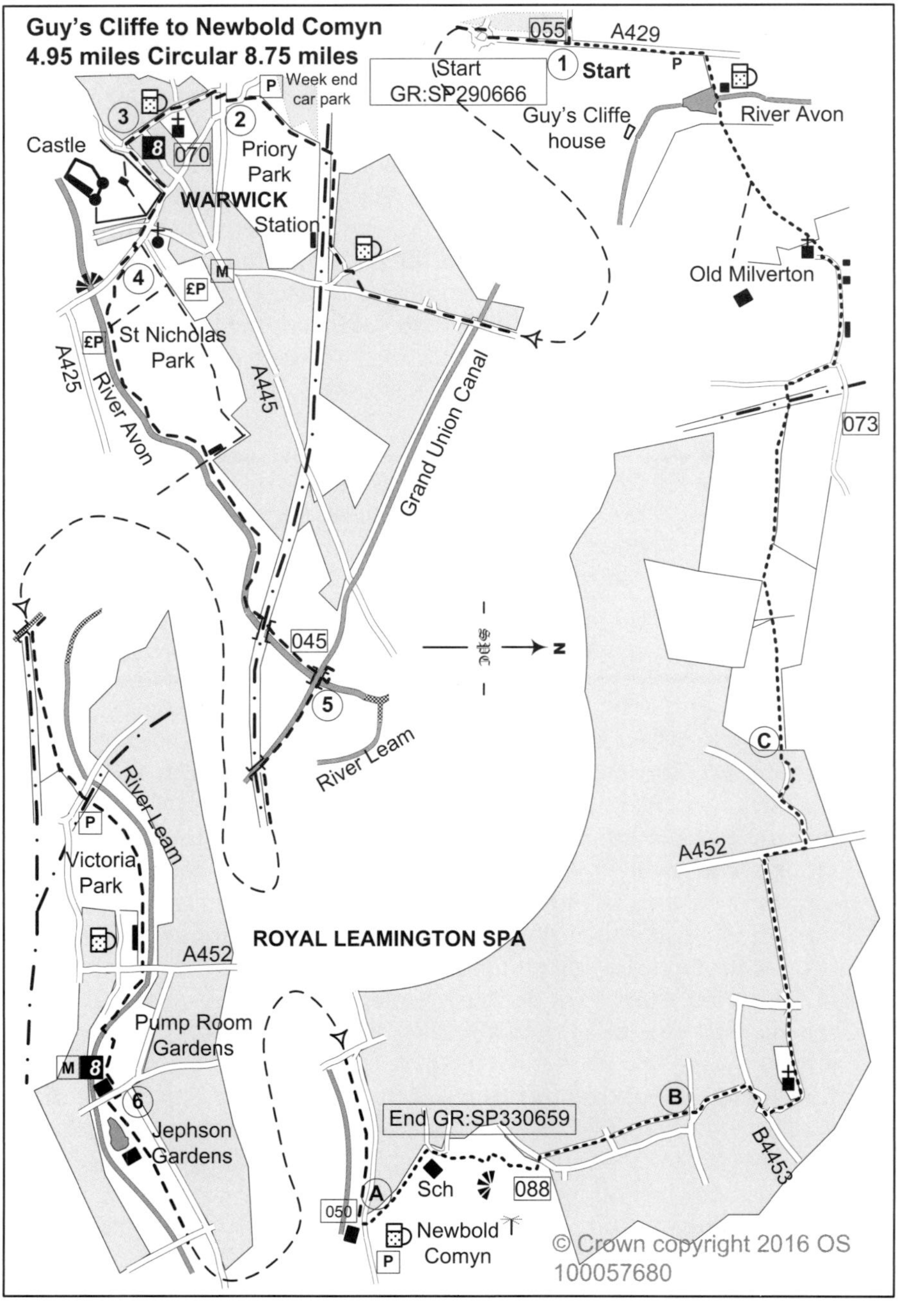

Guy's Cliffe to Newbold Comyn
4.95 miles Circular 8.75 miles
Start
GR:SP290666
1 Start
055
A429
P
Week end
car park
Guy's Cliffe
house
River Avon
3
2
Castle
8
070
Priory
Park
WARWICK
Station
Old Milverton
4
M
£P
£P
St Nicholas
Park
A425
River Avon
A445
Grand Union Canal
073
045
5
River Leam
N
C
P
River Leam
Victoria
Park
A452
A452
ROYAL LEAMINGTON SPA
Pump Room
Gardens
M 8
6
Jephson
Gardens
B
End GR:SP330659
B4453
A
Sch
088
050
Newbold
Comyn
P
© Crown copyright 2016 OS
100057680

3. Carry on along Castle Street and turn left along Castle Lane. If the Castle car park is open, to your right, you can turn in and take the steps ahead to follow the path through to the exit onto Mill Street, otherwise at the end of Castle Lane turn right along Castle Hill to cross Mill Street and reach the pedestrian crossing. To enjoy the view of the Castle from the bridge carry on, otherwise cross at the pedestrian crossing and continue towards the river.

4. At the main gates turn into St Nicholas Park, taking the wide footpath and then turning right to the bank of the River Avon. Turn left to follow the riverside path to eventually pass the old boat house and cross the cycle/footpath. Continue along the top of the grass bank to join a footpath which bends right and continues alongside the curves of the river. In 400 metres the path goes first under the railway and then next the Ground Union Canal aqueduct, with its continuous pressure relief valve discharging from the soffit of the structure. On the other side of the structure turn left to reach and climb the steps up to the canal.

5. Turn left along the tow path, and continue to reach and take the signed 'Link to Princes Drive' alongside the railway line cutting. Follow the path, which joins the side of the River Leam at a narrow point next to the water reclamation works and the boundary between Warwick and Royal Leamington Spa, continuing to emerge on Princes Way. Cross the road, at the pedestrian crossing, go under the railway viaduct to follow the path alongside the Leam around the edge of Victoria Park. Pass the Bowls Club, which hosts the English National Championships each August. Continue along the path, under the road and then take the steps down and turn left over the river into the Pump Room Gardens. Take the path right to the Royal Pump Rooms.

6. If you wish to taste the waters then turn in front of the colonnaded frontage to the far side of the building, to a plinth with a tap, otherwise cross 'The Parade' and go right then left through the gates into Jephson's Gardens. Follow the main path through the impressive gardens, passing the Temperate House, to the exit at Willes Road. Cross the road and follow the footpath to the side of the woods to join the surfaced path alongside the road into Newbold Comyn and reach the Leisure Centre.

A. *To return to Guy's Cliffe, at the first 'speed hump' cross the road and follow a path through the trees. Turn left around the edge of the pitch and putt course and take the footpath between the houses and the school and reach the road. Turn right go past the school and as the road bends right go straight ahead to take the footpath. After 50 metres take the right turn which snakes to the top of Campion Hill. Follow the path to the exit at Leicester Street. Cross the road turn right then left to follow a path behind the properties. The path then follows Gresham Place crosses Whitethorn Drive and continues behind the properties to reach and turn left along Pound Lane.*

B. *Follow the road to reach and turn right along the Cubbington Road and then turn left along Vicarage Road and pass the church of St Mary Magdalene. Turn left along Church Lane and then cross Lillington Road to walk the length of the tree lined Cloister Crofts and reach Kenilworth Road. Now turn right then left into Northumberland Road. Follow this tree lined avenue to reach and turn right along the modern development of Bamburgh Grove. At the end of this cul de sac take the gate into open fields.*

C. *Follow the well trodden path along the right field perimeter through a hedge gap to next field corner. Cross the field ¼ left continuing to the next field corner and continue straight ahead to cross the field to the next field hedge line. Follow the hedge line to cross the railway and turn right along Old Milverton Road. Follow the road and turn left at the T-junction. Continue through the hamlet of Old Milverton to enter the churchyard of St James the Great. Follow the path right of the church and take the gate into the field. Cross the field, following the footpath, down the hill to take the gate and cross the River Avon at the Saxon Mill pub. Walk through the terrace area and follow the path to the Coventry Road and turn left to reach the starting point.*

# CHAPTER 7

## Section 18: Newbold Comyn to Longhole Bridge

The 'Way' continues through Newbold Comyn and drops down to follow the River Leam. A short walk along the road leads us back on to the Warwick to Napton canal. A 1794 Act of Parliament granted the licence for the construction of a canal from Warwick to Braunston. However this act was amended in 1796, when the companies engineer recommended that the canal should terminate at a junction with the Oxford canal at Napton, and save £50,000. When the canal opened, in 1800, it linked Birmingham to London via the River Thames at Brentford.

Railway viaduct of the Grand Union Canal

Despite the competition from the railways in 1929 the Grand Union Canal Company was formed with the Regents Canal Company purchasing all of the separate companies between London and Birmingham. This was the first stage to make operating the system more efficient. The next stage was the equivalent to the modern dualing of our single carriageway roads. The Government funded the doubling of the lock width from Braunston to Birmingham. This was completed in 1934, although the final flight into Birmingham was judged too costly and not undertaken. The intention of the project was to enable bigger 12'6" wide boats to operate along the canal, but it did not happen. Instead it did enable two pairs of the traditional boats travelling together to negotiate the locks at the same time and quicken their journey.

At all the locks the original lock channel remains at one side as you will see from the first lock. Beyond the first lock is the viaduct that carried the London and North Western Railway's line between Milverton, Leamington and Rugby. A footpath from the towpath joins the old line which is now a 'greenway' as far as Welsh Road.

From Longhole Bridge the return path joins Welsh Road and then follows a cross country path leading to the outskirts of Offchurch. There is a legend that surrounds the village which originates from its name and its relationship with King Offa. Offa was the Saxon King who built Offa's Dyke to keep the Welsh out of England. Legend has it that Offa had a palace here and that his son Edmund was murdered and buried in its grounds. But no records or evidence of a palace has been found, just traces of an Anglo Saxon cemetery.

The Grade II* listed Church of St Gregory's nave and chancel are both original from the turn of the 11/12th century. We leave the village via a path leading through the parkland of Offchurch Bury. The estate, previously the seat of the Earls of Aylesford, is privately owned and the manor house, which is not accessible, has it origins from the time of Henry VIII. The park hosts equestrian events, which include cross-country, as can be seen from the jumps, but include three day eventing as well as polo, and carriage driving

After crossing the River Leam, the path takes us via fields and across the Comyn back to our starting point.

## Walk Directions

| | |
|---|---|
| Joining points | Newbold Comyn – free car parking: Longhole Bridge – 480 metres from the bridge at Welsh Road there is a 'casual' lay by: Offchurch – kerbside parking |
| Pubs | Newbold Comyn – Newbold Comyn Arms: Offchurch – the Stag (P) |

1. From the Leisure Centre continue straight ahead along the road for about 500 metres to reach the road barrier. Turn right, through the play area, to the far left corner to a way mark post. Take the footpath downhill through the trees and take the gate to the River Leam. Follow the riverside path to reach and turn right along a footpath via a bridge over the river. Continue through the car park to the A425 and turn left. Cross the road at a pedestrian refuge, continue past the last house and take the steps to the canal and turn left along the tow path.

2. Continue for just over a mile passing under the old railway viaduct numbered 33a, where the Offchurch Greenway branches off. (If you wish you can take this to complete a short circular route intercepting the main return route at the footbridge.) Otherwise continue along the tow path going under bridge no. 32, at the Fosse Way. The canal now climbs through three locks to reach Longhole Bridge no. 31. Turn right across the bridge to continue along the 'Way' or left to return to Newbold Comyn.

*A. Follow the track to reach Welsh Road and turn left following the road past Welsh Road Farm for 100 metres to take the marked footpath on the left through the hedge gap. Turn right following the right hedge and at the top of the field turn left to continue to the corner of the field. Turn right through the hedge gap and cross the drive to continue straight ahead with the left hedge. At the end of the field, turn left and right through the hedge gap and continue along the right hedge, to reach the Fosse Way. Cross this busy road with care and take the hedge gap slightly left opposite.*

*B. Cross the field, straight ahead, to the right of Fosseway Cottage, and continue along the left hedge through the next hedge gap. Follow the right hedge to go through the next hedge gap. Cross the field ½ right to the corner (crops) and continue on the same line to the hedge gap and the bridge over the Offchurch Greenway. Cross the bridge and reach the road crossing over to go along Village Street then turn right down School Hill. At the junction, unless diverting to the Stag pub on the right, turn left and just past the White Cottage on the left take the stile.*

*C. Follow the left fence and then continue straight ahead across the field and take the stile. Follow the right edge of the field and then swing left at the way mark post to cross to a drive and turn right. Follow the drive downhill to a band of trees and turn left to walk between a fence and the trees. Cross the next drive, adjacent to the horse eventing jump, to continue straight*

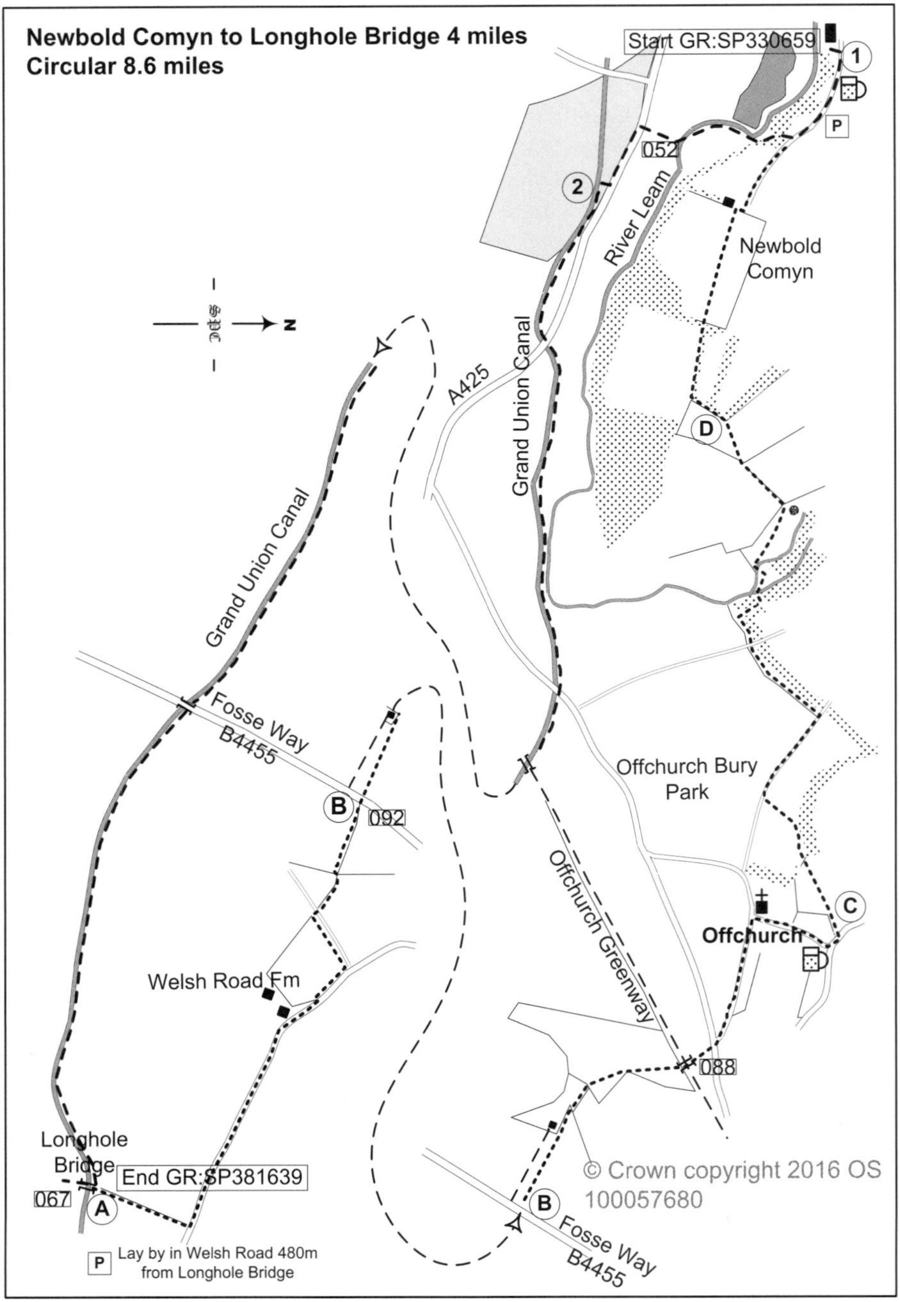
Newbold Comyn to Longhole Bridge 4 miles
Circular 8.6 miles
Start GR:SP330659
1
P
052
2
River Leam
Newbold
Comyn
N
A425
Grand Union Canal
D
Grand Union Canal
Fosse Way
B4455
B
092
Offchurch Bury
Park
Offchurch Greenway
C
Offchurch
Welsh Road Fm
088
Longhole
Bridge
End GR:SP381639
067
A
B
Fosse Way
B4455
P
Lay by in Welsh Road 480m
from Longhole Bridge
© Crown copyright 2016 OS
100057680

*ahead and then around to the right to join and turn left along the next track. Take the stile and cross the bridge over the River Leam and turn right following the footpath to take a second bridge over another arm of the Leam. From the bridge turn sharp right up the centre of the field heading left of a large tree to take a stile on the left. Follow the right hedge to a gap in the hedge and go through it and cross the next field ½ left and take the gate back into Newbold Comyn.*

D. *Continue left along a path, passing the end of the golf course on the right, to a large open area. Turn right follow the hedge line and go straight ahead through the band of trees and take a gate. Cross the area of football pitches aiming to the right of the distant changing rooms. Turn right and left from the building to follow the road which leads back to the Leisure Centre.*

## Section 19: Longhole Bridge to Harbury

After the canal we turn south and enter the south Warwickshire Lower Lias Claylands. In the medieval period these were intensively cultivated and became known as the 'Feldon' or field land. However in the 15th and 16th centuries, social and economic pressures were driving changes to farming and land management practices. In the Feldon, estates were enclosed and the land turned over to pasture for sheep and cattle. Today much of the land once again supports cereal crops growing in prairie size fields.

The approach to Ufton is a steep climb up the face of a glacial escarpment to the summit and the Church of St Michael (GII*). A church has stood here since the 13th century but was then only a nave and a chancel. The greater part of the building is 14th and 15th century. Before that, in 1043, the Earl of Leofric granted Ufton to the Coventry Priory and it remained in their hands until the Reformation. By 1291 the monks derived an annual revenue of £21 6*s* plus 6*s* 8*d* for a windmill.

After the reformation the manor changed hands a number of times until it was purchased by John Snell, a Scotsman and graduate of Glasgow University. On his death, in 1679, he bequeathed the manor and lands, then worth £450 per year, for the maintenance of Scottish students at the University of Oxford. In 1693 the Court of Chancery directed that Snell's bequest should be vested in the interests of Balliol College. Helpfully the village website confirms that the fund still exists and that the economist Adam Smith (1723-1790) was one of the first benefactors of John Snell's scholarships. Smith appears on some £20 notes and is considered to be the father of modern economics.

Leaving Ufton, the 'Way' goes through the edge of the Ufton Fields Nature

Reserve. This 100 acre site is managed by the Warwickshire Wildlife Trust and is a SSSI. The area was a 1950s limestone quarry which was haphazardly backfilled and surrounded by non native trees. The rest of the site was allowed to recolonise naturally. This has left a mixed landscape of grass, scrub, woodland and wetland that supports 41 rare species of invertebrates, butterflies, dragonfly, abundant water life as well as bird and mammal species.

From here the route is largely a gradual descent to the Birmingham Marylebone railway line which carries 50 freight trains and 80 passenger trains a day. The cutting to the left was a major feat of engineering when Brunel built the line in 1847. The excavation was undertaken entirely by hand and at 34 metres deep it was then the largest man-made cutting in the world. It took 5 years to complete although the original intention was to have built a tunnel but the underlying Blue Lias clay proved too unstable.

This lack of stability has proven an ongoing problem ever since. From time to time there has been subsidence but on the 31st of January 2015 there was an enormous landslip extending 150 metres from the tunnel entrance and 350,000 tonnes of material cascaded down towards the tracks. Network Rail had the line re-opened in six weeks. However civil engineering works continued for many months, both to remove the total of 560,000 tonnes of material and to create a better slope profile and undertake all of the remedial works.

Harbury Mill

The path now enters Bull Ring Farm Road and climbs steeply into Harbury the names origin is Saxon, that of 'a fortified place belonging to a woman named Hereburgh'. It is quite a large village, which even in 1730 had 148 houses many of which today are 17th and 18th century, built of either stone or brick. It also had a reputation for having the most public houses of any village which was created by the 'temporary' population of so many thirsty railway navvies.

All Saints Church (GII) is 13th century, but much altered and it seems that the West Tower suffered subsidence from early on, judging by underpinning buttresses at the west corner. Next to the church is the school house (GII) founded by Thomas Wagstaffe in 1611. The Wagstaffe's were a prominent Harbury family of some generations. The most widely known family member was Sir Joseph Wagstaffe 'a soldier of fortune'. In the civil war he fought for Cromwell, however, after his capture and imprisonment by the royalists in January 1643, he changed sides. It seems his flexible attitude was accepted as he was promoted to Major-General and then knighted for his soldierly retreat in the disastrous Battle of Langport. In 1655 the western royalists asked Wagstaffe to lead them in a rebellion against Cromwell. He led the Penruddock uprising, entering Salisbury and declared it for Charles II. This success was not sustained and as he led his troops into Somerset they were taken or dispersed. Wagstaffe escaped to Holland and after the restoration he sought reinstatement by the King, but only received a small pension.

Leaving Harbury, after crossing the railway line, it is a cross-country route which, after passing Ufton Hill Farm, circles Stratford upon Avon's main landfill site. After crossing the A425 the path goes through the parkland of Stoney Thorpe Hall, and the adjacent Polo Club. The whole estate was purchased by Dr Dallas Burston who developed the polo complex and renovated the Grade II listed hall. The source of his wealth is pharmaceuticals and he can be found in the Sunday Times Rich List.

After leaving the estate and crossing Welsh Road the route crosses a few fields and via a lane and the Grand Union Canal towpath returns to Longhole Bridge.

If you decide to undertake this walk as two circles then the path follows the southern edge of Long Itchington and Ufton Wood. The wood which has an area of 79ha has SSSI status. It is described as one of the better oak-hazel coppice woodlands in the Midlands. The wood has a mixture of flora as well as species not commonly found in Warwickshire and is also noted for its fungi. The coppice re-growth is also important habitat for breeding birds, including warblers, green and great spotted woodpeckers and tawny owls.

## Walk Directions

| | |
|---|---|
| Joining points | Longhole Bridge – 480 metres from the bridge at Welsh Road there is a 'casual' lay by: Ufton and Harbury – kerbside parking |
| Pubs | Ufton – the White Hart (P): Harbury – the Crown, Gamecock and the Shakespeare Inn (all close by) |

**Longhole Bridge to Harbury 2.9 miles**
**North Circuit 5.6 miles, Overall outer circuit 8.3 miles**
**Map 1 of 2**

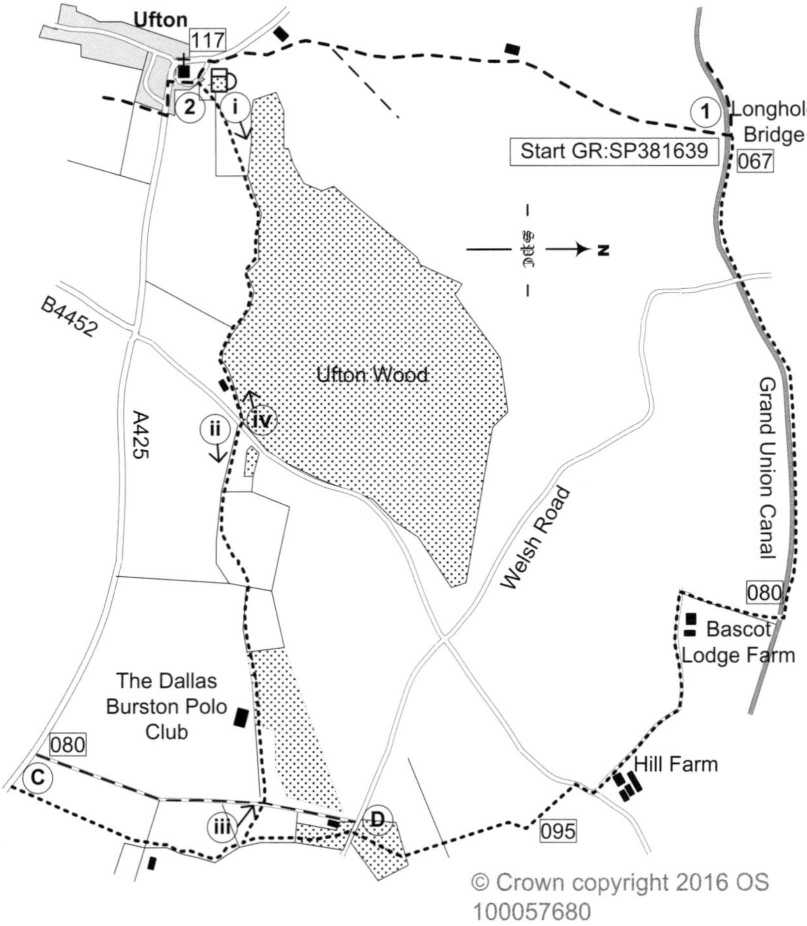

1. At Longhole Bridge, numbered 31, cross over the canal and follow the wide unsurfaced 'County Road'. Continue for one mile to reach the A425 road and turn left. Climb the hill turning left, as the footway stops, into White Hart Lane between the pub and the Church of St Michaels at Ufton. To return to Longhole Bridge go to paragraph (i) otherwise, to continue along the 'Way,' follow the lane and cross over the A425 and turn left then, just after St Michael's Close, turn right into the drive leading to the allotments.

2. Keep straight ahead continuing along a footpath and take a gate. Follow right perimeter, take a gate and follow the path right through Ufton Fields Nature Reserve. Take the next gate keeping to the right and then take a gate to the lane. Turn right follow the road to the bend and take the gate on the left. Cross the field, towards a wide hedge, take the gate to continue along the right side of the hedge. Continue through four gates and pick up a track following it towards the farm complex. Just before the farm take the gate left to follow the footpath and join Bull Ring Farm Lane crossing the railway bridge. Continue up the lane to reach Hall Lane and Harbury.

A. *Turn left along Hall Lane and continue to the B4452 and turn left, crossing the unseen railway far below. Immediately after 'Water Tower Buildings', take the footpath on the right and follow the right hedge to a gap. Turn right and left to follow the left hedge to take the stile on the left. Cross the field towards the distant barns of Ufton Hill Farm to the right of the pylon. Leave the field via the gate and follow the seasonally wet farm perimeter then hedge to take a gate. Continue ½ left, take a gate then follow the ditch downhill to and take a gate into an open area.*

B. *Turn left and follow the left perimeter to join a track passing a derelict 'shed'. Just before the track reaches a locked gate bear right along a worn wet path through woods. Leaving the trees continue to take a stile/gate and through another band of trees. Take the next stile/gate and cross the field, downhill, to the left of a large tree. Take the gate and follow the right hedge to reach and cross over the A425.*

C. *Entering the Polo Club Estate, cross the parkland slightly left of the distant large house and pick up the marker posts leading alongside a steel fence to take a gate. Continue straight ahead and cross the field and take the next gate. If returning to Ufton go to para. (iii) otherwise, continue along the bottom of the field and take the next gate. Follow the footpath through the woods to cross the road.*

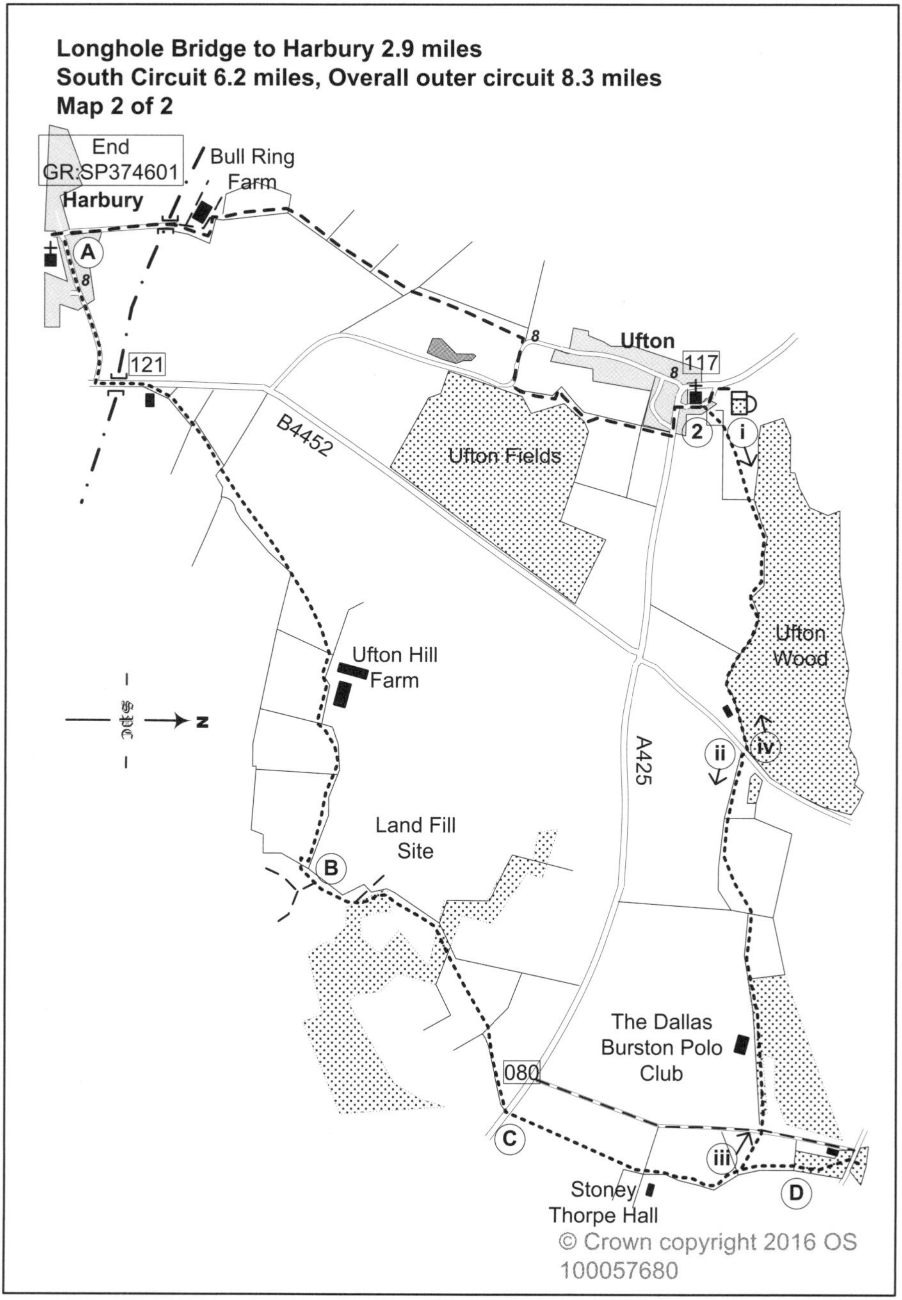

Longhole Bridge to Harbury 2.9 miles
South Circuit 6.2 miles, Overall outer circuit 8.3 miles
Map 2 of 2
End
GR:SP374601
Bull Ring
Farm
Harbury
A
8
121
B4452
8
Ufton
117
8
2
i
Ufton Fields
Ufton Hill
Farm
Ufton
Wood
N
A425
ii
iv
Land Fill
Site
B
The Dallas
Burston Polo
Club
080
C
iii
D
Stoney
Thorpe Hall
© Crown copyright 2016 OS
100057680

D. *Take the footpath through the wood and now cross the field on the same line to a marker post. Keep straight on to join track turning right to reach the road. Turn right then left into 'Pudding Bag Lane'. Continue along the lane then track passing Bascot Lodge Farm. Take the right turn along the track to the Toll House and join the Grand Union Canal, via a path on the left, at the Bascote Lock flight. Continue west along the canal to return to Longhole Bridge.*

i. ***Return to Longhole Bridge.*** *Pass the White Hart and turn left, through their overflow car park, take the gate and continue between the fences to take another gate. Cross the field ½ right and take the gate continuing around the perimeter of Ufton Wood. Take the next gate and continue between the fence and ditches through the gates to reach the road. Cross the road right and left and take the gate into the field.*

ii. *Cross the field following the right hedge line and take the gate. Follow the path line around the field and take the gate. Continue straight ahead with the hedge line and take the next gate into the wood. Follow the path along the right fence line of the polo grounds via a gate now take another gate into the open, continuing straight ahead to reach and cross a wide track via two gates. Now go straight ahead down the field and turn left at the bottom, follow the field edge and take a gate. Follow the path through the woods and cross the road* ***to continue at para. D.***

iii. ***Return to Ufton.*** *From the gate go ½ left up the field to reach and cross a wide track via two gates. Follow the path along the left fence line of the polo grounds to take a gate into the woods. Go through the wood, via gate, and take another gate into a field. Continue straight ahead with the hedge line and take the next gate, now follow the path line left around the field and take a gate. Cross the field with the left hedge line, reach the road and take the gate.*

iv. *Cross right and left to take the gate and continue between the fence and ditches through the gates to reach an open field. Continue following the perimeter of Ufton Wood to take a gate. Cross the field ½ left, take the gate and continue straight ahead via a gate to the overflow car park of the White Hart and the road.*

## Section: 20 Harbury to Knightcote Bottom

The 'Way' from Harbury soon takes us cross-country with wide, open views to the west. The bridleway continues without interruption and for the last ½ mile follows the western edge of Itchington Holt Wood. The peace of the countryside becomes increasingly disturbed by the M40 but between 1942 and 1971 our walk from Harbury may have been disturbed by a different airborne sound.

Walking alongside the wood we would have been just off the line of the flight path into RAF Gaydon. From our turning point at the corner of the wood the runway threshold would have been just another mile distant. The station opened in 1942 and operated for most of its life as an Operational Conversion Unit (OCU), training qualified pilots for operational duties. Initially, the pilots were converted to fly Wellington bombers but during the cold war period the aircraft were the Vickers Valiant and then the Handley Page Victor, which with the Vulcan formed Britain's V-bomber fleet.

The station closed in 1974 and today the site is shared by two companies. Aston Martin's headquarters and production plant have been established there since 2003 and Jaguar-Landrover's engineering research and product development are also based here. The old 1.7 mile long runway is part of the vehicle road testing facility.

Turning towards the B4451 Gaydon Road whilst the 'Way' continues across the road we return along the eastern side of the wood towards Bishop's Itchington. The landscape now changes to the more traditional pattern of smaller interlocking fields, as we enjoy the views east from the ridge. Before dropping down the slope to the village the path passes close to the Elms Park solar farm. The site generates 29 mega watts and was connected to the grid in March 2015.

Planning permission for the site was given on condition that an archaeological survey of the site area was conducted. Unfortunately no historical material or evidence was discovered. However, the report did state that Bishops Itchington was probably established around 500 AD and the origin of its name was 'the farmstead by the Itchen'. The Bishop prefix was added in the 12th century when it became part of the Bishop of Coventry's estates.

Leaving the village and crossing the fields we pass close to the old site of the Bishop's Bowl Quarry where Blue Lias was quarried. Geologically the material consists of limestone and shale layers laid down in the Triassic and early Jurassic periods between 195 and 200 million years ago. It is the same material that forms the Jurassic Coast in Dorset between Lyme Regis and Charmouth.

In 1820 Richard Greaves saw the potential of the underlying strata and installed the first kiln to produce cement and lime. The success of his entrepreneurship was handicapped by the lack of a canal and his reliance on horse-drawn transport. However the opening of the Birmingham-Oxford railway, passing right by the site, changed that and the business expanded. Greaves gained two new partners, railway tracks were laid into the works and by 1882 four bottle kilns were producing 120 tons of Portland cement a week. By 1907 eighteen chamber kilns were producing 600 tons a week. Needless to say the business became a major employer and generated expansion in the surrounding villages.

The facility continued to expand, as technology improved, and in 1924 with three rotary kilns, having a total production length of 368 feet, daily production of 343 tons of cement was achieved. Blue Circle Industries bought the company in 1932 and production levels of 250,000 tonnes a year were achieved before production ceased in 1970. During the lifetime of the operations it is estimated that 9.7 million tonnes of material were produced.

It is just a further short walk across the fields to return to Harbury.

## Walk Directions

| | |
|---|---|
| Joining points | Harbury – kerbside parking: Knightcote Bottoms – no parking: Bishops Itchington – kerbside parking |
| Pubs | Harbury – the Crown, Gamecock, Shakespeare Inn (all close by): Bishops Itchington – the Butchers Arms (P) |

1. At Hall Lane continue straight ahead along Church Terrace then right and left along Ivy Lane to the junction with South Parade. Turn left then right and follow the footpath along side the play area. Continue through the allotments and take s stile into the open field as far as the marker post then turn left. Cross the field take the gate and follow the hedge and take the gate to the road. Turn right and follow the road to the crossroads and take the drive way straight ahead to Kingston Farm. Follow the drive turning left at a junction to take a gate left and follow the footpath. The path continues straight ahead along side the left boundary hedge/fence eventually reaching and continuing alongside Itchington Holt Wood.

2. Reaching the south west corner, with the M40 in sight, turn left and continue to follow the boundary of the edge of the wood then field edge to take the gate to the road. The 'Way' crosses over the road to continue along Knightcote Bottoms.

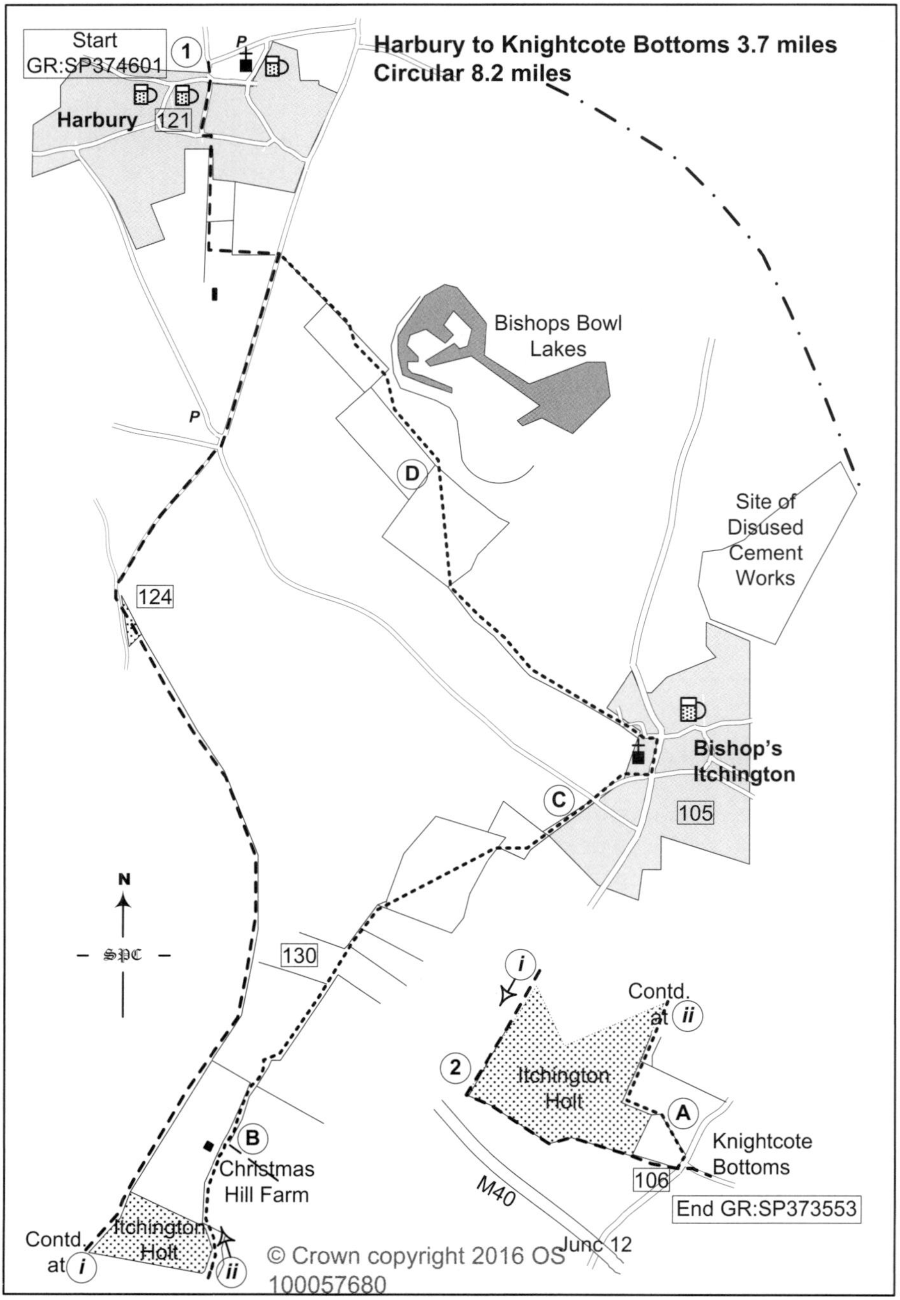

Harbury to Knightcote Bottoms 3.7 miles
Circular 8.2 miles
Start
GR:SP374601
1
P
Harbury
121
Bishops Bowl
Lakes
P
D
Site of
Disused
Cement
Works
124
Bishop's
Itchington
C
105
N
SPC
130
i
Contd.
at ii
2
Itchington
Holt
A
Knightcote
Bottoms
B
Christmas
Hill Farm
106
M40
End GR:SP373553
Itchington
Holt
Contd.
at i
ii
Junc 12

A. *To return to Harbury turn left along the B4451 Gaydon Road for 50 metres and take the stile on the left. Follow the edge of the wood, turning right at the corner and continue to take a gate. Continue straight ahead through the narrow 'paddock' to bear left at the north east corner of the wood and take a stile. Go straight ahead, along the left hedge, to take a gate then stile at Christmas Hill Farm.*

B. *Go straight ahead to follow a track between the hedges and take a gate. Continue along the track to reach and cross an open field to take a stile. Follow the left hedge take a stile, then continue to take a stile left into a copse. Turn right and follow the path to take a stile into a large field. Cross the field ½ right to the far corner and take two stiles. Cross the field right of the derelict building then turn left with the fence to take the gate. Continue straight ahead to take the gate to the road.*

C. *Cross over the road to continue along Manor Road, passing the church of St Michael, and turn left along the Gaydon Road. Continue to turn left along Mount Pleasant, unless a visit to the Butchers Arms Pub is desired which is right turn along Fisher Road. Continuing the route to Harbury, as Mount Pleasant bends right, take the footpath left at the edge of the development. The path soon enters a field and continues along the left field edge via two stiles when it crosses a field ½ right to reach the far corner.*

D. *Take the stile and follow the left field edge until the right of way crosses ½ right across the end of the field to the right hand corner. Glance over at the now water filled old quarry workings before taking a stile then the gate. Continue along the right hedge line across a bridge before turn right via two stiles through the hedge line. Turn left to follow the hedge line to the road. Cross the road and take the gate and retrace your route to the starting point in Harbury.*

# CHAPTER 8

## Section 21: Knightcote Bottoms to Burton Dassett Hills Country Park

Two-thirds of this circular route, I am afraid, is along fairly quiet lanes. This section of the 'Way' does however finish on top of the Burton Dassett Hills giving a very invigorating climb of 50m to the summit.

The route crosses a single track railway line opened by the East & West Railway Company (E&W) in 1871, linking Evesham, Stratford and Towcester. In 1909 the E&W amalgamated with the Stratford upon Avon Midland Junction Railway (SMJ), which promoted itself as the 'Shakespeare Route'. However, it was apparently usually referred to as the 'Slow Miserable and Jolty', reflecting its careworn and 'make do' approach to survival. By 1923 the railway became part of the London Midland Scottish and the old SMJ network closed for traffic in July 1965, except for this section of line.

The remaining four miles of single track, from the old Fenny Compton junction on the Birmingham-Marylebone line, serves, what was known as the Kineton Central Ammunition Depot which was constructed during World War II. The Historic England web site states that it is the largest ammunition store in Western Europe. The site is vast, having a perimeter of just under 10 miles covering an area of 4 mile$^2$ served by an internal railway track of many miles.

Today, from the Army website, the official title of the base is the DEMS Training Regiment, Marlborough Barracks or to give its full title the Defence Explosive Ordnance Disposal, Munitions and Search Training Regiment. In simple language, it teaches both our own and various international military personnel every aspect of dealing with the safe handling of explosives. This also includes training in all aspects of Improvised Explosive Device Disposal. The barracks has its own memorial to all the bomb disposal officers that have lost their lives in service.

Within the Army the official title of the base is the Kineton Military Station and on the 18th May 2012 the base was honoured with the freedom of Warwick. The parade commenced from Warwick Castle and 200 soldiers exercised their right to march through the town with bayonets fixed and colours flying. Distant views of the complex can be seen both from the top of Burton Dassett Hill and Edge Hill.

Since I parked my car at the summit for both this and the next circular walk I enjoyed the climb at the end of both walks. My description of Northend's part of the local history is described in the next section. Returning to the starting point we follow a cross-country route to Knightcote.

The Doomsday Survey records that Knightcote, although part of Dassett, had its own Lord of the Manor, three attendant knights and a clergyman. Today the members of the community describe the hamlet as being distinctive because of its smallness. Given the proximity to the hills to the south it is not surprising that this provided several natural sources of water. At the eastern end of the hamlet is Stockwell Spring which no doubt is historically why the settlement was established.

## Walk Directions

| | |
|---|---|
| Joining points | This is a circuit where the only start and finish point is either kerbside in Northend or in the pay and display car park(s) in the Country Park |
| Pubs | Northend – the Red Lion (P) |

1. Cross the B4451, Gaydon Road, and follow the lane opposite. After about 500 metres, take the gate on the right and follow the left hedge and then a track, between fences. At the double gates, bear left to follow the path at the bottom of the road embankment to take a gate. Continue between the fences to take a gate and turn left along the lane. Follow the lane and shortly after crossing the railway, serving Kineton Military Station, reach a junction and turn right along Blacksmiths Lane.

2. Follow Blacksmiths Lane into Northend and at the Red Lion pub take the left turn into 'Peartrees'. Climb the hill and at the left hand bend keep straight on up the hill passing the last house to follow the continuing track. Take the gate and continue up the track, following the left fork to reach the summit in Burton Dassett Hills Country Park.

A. *From the summit, to return to the B4451, retrace your steps back down the hill but bear right below two large bushes to follow a path to take a stile. Cross the field, following the contour, to take the next stile, followed by two more, then take the gate and follow the drive to the road. Turn right along the road and shortly after the last house take the stile on the right. The right*

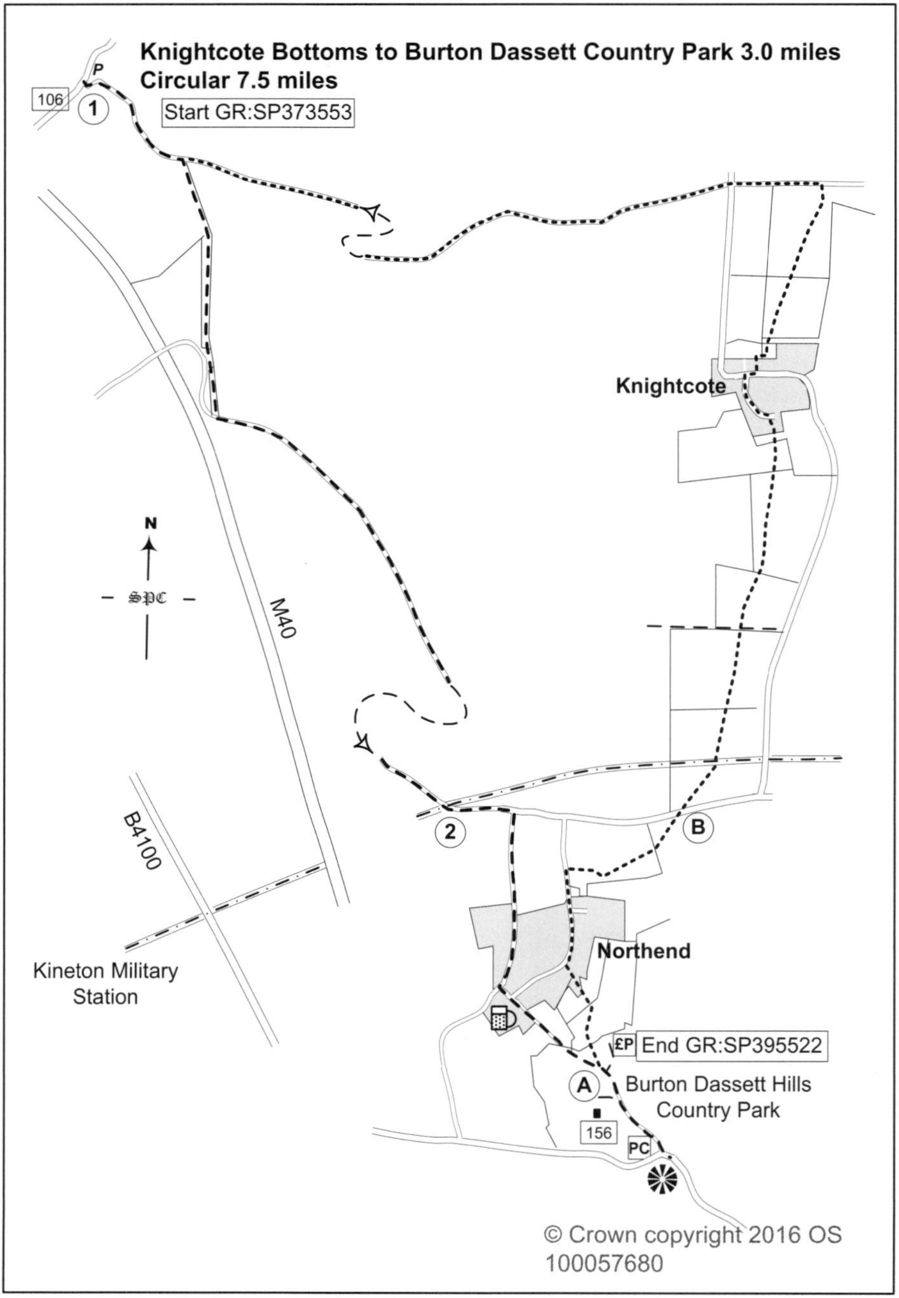

Knightcote Bottoms to Burton Dassett Country Park 3.0 miles
Circular 7.5 miles
Start GR:SP373553
106
P
1
N
SPC
M40
B4100
Kineton Military
Station
Knightcote
2
B
Northend
£P
End GR:SP395522
A
Burton Dassett Hills
Country Park
156
PC
© Crown copyright 2016 OS
100057680

*of way, despite a mature cereal crop, crossed the field and turned ½ left to a stile. Take the stile then go ½ left to cut across the field corner and take the stile to the road.*

B. *Cross the road right and left to take the stile. Cross the field ½ right to reach and cross the railway, via the stiles. Continue ¼ right, cross the field and take the stile; now continue on the same line through the next three fields via a hedge gap and stile to reach a band of trees. Take the two stiles and cross the field and take the gate continuing straight ahead to reach a road. Turn left along 'Kimble Close' to reach the main village road and turn right, for about 75 metres, and take the gate signed 'Knightcote House'. Walk up the drive and turn right behind the garage, take the gate and follow the path, to take the stile. Cross the field and take the two stiles and cross the next field ¼ right, to take the next stile. Cross the field ¼ right to take the hedge gap and turn left along the lane. Follow this quiet lane, named 'Knightcote Bottoms', straight ahead for 1.85 miles to reach the start.*

## Section 22: Burton Dassett Hills Country Park to Avon Dassett

Starting at the top of the Burton Dassett Hills Country Park from the view point at Magpie Hill summit it is the widest vista so far on our journey.

The hills are capped with Marlstone but underneath sits 'Hornton Stone', the local name for the organgey-yellow Middle Lias ironstone. This has been quarried throughout the centuries, providing the masonry for many of the properties in the area. In 1908, a discovery made by quarrymen on Pleasant Hill, at the northeast corner of the ridge, dated the earliest recorded human activity in the area. A Saxon burial was unearthed in two trenches containing thirty-five skeletons and their injuries indicated violent death. With them was a sword and pottery dated to the 6th or 7th century indicating the period when they presumably died in battle.

Under Norman rule the Burton Dassett parish had a population of about 350 and included Great and Little Dassett and Northend which extended into Southend, Knightcote and Hardwick. By the time of the 13th century the prosperity of the parish had continued to improve and the population of Burton Dassett had spread down to Northend and Southend. The manor was in the hands of the de Sudeley family, who had excellent relations with royalty and, in 1267, King Henry III granted them a weekly Friday market and a three day annual fair. The royal connection continued for in 1299 King Edward I elevated John de Sudeley to Baron and the parish was granted more privileges, including the holding of a Court Leet.

Prosperity continued and by 1332 the taxes paid to the King's Treasury were the third highest in the County, equalling a quarter of those paid by Coventry. The estates eventually passed to a de Sudeley nephew, Thomas Boteler, but the royal connection was not disrupted when his grandson became King Henry VI's bodyguard, Standard Bearer and then Lord Treasurer of England. He died childless and through his sisters marriage the estates passed to the Belknap family.

Nothing further is recorded until the end of the 15th century when Sir Edward Belknap, who lived at Western under Wetherley, decided to maximise his income from the Dassett hills. The hills were ideal for sheep grazing so he evicted the twelve tenant farmers and their families, 60 people in total, and enclosed 600 acres for sheep grazing. The area was already depleted by the Black Death and his actions only served to increase the migration and economic decline of the area. Belknap's lasting monument was the stone Beacon Tower built by him, presumably to replace a less permanent structure, which in times of emergency would have had a lit warning beacon.

Following the path down the hill we enter the churchyard of the 12th century Grade I listed Church of All Saints, described as one of the finest in South Warwickshire. The first building was just a chancel and a short aisle-nave but during the 13th century several phases of extension and improvement were undertaken by the de Sudeley's. Clearly they were happy to expend their wealth, to ensure that it was reflected in the status of the church. In later years alteration and repair has been undertaken but largely in sympathy and without compromising the original structure and features.

From the church the 'Way' roughly follows the 160m contour to Avon Dassett. The village's recorded history starts from the Norman period but clearly its Lords of the Manor did not have either the wealth or connections of their neighbours.

One 20th century resident in the village was John Profumo, he resigned as Secretary of State for War in 1963, after admitting to an affair with a model. He was MP for Stratford and his home in the village was 'Avon Carrow', which is behind the main street and now apartments. For the rest of his life he sought his own redemption and worked tirelessly for the Toynbee Hall charity in East London, starting as a volunteer and later becoming Chairman. In recognition of his work he was created CBE on the advice of Harold Wilson. He died at the age of 91, in 2006, having never re-entered public life.

Climbing the main street, we pass the church and follow undulating, cross country paths to Fenny Compton. The explanation for the delightful name is the slightly less poetic description 'a settlement in a marshy valley'. Certainly our first view of the village presents a picture of the church centre foreground in a pleasant landscape despite a potentially 'soft' approach.

The parish church of St Peter and St Clare's (GII*) earliest features, the chancel arch and part of the north arcade, were built between 1320 and 1330. It was in the late 14th century that considerable rebuilding was undertaken and the tower and spire were added. A tour of the village, with its great number of historical listed buildings, including the pub is most worthwhile.

The walk to Northend is a straight level path across the fields before a slight climb and contour around to Northend. The total climb through Northend to the top of the Burton Hills is 70m, and the last vertical slope is very short!

The church of St Peter & St Clare

## Walk Directions

| | |
|---|---|
| Joining points | County Park – pay & display: Avon Dassett – car park adjacent the play area: Fenny Compton – kerbside parking |
| Pubs | Avon Dassett – the Avon: Fenny Compton – the Merrie Lion (P): Northend – the Red Lion (P) |

1. From the most north-eastern car park you can either follow the road or explore the summits of Beacon Hill and Magpie Hill, with its viewing plate. Given a clear day the landscape from this view point is impressive. Whichever route you choose, after Magpie Hill from the ridge way road, take the narrow road right downhill to the Church. Cross the cattle grid and keep left to enter the churchyard of All Saints Church. Go right of the church to exit via the gate and follow the fenced path and take the gate and stile. Cross the field to the right, taking the gate in the fence and continue past the corner of the wood to take the gate and stile in the corner of the field.

2. Cross the field and take the bridge and stile, continue following the left hedge line to reach and take the second stile. Continue along the fence

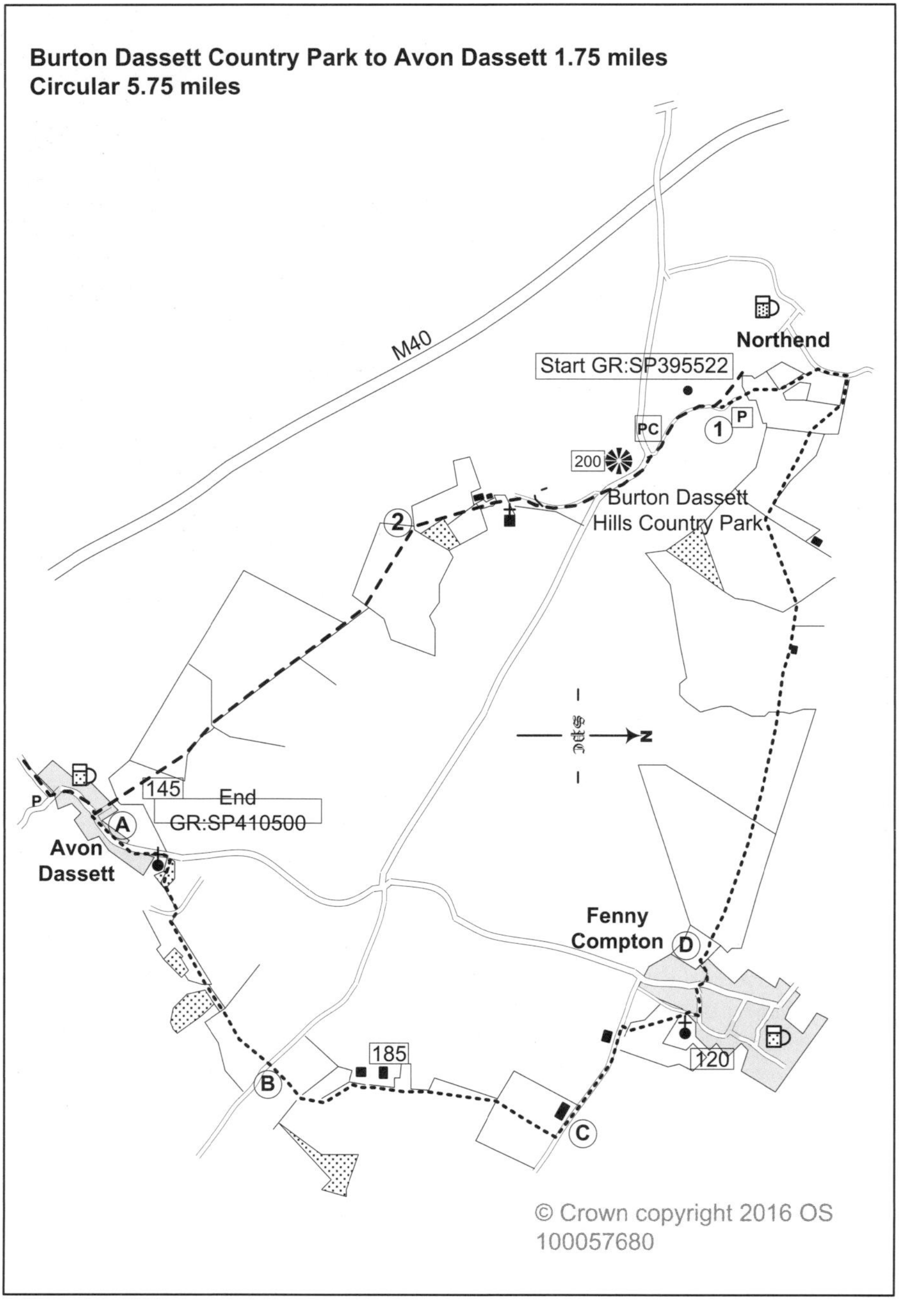

Burton Dassett Country Park to Avon Dassett 1.75 miles
Circular 5.75 miles
M40
Northend
Start GR:SP395522
PC
P
1
200
Burton Dassett
Hills Country Park
2
145
End
GR:SP410500
P
A
Avon
Dassett
N
Fenny
Compton
D
120
185
B
C
© Crown copyright 2016 OS
100057680

line, taking a stile and, as the fence bends left, cross the field ½ right to take the stile. Continue on the same line across the next field to take a gate to join a track. Follow the track via another gate and through Park Close to turn right along the main road to continue along the 'Way'.

A. *To return to the start of this section turn left up the hill through the village to go past the church of St John the Baptist. At the end of the churchyard take the path on the right up the hill. Continue to go between the box hedges and reach a lane and turn right. Take the stile on the left, follow the left fence, as it turns left, and continue to reach the end of the field. Take the gate, follow the short track and take the stile. Cross the field straight ahead and take the stile and cross the lane to take the stile.*

B. *Go straight ahead to cross the field and through the hedge gap. Now go ½ left across the field to aim to the right of the projecting hedge. Follow the hedge line around to the right, passing the gap through to the farm yard, to reach the corner of the hedge. Cross the field straight ahead, to follow the hedge line to a marker post. From the post go down the hill aiming for the far left corner of the field and take the stile. Continue straight across the next field taking the gate and bridge to turn left along the lane.*

C. *Follow the lane down the hill and, just after Grange Farm, take the gate right. Take the next gate and cross the field around to the left and take the gate to the lane. Turn right, passing the church of St Peter & St Clare to the junction with Church Street. Now either turn left to continue directly on, or turn right to tour the village and pass the Merrie Lion Pub. From the bottom of Church Street turn right along the 'main' road and as it turns right take the track left adjacent the lamp post. Follow the track around to the left and in front of the barn take the gate and turn right.*

D. *Follow the right perimeter and around to the left take the stile. This next vast field crossing is about 780 metres straight ahead, via a hedge gap, to reach and take a bridge crossing. Continue straight ahead to the left of a shed to take a stile. Now go ½ left across the field to take the gate and follow the right fence line and then, bearing left, to take the next gate. Cross the field ½ right, to take the gate in the corner and follow the track left to road. Turn left and at Stone Cottage turn left up the hill continuing straight on via a path and then a stile into the Country Park. Now take your best route to climb the final 40m to the ridge.*

## Section 23: Avon Dassett to Ratley

The walk from Avon Dassett is downhill and along the road which after crossing the Banbury road becomes a pleasant lane leading us to Arlescote. Arlescote is a small hamlet with a few scattered houses sitting back from the road. However, as the lane curves left, a long wall presents itself and behind is the end elevation of Arlescote House. As the lane bends right the full impact of this late 17th century Grade II* listed manor house is revealed. As Arlescote was within the Parish of Warmington there is no record of the original owner despite his obvious wealth. However the sale particulars, when the house was on the market in 2014, state that Indigo Jones was in the area and thought to have lent his genius to the house. It is also said that during the battle of Edge Hill, both the King's two sons stayed in the house with their tutor.

At the end of the hamlet we leave the road and take a path climbing steeply 46m to provide a view back to the Burton Dassett Hills. We now make a steep descent before making a gentler assent to the 200m contour and the Parish of Ratley and Upton which declares itself the highest parish in Warwickshire.

Arlescote House

At the crossroads the 'Way' turns right to Edge Hill, through the modern part of the village. But to return to Avon Dassett we turn left along High Street descending a very picturesque street to the Grade II* listed church of St Peter Ad Vincula. Its name is unusual and only shared by a few other churches, notably the Tower of London chapel. The whole fabric of the church dates from 1340 and development continued through various stages to the completion of the top of the tower in the late 14th century. It is considered remarkable for the variety of its window tracery, the progress of which may have been disrupted by the Black Death. A wider tour of the village would reveal other noted buildings but the Rose and Crown, which we pass as we leave the village, could also provide a 17th century, Grade II listed distraction.

The cross-country route to Warmington is undulating and provides a total climb of 50m back to the scarp slope of Edge Hill. The last short section, along a narrow path right at the top of the slope, certainly provides a surprise as we emerge from the trees. From the B4100 my route turns left and right along the bottom of the hill through Warmington. However if you can face the hill there is a reward. After passing the church of St Phillips (GI), the view along the main street unfolds to reveal the unique aspect of the village green and pond overlooked by the Manor House (GII*) dated 1603. If you need further encouragement before reaching the pond we pass the 17th century Plough Inn (GII). The remaining part of the walk includes a left and right to cross the M40 and then field-crossings to reach Avon Dassett.

## Walk Directions

| | |
|---|---|
| Joining points | Avon Dassett – car park adjacent the play area: Ratley and Warmington – kerbside parking |
| Pubs | Avon Dassett – the Avon, Ratley – the Rose & Crown and Warmington – the Plough Inn |

1. Follow the road downhill crossing the M40 and then the B4100. Continue along the lane into the hamlet of Arlescote, with its impressive 17th century manor house. Follow the lane for about 200 metres and just after Pond Farm take the stile on the left. Follow the fence on the left and continue straight ahead and cross the field to take the stile. Follow the left fence up the steep incline and then go around to the right and left to take the stile to the road.

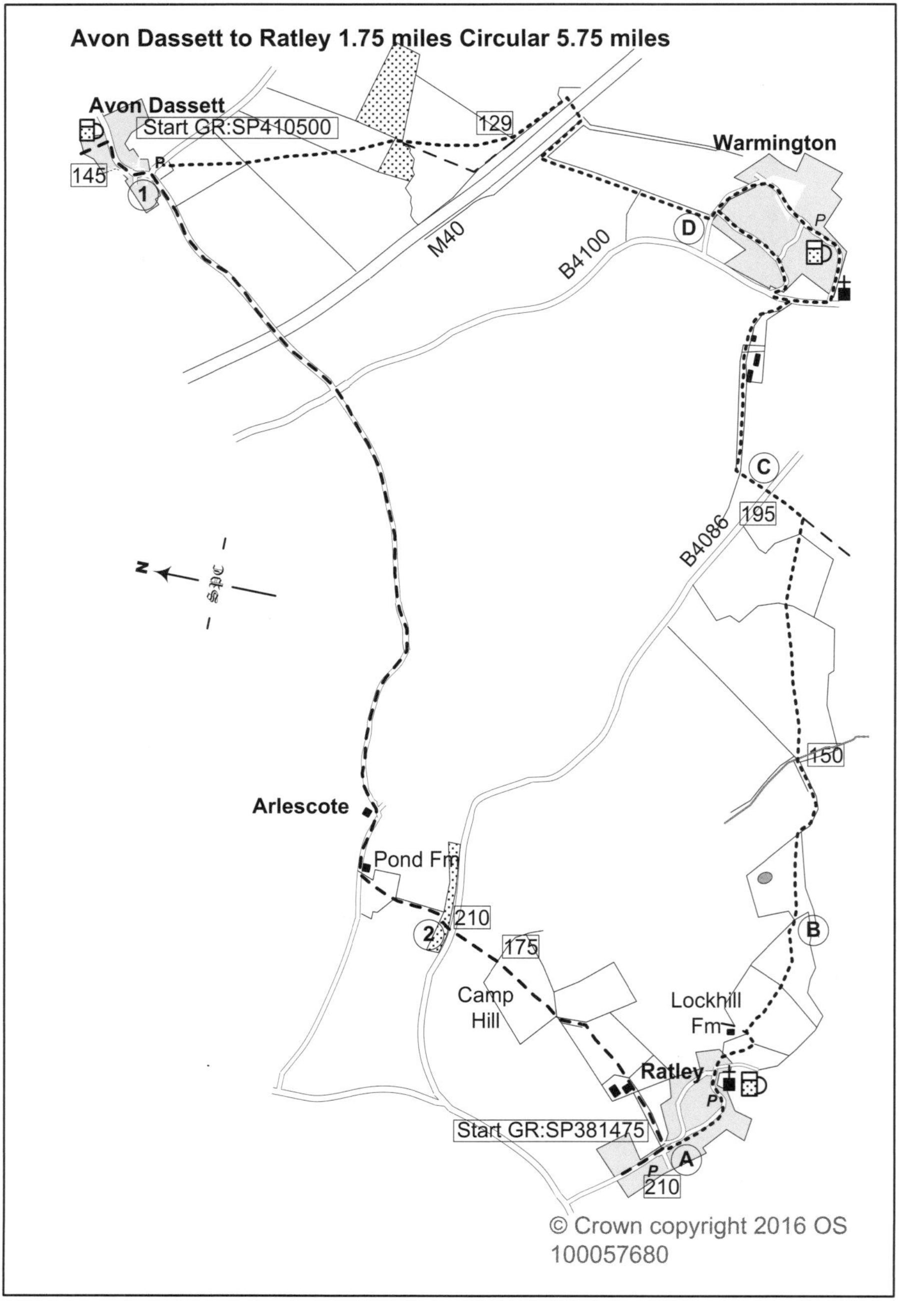
Avon Dassett to Ratley 1.75 miles Circular 5.75 miles
Avon Dassett
Start GR:SP410500
145
1
129
M40
B4100
Warmington
D
C
195
B4086
N
150
Arlescote
Pond Fm
210
2
175
Camp Hill
Lockhill Fm
B
Ratley
Start GR:SP381475
A
210
© Crown copyright 2016 OS 100057680

2. Cross the road through the hedge gap and go straight down and across the field to take the bridge. Now cross the next field up hill to the left corner. Take the stile and follow the fenced path to the end of the right fence. Now turn right to cross the field and take the gate. Follow the track to reach Ratley and the Old Road/High Street and turn right to follow the 'Way'.

A. *Returning to Avon Dassett turn left downhill along High Street passing the church of St Peter ad Vincula and then the Rose & Crown Pub. Follow the road up hill to reach a gate on right and a way mark post. The path to Warmington follows the way marked route the 'Macmillan Way'. Take the gate and cross ¼ left down the field to take a gate. Now turning left curve right with the contour before climbing the bank up hill to the left and the top corner of the field to take a gate.*

B. *Go downhill slightly right to pick up the hedge and continue to the gate. Take the gate and follow the hedge around to the right as it becomes a track between hedges. Continue to the bottom of the gradient and take the gate/gap on the right into the field. Cross the field ½ left and through the gap in the hedge to climb the steep gradient taking a stile. Almost at the top there is a redundant stile before the track. Turn left along the track through a storage area to the B4086.*

C. *Cross the road to the left, take the stile and cross the field. Take the stile on the right and follow the path between the hedges to reach a barn. Take the left of two gates and continue along the path to take a stile and then a gate. Continue along the scarp edge to take a stile and turn left along the drive to the B4100 road. From here you have a choice either turning right or left. Turn right and then left to walk through the picturesque centre of Warmington village and the Plough Inn, or turn left then right to follow School Lane. If you have walked through the village centre take the left fork at the end of the village green and continue to the end of School Lane. From School Lane turn left for a few metres to take the way marked gate on the right.*

D. *Follow the track to the M40 embankment hedge and turn right through the gates. Follow the track and cross the bridge over the motorway and on the opposite side turn left to follow the track along the opposite side. At the end of the track enter a field (crops). Here, the the right of way continues along the hedge line to turn right across the field. However the preferred line goes*

*½ right to the first overhead power cable pole and on to the far field corner, which is the path I have shown. Take the bridge (crops) and go ½ left across the field to a plank bridge.Take the bridge and cross the next field ½ right to take a stile. Continue on the same line across the next field to take a gate into the play area and another gate to the road.*

# CHAPTER 9

## Section 24: Ratley to Tysoe

Leaving Ratley we quickly descend the scarp face of Edge Hill and follow another undulating path along it. The path passes just below the Castle Inn and provides an early opportunity to view the plain below, from its garden. The Inn's Grade II* listed, ornate tower is a sham castle designed and built in 1747 by Sanderson Miller, pioneers of Gothic revival architecture. In the garden there is also an interpretation board of the Battle of Edgehill which took place on 23 October 1642, the first battle of our Civil War.

The Castle Inn Folly

Naturally there is a great deal of fascinating information about the battle and I could not let us pass without attempting to provide you with sufficient information to whet your appetites.

On 22 August 1642 King Charles I raised his standard in Nottingham and made his declaration of war against Parliament. By October he was leading his forces to London and Parliaments forces, lead by the Earl of Essex, were marching from Worcester to block them. The Royalists arrived at Edge Hill and realised that the opposition were close by. They could have crept by but decided it was an opportunity not to be missed. They amassed at the top of Edge Hill and the opposition, camping at Kineton and belatedly realising the King and his army were on their doorstep, came out to meet them.

In the early morning the Royalist army had been allowed to find their way down the steep slope of the hill undisturbed and present themselves for battle. The battle commenced at about 2pm with an initial cannonade exchange. The Royalist right and left wings of cavalry then struck first, so successfully they continued through the battle line attacking the retreating opposition. The next attack was made by the centre Royalist 'foot' against the stationary centre of the opposition force. However the Parliamentarians were supported by units of cavalry that had been kept centrally in reserve and they counter attacked creating havoc amongst the unsupported Royalists.

With 13,500 King's men and a force of 12,500 Parliamentarians the battle fragmented into many individual fights across the battlefield. With dusk gathering at 6pm, the fighting largely ground to a halt. Throughout the night, those that were able returned to their original positions at the top of Edge Hill or in Kineton.

The outcome was considered a draw, with estimates between 1,000 and 1,500 dead on the battlefield and 2-3,000 injured, which probably means a total eventual number of at least 3,000 deaths. After the battle the King took Banbury but failed to reach London ahead of the Earl of Essex army and retired to Oxford for the winter.

However, just before Christmas, back at the battle site, as rural normality returned, local shepherds reported hearing noises; the screams of battle, clash of armour, the cries of the dying; and of seeing ghostly figures re-enacting the battle in the night sky. News of the terrifying apparitions reached the King, so he sent a Royal Commission to investigate and they also witnessed the ghostly battle, even recognising some of the soldiers who had taken part. The villagers decided that to stop the apparitions, they would give a Christian burial to all of the dead still lying on the battlefield.

The Royal Commission's investigation and report is still held by the Public Record Office, their findings remain a matter of established fact. Not surprisingly, even today, there are reports of ghostly events, which should be of concern, as most of the battle took place within what is now a massive ammunition store.

We continue along the top of the hill crossing the Banbury Road at Sun Rising Hill, where you may decide to take the shortened route via Upton House back to Ratley. We continue along the summit and reach the open area of Spring Hill. The bench could provide a resting place from which to enjoy again the vista of south Warwickshire. After a short distance we pass the return route on the left and take the bridleway, down to Tysoe.

The origin of the village name is refined from the name 'Tig', the Saxon god of war, and 'hoh' the name for hill. It is interesting to contemplate how the settlement gained the dubious privilege and potential of hosting this Saxon visitor attraction. Presumably if you intended to start a war you popped over or made a regular visit as insurance just in case of the event arising.

On the map, for brevity, I have not identified the separate entities of Upper and Middle, which is where we arrive and is essentially the centre of the village. We walk along the Main Street and pass the Grade I listed Church of the Assumption of the Blessed Virgin Mary. The church dates from the 11th century and it was extended and the tower added through to the 14/15th centuries. Since then except for minor alterations and structural restoration, it has remained unchanged. As with all the villages the church is surrounded by a number of historical and listed properties.

Continuing through the village, to the centre, note the old drinking well to the left of the entrance to the Health Care Centre. At the end of this section is the Peacock Pub but beyond it the village is also served by a convenience store.

We return to Ratley through the churchyard and across the fields to Lower Tysoe and then retrace the route back up Spring Hill. The path across the fields is flat with just a short climb at Home Farm to reach the car park at Upton House. The house is National Trust Property and was built for Sir Rushout Cullen in 1695 and was possibly designed by one of the Smiths of Warwick. Alterations and additions were made in 1735 for William Bumstead. Today the house bears the stamp of the 2nd Viscount Bearsted, who owned the house from 1927 until 1948, when it was gifted to the Trust, although the family continued living there until 1988.

The last section of the walk has two alternative routes to Ratley. Choose either the flat route along the lane or, after a short walk along the Banbury Road, the more physical and enjoyable cross-country route. Following the latter route look out for the early 19th century Grade II listed mile stone, opposite the second entrance gates, inscribed 'London 80 Banbury 7 miles'.

## Walk Directions

The complete circular walk is 8.7 miles long with a total climb of approximately 245m overall. There is an opportunity to complete the walk in two circles or shorten the return leg by a ½ mile and reduce the overall climb by 75m.

| | |
|---|---|
| Joining points | Ratley and Tysoe – kerbside parking: Upton House – NT membership parking |
| Pubs | Ratley – the Rose & Crown, Edge Hill – the Castle Inn and at Tysoe – the Peacock Inn (P) |

1. Continue along Old Road to the T junction, turn left and cross the road and go through the gap in the hedge. Take the steps and continue down

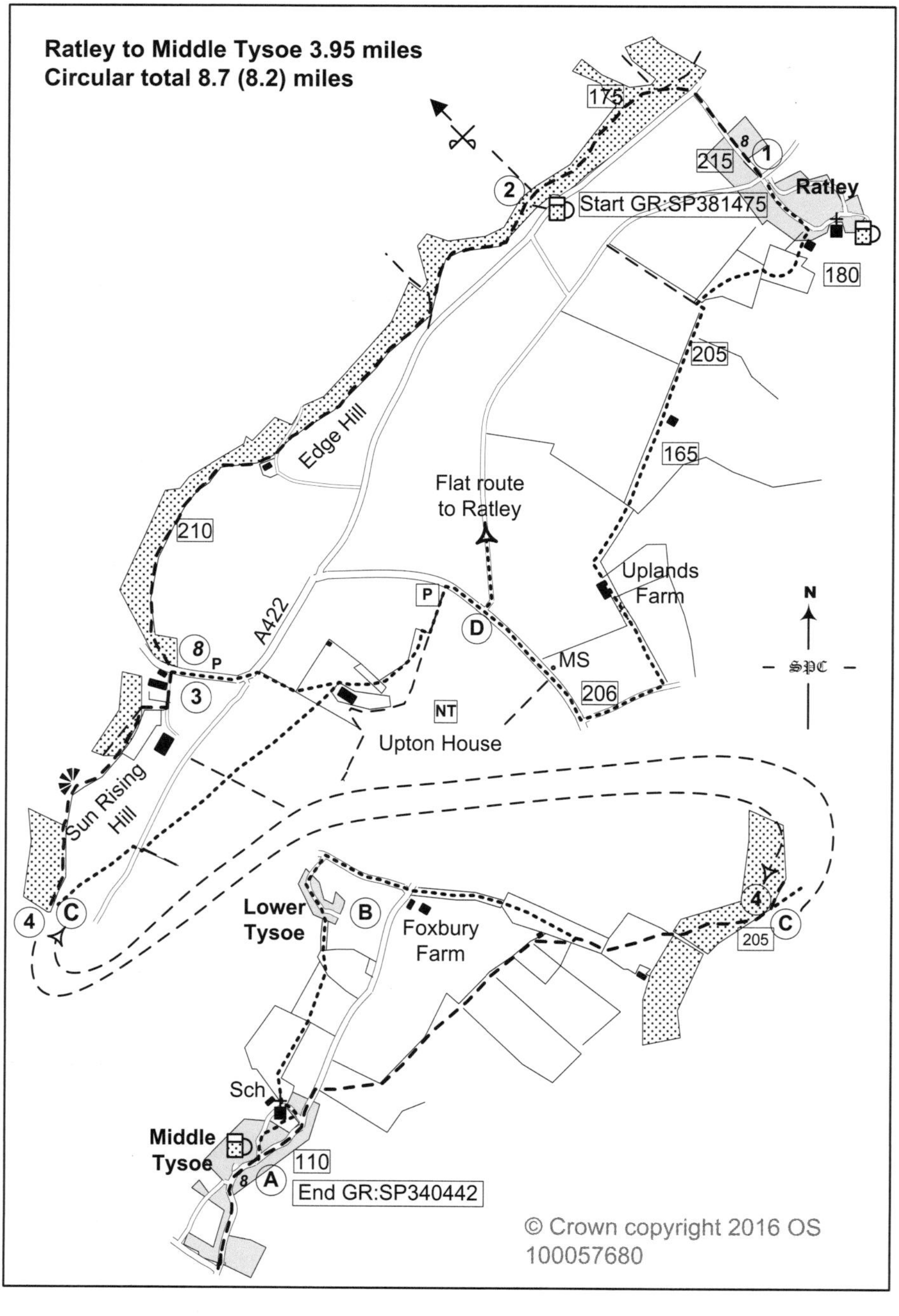
Ratley to Middle Tysoe 3.95 miles
Circular total 8.7 (8.2) miles
175
215
1
8
Ratley
2
Start GR:SP381475
180
205
Edge Hill
165
Flat route
to Ratley
210
Uplands
Farm
N
P
A422
D
8
P
3
MS
206
NT
Upton House
Sun Rising
Hill
4
C
Lower
Tysoe
B
Foxbury
Farm
4
C
205
Sch
Middle
Tysoe
110
8
A
End GR:SP340442
© Crown copyright 2016 OS
100057680

the slope to join a footpath and turn left. Ignore a gate on the right, to continue inside the edge of the wood. Keep right at the next marker post, where a stony track goes left up the hill. This leads to the Castle Inn but, if you wish to visit it, the better path is the next left turn which is an easier and shorter.

2. Continuing along the main path it gradually curves left and climbs back to the top of the escarpment. The path now runs inside the fence line at the edge of the wood and crosses a bridle way descending across our line. The path continues winding along the edge of the wooded summit and joins and meets a surfaced drive. Turn left and then right, alongside a stone wall, continuing for about ¾ mile to reach a marker post. Ignore the direction to go straight on and go ½ left to follow the path through the trees. This leads to the top of the hill and avoids walking along the busy A422. (To return to the start at this point see instruction (*i*) below.)

3. Cross the road and follow the concrete drive and turn right into the equestrian centre and then left between the fences to follow the path the woods, left of the marker post. Take the gate at the edge of the woods and continue along the escarpment edge and in kind weather enjoy the magnificent views. As you follow the fence line take the opportunity to cross the stile on the left to view the Battle of Edge Hill interpretation board. Continue along the edge and take the gate into the wood. Follow the path, passing a gate on the left which is the crossover point of the return route.

4. Just beyond the gate the path descends along a wide path, which can be very 'sticky', to the bottom of the escarpment. Take the gate and cross the field ½ left and take the gate. Follow the left hedge for 100 metres and take the gate on the left and cross the field ½ right, to the end of the line of Willow trees. Now follow the right hedge line, take the gate and continue to the second hedge gap. Cross the field ¼ right to a marker post in the hedge line, and follow the hedge to the corner. Turn ½ right and cross the field to take the gate to the road. Turn left along 'Main Street' passing St Mary's Church to reach the Peacock Inn and the village centre of Middle Tysoe.

*A. Returning to Ratley turn right into Saddledon Street following the road around to the right through the churchyard. Leave by the opposite gate and turn left along the lane to take the footpath to the right of the school. Take the gate and enter the field bearing right to follow the right fence line crossing the field to take the next gate. Cross the field slightly left and take the gate under the willow trees. Cross the field ½ left and take the gate and follow a hedged path between the houses.*

B. *Turn left along Badgers Road and then right along the Tysoe Road. Continue to the road junction and cross straight over and take the gate into Foxbury Farm. Follow the track straight ahead to take a gate. Cross the field to take a gate and rejoin the outward route. Cross the field ½ left take the gate and follow the path up the escarpment and turn left at the top to reach a gate on the right.*

C. *Take the gate and cross the field ½ left to take a gate and cross the road. Take the track opposite but turn immediately ½ left to cross the large field to the middle of the far side and take the stile. Go straight ahead around the end of the fenced enclosure surrounding Home Farm (GII) and turn right and bear left up the slope. Take two gates and follow the fenced path to take either the gate or stile into the Upton House National Trust car park. Go through the car park to the exit at the A422, Stratford Road. Turn right and the first option is to take the ½ mile shorter, flatter route turning first left along the lane signed for Edgehill and Ratley.*

D. *The second option is to continue along the wide verge of the A422 for a further 470 metres to take the next left, along Quarry Road. Follow the road to where overhead power lines cross and turn left to follow them and the right hedge line. At the corner of the field the path continues through a corridor of trees and then continues along side a large barn. Continue with the right hedge line around to the right to follow a track down the field to take a stile. Follow the left hedge line continuing downhill then climbing past a derelict building to the summit and through a large hedge gap. Continue for a further 100 metres to go through a hedge gap on the left and take the stile on the right. Go through the narrow neck between the fences and, as the field widens, turn ½ right across the field to take a stile. Follow the track around the field to take a gate and continue straight ahead to the road at the bottom of Ratley. Turn right for the Rose and Crown or left to reach the starting point.*

i. *To return to Ratley at this point turn left up the A422, Stratford Road, passing the lay by on the left and the lane on the right to take the gate on the right. Follow the left hedge and take the stile on the left. Cross the field to the corner of the left side of the fenced enclosure and bear left up the slope. Take two gates and follow the fenced path to take either the gate or stile into the Upton House National Trust car park. Go through the car park to the exit at the A422 Stratford Road. Turn right and the first option is to take the ½ mile shorter, flatter route turning first left along the lane signed for Edgehill and Ratley or to follow the instructions at D above.*

## Section 25: Tysoe to Whatcote

Leaving Middle Tysoe we follow the road through Upper Tysoe and turn right along the Shipston Road. A little way along we pass a pair of unmatched Grade II semi-detached thatched cottages, which are examples of the basic workers cottage of the late 17th century.

We leave the road through the entrance gates to the 14th century Grade II* listed Manor House. Unfortunately the house is hidden, but its entry on the Airbnb web site suggests it is still fit to entertain the 21st century lady and gentleman.

'The Way' now follows field paths to the hamlet of Whatcote which is certainly best described as very quiet. The church of St Peter is Grade II* listed and the Historic England web site notes the buildings origins as; '12-14c, restorations 1820, repairs circa 1940'. The latter note, I assume, refers to the 1941 incident when a stray bomb landed, presumably one of 'theirs', and destroyed the porch and most of the south wall west of it. The only casualty was a sheep – I wonder if they needed their ration cards to recycle it? If the church is open there is a mural monument to the Reverend John Davenport, who was rector for 70 years and 6 months and died at the age of 101 in 1668.

From the churchyard the 'Way' continues across the fields but returning to the start we leave the churchyard and follow the road north-west, passing the Royal Oak Grade II listed pub, which was undergoing refurbishment and due to re-open in late 2017. After a few minutes walk along the road the path to Oxhill follows field paths before joining the road at the edge of the village.

The village of Oxhill presents another quiet backwater with a mix of historical, listed and more modern buildings, including another Peacock Inn pub. We pass the Grade I listed 12th century church of St Lawrence and like many of the churches it has a multi listing for tomb stones and churchyard crosses. However it was the grade II* listing for: 'The tomb of Myrtilla is one of the earliest known to have been established in England commemorating a person of African descent'. She died January 6th 1705. The inscription on the stone refers to Myrtilla as 'a slave of Thomas Beauchamp' but the church burial register describes her as 'a negro girl of Mrs Beauchamp'. The history of the 'girl' is uncertain but research has concluded that the Beauchamp

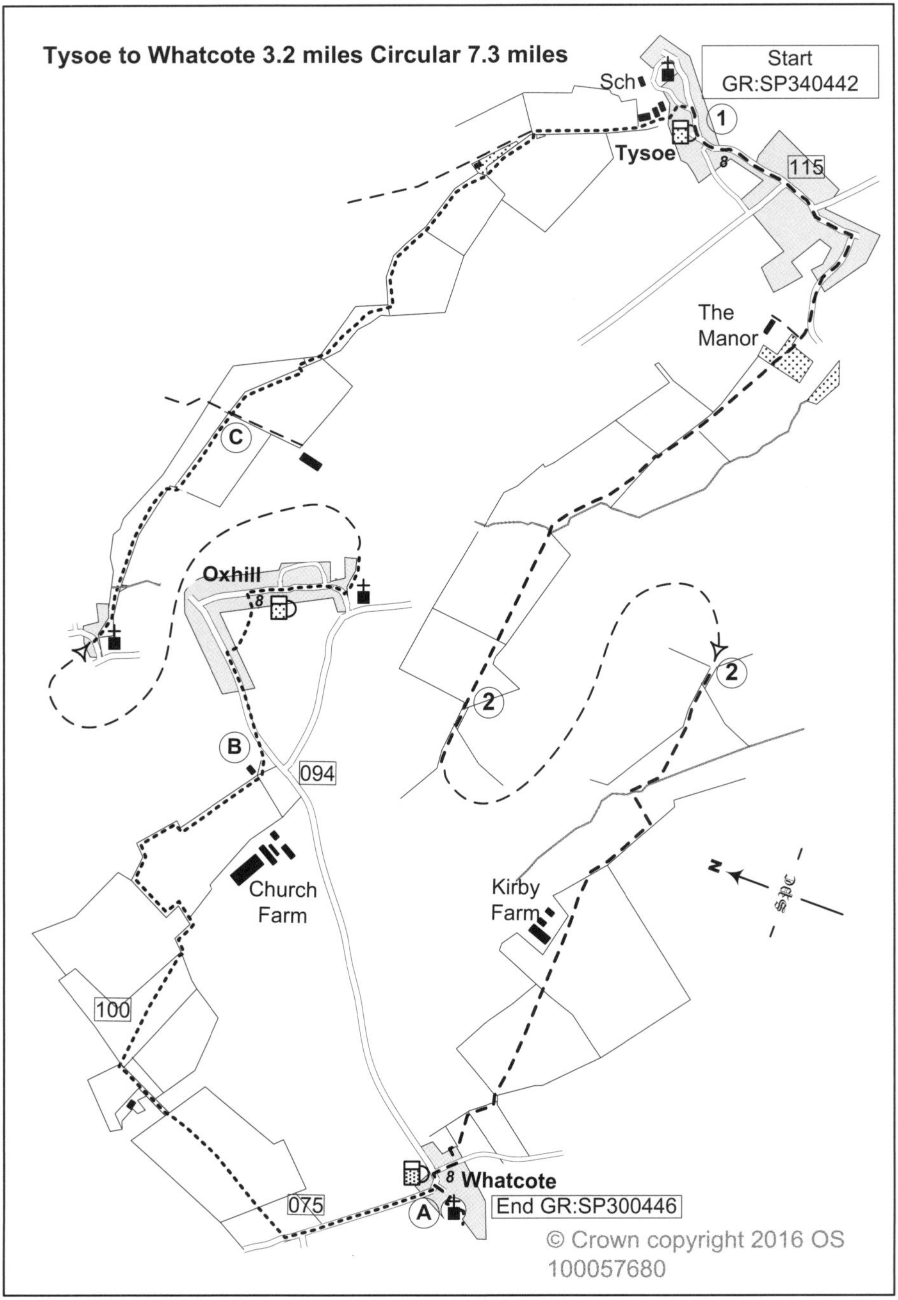
Tysoe to Whatcote 3.2 miles Circular 7.3 miles
Start
GR:SP340442
Sch
1
Tysoe
8
115
The
Manor
C
Oxhill
8
2
2
B
094
Church
Farm
Kirby
Farm
N
SDC
100
075
8 Whatcote
A
End GR:SP300446
© Crown copyright 2016 OS
100057680

family had business interests on the island of Bevis in the West Indies, where the main industry was sugar. It is speculated that Myrtilla may have been brought to England to look after her master's first born child. It was not uncommon for West Indian planters to bring back a favourite slave to work for them in a domestic capacity. In the parish record Myrtilla was baptised only a few months before she died, possibly soon after her arrival from Bevis. She was clearly valued by the family given the dignified grave and decoratively carved headstone she was granted. The tomb stone is on the south side of the church a few yards from the south door, which is also worth examining. The stonework jamb and arch is the original 12th century craftsmanship.

We take the path from the eastern end of the churchyard, passing the attractive white rendered 17th century listed Bilton Cottage. The path continues through the fields to eventually join a track leading us back to Middle Tysoe.

## Walk Directions

| | |
|---|---|
| Joining points | Tysoe, Whatcote & Oxhill: kerbside parking in and with care in Whatcote |
| Pubs | Tysoe – the Peacock Inn (P), Whatcote – the Royal Oak (P), Oxhill – the Peacock |

1. From the Peacock Pub continue along Main Street through the village, eventually walking along the grass verge and turning right into the drive of Tysoe Manor. Pass the multi-armed elephant, at the bend in the drive, and follow the path straight ahead alongside the wall and then through the wood and take the gate. Cross the field ½ right to the hedge and follow it to reach a marker post. Go through the gap and turn left following the hedge, then bear ¼ right to follow the line of the more substantial hedge to the end of a field to cross a bridge and take a gate. Continue straight ahead across the field to a gap in the hedge and take the gate and cross the next field on the same line to the corner.

2. Continue between the hedges to next field. Now follow the right hedge to a marker post and turn ½ left to cross the field and turn right with the hedge. Follow the hedge and turn left and take the bridge through the hedge. Cross the field aiming for the tall tree and turn right with the hedge to take a stile on the left. Now go ½ right and cross the field to the fence

corner at Kirby Farm continuing straight ahead to take the fence gap and cross the next field on the same line. Take the stile and bridge, then the next stile and follow the right hedge. Take the stile and cross the field ½ left to take another stile and go straight ahead to take a gate on the left and continue to the road. Turn right then left at the junction and then left along Church Lane to continue on the 'Way' or keep straight on to return to Tysoe.

A. *Walk along the lane for a ¼ mile, past the left turn, and take the gate on the right. Follow the track across the field through the gap in the hedge. Cross the field slightly left to take a bridge and a gate adjacent a power line pole. Keep straight ahead up the hill along the track and take two gates. Continue with the right hedge to almost the corner of the field and take the stile on the right. A maze of tractor tracks lead to the top left corner of the field but if no cross field route is available follow the right hedge around the field. At the corner take the bridge and the stile and turn left to follow the field perimeter and take the second gate left. Follow the left hedge line around two sides of the field and after the barn take the gate left. Follow the path, take the stile and turn left to reach the road.*

B. *Turn left along the road and take the way-marked gate on the right between the houses. Continue into the field and turn ½ left to go through the gap between the houses, then take the stile to the road. Turn right passing the Peacock Pub to the church of St Lawrence. At the side of the church take the gate to 'Church House' and turn left to take the gate in the hedge. Follow the path ½ right, take the gate and continue through the narrow meadow. Cross the gated bridge and continue along the right perimeter to take a gate on the right. Turn left around the field corner to turn left through a hedge gap and over a bridge and continue into the open field. Follow the left hedge and continue to take a gate and cross a bridge and track.*

C. *Continue following the left hedge and, before the end of the field, turn left and take the bridge and gate. Turn right, take the stile and follow the track to take the gate. Cross the next three fields, taking the gates. Continue with the left perimeter and take the stile on the left, leaving the field, to join and turn right along the track. Follow the track through the farmyard and turn left along the footpath to join Saddledon Street. Turn right to rejoin Main Street by the Peacock Pub.*

## Section 26: Whatcote to Honington

The 'Way' launches itself quietly from the churchyard but then, almost unnoticed, climbs from the 75m contour starting point to the summit of Idlicote Hill at 135m, close to Idlicote Hill Lodge.

The name Idlicote originates from Idli's cottages. My source of reference, British History online, declares that there is little of interest in the tiny village this, despite the fact that, it seems to have been the setting for the middle-ages precursor of *Midsommer Murders.*

The ownership of the Manor was held by the Earls of Stafford until 1393. It was then granted to Geoffrey de Clinton, Chamberlain to Henry I, who bestowed it upon his foundation at Kenilworth Priory. After the Dissolution the Manor passed through several hands and eventually, in 1570, William Underhill became the owner. It seems he had owned New Place in Stratford upon Avon and had sold it to William Shakespeare who may have been sufficiently closely connected to use the next event in one of his plays.

On 15th July 1597, William Underhill died, the cause of death - as the historical record bluntly states - poisoned by his eldest son Fulk, aged 18. He was subsequently executed and his brother Hercules, who died in 1658, succeeded him. The Manor now passed to his nephew William, who had been knighted at the Restoration.

However at some point, it appears that Sir William had suffered a disagreement with a man named Devereux, whom he had shot and wounded with a pistol. When the matter came to court Devereux was awarded £1,500 damages which Sir William refused to pay. The sheriff therefore granted Devereux full possession of Sir William's house and the lands at Idlicote. But Sir William was not prepared to concede defeat and he and his men 'forced entry' and reclaimed the property, killing one man. The lack of further details gives us much to speculate. I assume that Sir William, having reclaimed his estates, had full enjoyment of them as, at the age of 87 in 1710, they passed to his grandson.

To finally confound the quote 'there is little of interest in Idlicote', Elspeth Howe, widow of Geoffrey Howe, having, by virtue of her husband's knighthood and peerage, already being titled 'Lady', became three times a lady when in 2001 she became, Baroness Howe of Idlicote and after his death in 2015 also Dowager Lady Howe of Aberavon.

After the isolated Idlicote Hill Lodge farmhouse we commence a meandering path down to the Stour valley as the Feldon landscape unfolds before us. There are no records of when the enclosure of this area was undertaken. But, the isolated position of Idlicote Hill Lodge is typical of the post enclosure period. With bigger farm areas, the farm house and buildings were moved from the village to the centre of the farm and linked to the nearest public road by a long track. The 1885 OS map shows the farm split into large fields not much different to today's layout, providing efficient agricultural production and interspersed with woodland for hunting and shooting.

Honington is a small, very attractive village with a number of listed buildings but, I am afraid no pub. If you choose to make a tour of the village then at the bottom of the main street the view of the timber framed early 16th century (GII) Magpie House will not disappoint. Just after the Wren-style (GII) gate house, with its imposing gate and piers turn right in front of Magpie House to the church. The lane passes more attractive historical listed properties before arriving at the Grade I listed church of All Saints.

The Gatehouse to Honington Hall

The west tower of the church is circa 1275-1300 but the rest of the church was rebuilt in 1680. The intention was to model the church on a simpler Wren style church in the City of London. Next door to the church, but not really visible, is the Grade I listed Honington Hall built for Sir Henry Parker in 1685.

The return to walk to Whatcote starts with a gentle climb and then contours along the slopes, before turning up hill back to the summit.

## Walk Directions

| Joining points | Whatcote and Honington – kerbside parking |
|---|---|
| Pubs | Whatcote – the Royal Oak (P) |

1. Take the gate into the churchyard of St Peter's Church, turn left to the corner and take the gate and turn left and right to take the adjacent gate. Follow the right hedge line, to take the next three stiles, then a hedge gap to take a stile on the right as the field narrows, with the encroaching wood. Turn left to follow the hedge line around to the right, passing two marker posts to reach a third post and turn left to follow the track across the field. Continue along the track and at the approach to Idlicote Hill Cottage, turn left then right along its boundary hedge line.

2. Continue along the track, turning right along the perimeter of the wood to the next field. Continue to go through the next hedge gap, turn left along the hedge line with views to Campden and Meon Hills. At the far corner of the wood turn left through the hedge gap. Continue alongside the wood through the next hedge gap and turn right. Follow the right hedge line, passing the end of an island of wood, to the corner of the field. Turn left along the field edge to reach a marker post, continue past the pond on the right. Ignore the downhill track and cross the narrow neck of the field to a marker post. Turn right along the hedge line and at the corner turn left through the hedge gap.

3. Follow the right hedge to reach a junction with a track and turn right. (If you do not wish to visit Honington you can turn left along the track and follow the instructions below at 'B'.) Continue straight down the track and the edge of the field to the road via the gate to Fell Mill Lane. In continuing along the 'Way' the choice is yours. The next section description covers the route between here, at Honington, and Shipston on Stour the most southerly point and north to Tredington where the penultimate circular walk commences. Honington has no facilities but is an attractive hamlet. To return to Whatcote from this point turn left along the Lane.

*A. At the bend in the lane take the gate to the right of the drive to Bowback House. Cross the field ½ right and take the gate and continue straight across to take the next gate. Turn ½ left and take the stile and continue on the*

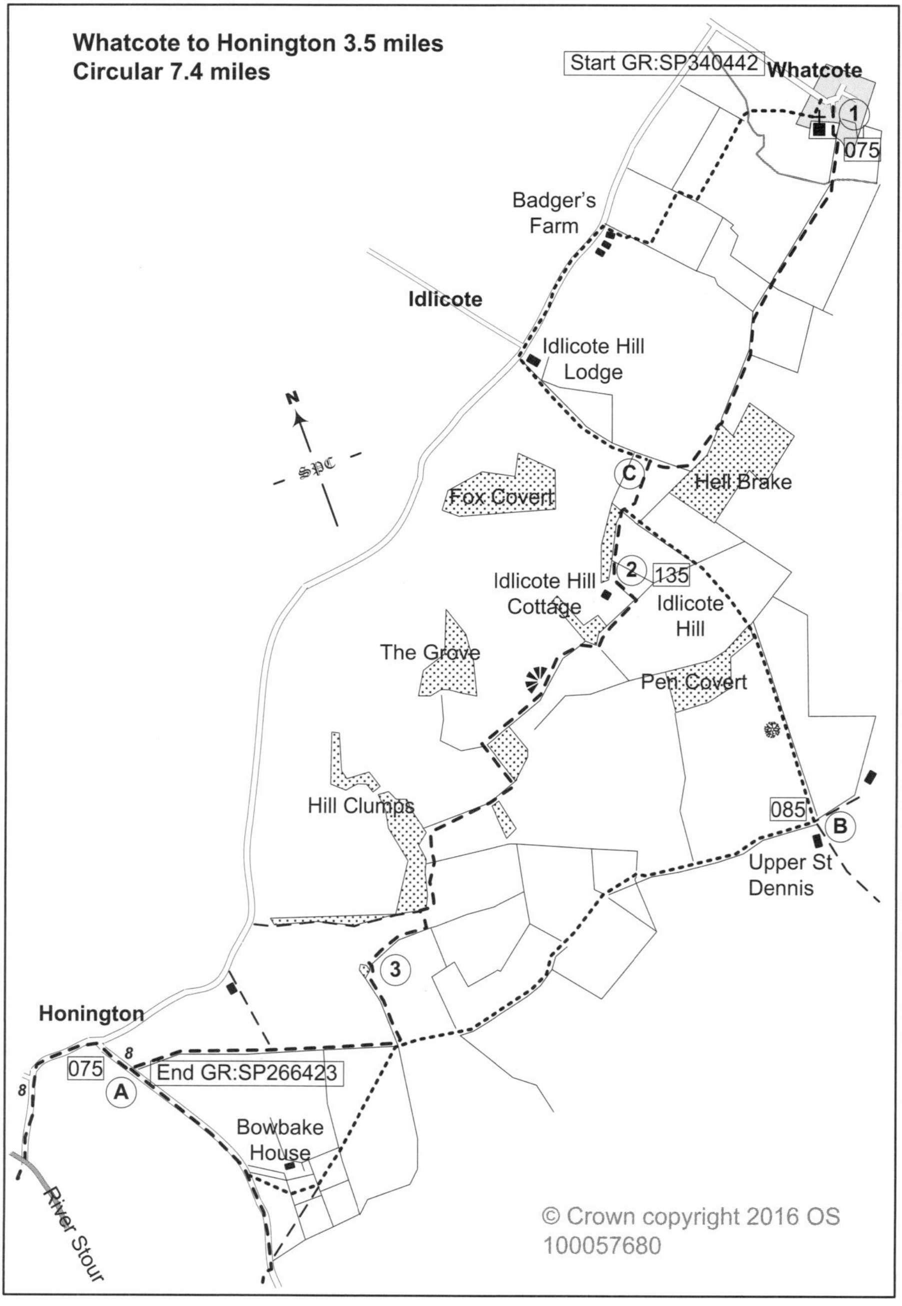
Whatcote to Honington 3.5 miles
Circular 7.4 miles
Start GR:SP340442
Whatcote
1
075
Badger's Farm
Idlicote
Idlicote Hill Lodge
N
SPC
C
Fox Covert
Hell Brake
2
135
Idlicote Hill Cottage
Idlicote Hill
The Grove
Pen Covert
Hill Clumps
085
B
Upper St Dennis
3
Honington
8
075
A
End GR:SP266423
8
Bowbake House
River Stour
© Crown copyright 2016 OS 100057680

*same line up the hill to the far corner and through the gap. Turn right to follow the track across the field which continues for about one mile. Continue through the hedge gaps including one further field crossing to reach a cottage at Upper St Dennis and a junction with another track.*

B. *Turn left up the hill, following the track, with the fence on the right. Go through a hedge gap, cross the next field, as the track continues along a fence line on the left to reach the summit and the route of the 'Way'. Turn right along the track to reach the left turn. From this point you can either turn right and follow the 'Way' and retrace your steps back to start or turn left along the track.*

C. *If you wish to take the alternative route follow the track downhill to a lane and turn right. Follow the lane to reach farm buildings and turn right through the gates (the stile was overgrown) and go left between the barn and the hedge. Continue along the hedge line to take the bridge and stile left and turn right along the right hedge. Continue to the field summit and at a point opposite the third power pole, cross the field towards it. Continue to go through the hedge gap and turn right for about 50 metres along the hedge line. Now turn left across the field through the hedge gap and bear right to cross a bridge. Continue straight ahead to follow the path between the house and reach Rectory Lane, turning right for the church or left for the village centre.*

# CHAPTER 10

## Section 27: Honington to Shipston on Stour and Tredington

The 'Way' makes a D-tour to visit and enjoy the most southern town in Warwickshire, Shipston on Stour. It is a typical country town which has kept its own identity and retains a vibrant town centre. From the Saxon records of 764 we know that the Saxon name for the town was *Scepeuu aeisctune* or in modern language Sheepwash farm on Stour.

As the name suggests it was the wool trade that underpinned its economic success. Its position close to the Fosse Way and on the crossroads between

High Street, Shipston on Stour

Stratford upon Avon and Oxford and the west-east road between the Cotswolds and Banbury would also have benefitted the trade. The town was also granted its Charter for an annual fair and a weekly market in 1268.

In the spring sheep were driven off the Cotswold Hills into the town where they were washed in the river before being moved onto their summer pasture after lambing. Later in the year they would be driven back into the town to the sheep market, the biggest in the country. The narrow alleys between Sheep Street and Telegraph Street were used to run the sheep so that they could be counted at the exit.

Even after demand for its wool began to diminish, given its road links it was also an important coaching town, reflected by the number of inns that still remain. But the next step forward was the railway. A man called William James, who lived in Henley in Arden, had an ambitious scheme to link the Midlands via canal to Stratford, tramway to Oxford and then barge along the Thames to London. William was ahead of his time and his 4' 8½" railway gauge tramway from Stratford to Moreton in the Marsh was operating by 1826, twelve years before any other railway in the County. Shipston's branch was delayed and did not open until 1836.

The intention was that the line would be worked by steam traction but even when the line was taken over by the Oxford, Worcester and Wolverhampton Railway Company in 1847, the tramway continued to be horse drawn. But, with the takeover by Great Western Railway, the line south of Darlingscott was abandoned as uneconomic and full steam train services were introduced to Shipston on the 1st July 1889. Passenger services continued until 1929 and the line was closed in 1960.

The centre of Shipston today retains its country town ambience with its many largely late 17th century and early 18th century Grade II listed properties and the Grade II* listed parish church of St Edmond. Depending upon the time of day refreshment can be enjoyed at a number of cafes and hostelries.

The distance to Tredington from Shipston, along the A3400 is two miles. This small village, which has seen very little change since Saxon times, gives its name to the Parish. Even its Saxon name Tredington, 'the farm of Trydda's people' is virtually unchanged. Within the parish boundary are Newbold on Stour, where there is a shop, Blackwell, Darlingscott and Armscote.

The church of St Gregory is Grade I listed notably because of the remains of the original Anglo-Danish origins and late 12th, 14th and 15th century additions. Past Rectors of St Gregory's include Humphrey Owen, 1744-1763, who became the Bodleian Librarian and Peter Vannes, in 1542, who was King Henry VIII and Edward VI's Latin Secretary before becoming Dean at Salisbury.

**Honington, Shipston on Stour, Tredington and Fosse Way**

Honington to Shipstone 1.6 miles, Honnington to the Fosse Way 2.15 miles, Shipstone to Fosse Way 2.6 miles

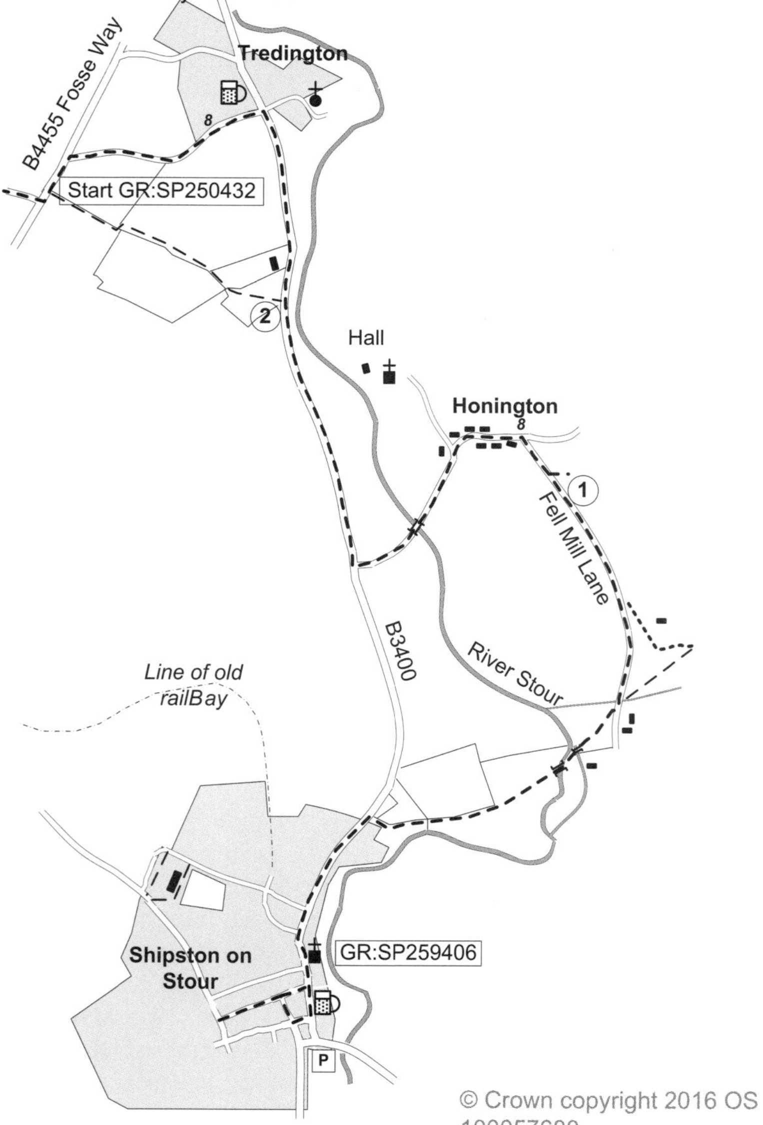

## Walk Directions

| Joining points | Honington and Tredington – kerbside parking: Shipston on Stour – free car park |
|---|---|
| Pubs | Shipstone on Stour – the Horseshoe Inn, George, Falcon, White Bear Inn and Coach & Horses; Tredington – the White Lion (P) |

**From Honington you may make your own decision as to whether or not to visit Shipston on Stour on foot or walk directly to Tredington and Blackwell.**

1. If you choose to walk directly to Tredington then from Honington turn right along Fell Mill Lane and left through the village to reach the A3400. Turn right and follow the road to the edge of Tredington (or take the shorter route at 2. if you wish) and turn left along Blackwell Road. Continue to the junction with the Fosse Way turn left along the footpath for 140 metres and turn right along the lane for Blackwell.

   Alternatively to walk to Shipston on Stour from Honington along Fell Mill Lane, continue to cross the bridge over a stream and take the gate on the right. Go ½ left over the mound to cross the bridge over the mill stream. Now follow the bank of the River Stour, cross the bridge and follow the track across the field. Continue along the left side of the hedge line passing a redundant gate, continuing to take a gate and then a gate to the road.

2. The alternative footpath, shortening the road route to the Fosse Way, leaves the A3400 down a bank to take a gate. Cross the field to the corner and take the gates as necessary into the next field. Follow the left hedge and take a gate and turn left to follow the field perimeter. Continue up the hill to reach the corner and turn left and right through the hedge gap to continue straight ahead. Follow the right hedge take a stile onto the B4455 Fosse Way and turn left and right along the lane to Blackwell.

## Section 28: Tredington to Ilmington

Leaving the Fosse Way for the last time we follow a lane through the hamlet of Blackwell. Once again the buildings range between modern 'des res' and listed buildings. Two examples of the latter are the Gables and Williams Farmhouses which are GII late 17th and 18th century respectively, just before the crossroads in the centre of the village. Following the road uphill we turn left next to the 18th century (GII) Blackwell Grange Barn, part of the Blackwell Grange Manor Estate.

For many years the Grange was a racehorse yard owned by the Vernon family and their biggest winner was 'Bighorn' in the 1971 Hennessy Gold Cup at Newbury. Today the 1604 Manor House is the centre piece of a 'thriving sheep and arable farming operation' as well as a Wedding Venue business.

Following Ilmington Lane the field on the right has a well pronounced ridge and furrow pattern. We turn right then left to follow the 'Way' through the fields and then reach the lane which links the north end of Ilmington with Shipston. Parallel with the lane is the line of the railway line that linked Stratford and Shipston. The last section takes a steep, cross field path climbing to the summit at the north-east corner of Ilmington.

The peculiarities of the ecclesiastical boundaries and land ownership meant that until 1931 the parish of Ilmington was effectively an offshore island separated from Warwickshire by Worcestershire and Gloucestershire. The situation was rectified with the 1931 boundary adjustments eliminating the gap. Notwithstanding the claim made by Ratley that they are the highest parish in the county, Ilmington has the highest summit on Ebrington Hill at 261m.

However Ilmington is classified as a Cotswold village positioned on the rising northern slopes of the Cotswold Hills. The hills have a number of worked out quarries which would have provided the Campden Stone, the traditional honey coloured material used in many of the village's buildings.

The village is long and narrow with three main thoroughfares, helpfully named Front, Middle and Back Street. We start by turning left 'up' Front Street and turn right into Middle Street in front of the 18th century (GII) Howard Arms Inn. As the street swings left, it reduces to a path alongside the stream that runs through the village. However despite the lack of vehicular access it is still very much the main street to some of the properties along it. Opposite the pond we pass the rear of the listed Manor House and continue to turn left and right into the churchyard of the mid 12th century (GI) church of St Mary. Like many of the churches we have passed, the nave is the oldest part, with the tower and chancel added during the late 13th and 14th century. The north and south transepts were added in the 15th century.

Following the 'Way' we turn right around the church to Back Street and the return route turns left to Front Street. We pass the uniquely named Valenders Lane and then walk beside the stone wall and the ornate entrance

The Dower House, Back Street

pillars of the early 16th century (GII*) Ilmington Manor House to reach the Red Lion. This pub is worth noting as it is part of the Hook Norton Brewery estate which includes both the Castle at Edge Hill and the Coach and Horses in Shipston. The brewery was established in 1849 at Hook Norton, just over the border in Oxfordshire.

We turn right, opposite the pub, to follow the lane back to the old railway line. From the intersection with the 'Way' we take the field path to Darlingscott. The hamlet has a number of listed properties but we pass three, all 17th century Grade II* listed. Along the main street the Manor House and Camperdown Farmhouse and turning into the lane to Blackwell on the first bend there is Darlingscott Farmhouse.

Leaving the lane it is a cross-country path back to the start.

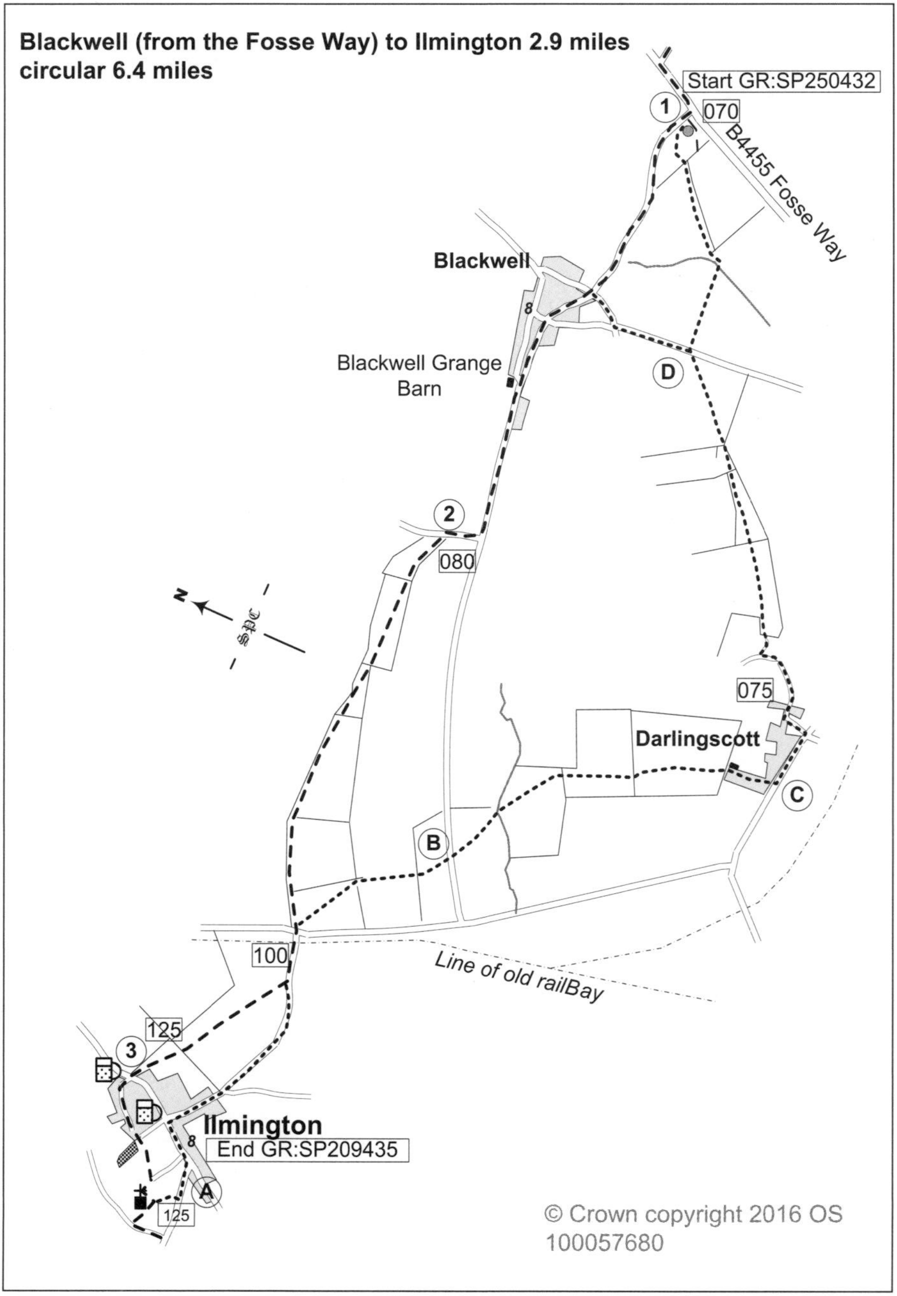
Blackwell (from the Fosse Way) to Ilmington 2.9 miles
circular 6.4 miles
Start GR:SP250432
1
070
B4455 Fosse Way
Blackwell
8
Blackwell Grange
Barn
D
2
080
N
075
Darlingscott
C
B
100
Line of old railBay
125
3
Ilmington
8
End GR:SP209435
A
125
© Crown copyright 2016 OS
100057680

## Walk Directions

| | |
|---|---|
| Joining points | Tredington, Blackwell and Ilmington – kerbside parking |
| Pubs | Tredington – the White Lion (P): Ilmington the Red Lion and Howard Arms (P) |

1. Having turned right from the A429 Fosse Way follow the lane to Blackwell. At the edge of the village keep straight on at the crossroads. Follow the lane climbing slightly through the village, ignoring left and right turns. At the ancient thatched barn of Blackwell Grange continue past the last houses on the left and the a ridge and furrow field on the right. Now take the right turn along a lane for a short distance to a gate on the left and take the adjacent stile.

2. Follow the left perimeter and take the stile. Cross the field, aiming for the power pylon, and take the stile. Keeping to the right follow the right field perimeter and take the next stile. Continue through the next three fields, via a stile then hedge gap to take a bridge/stile to the road. Turn left and right along the lane for Ilmington for 130 metres to reach a marker post on the right. Cross the field aiming aiming for the right power line pole on the summit and continue to take the stile. Cross the field straight ahead, take the stile to the right of the houses and continue to the road.

3. Cross the road and follow 'Lower Green' opposite the 'Howard Arms' around to the left to join 'Middle Street'. Follow the road and then the continuing footpath, which curves right across the end of a lane from the left, to reach the churchyard of St Mary the Virgin. To continue along the 'Way' turn right in the corner of the churchyard to Back Street and to return to the start of this section turn left to Front Street.

A. *Turn left along Front Street and opposite the Red Lion turn right into Ballards Lane following it to connect with the 'Way'. At the T-junction turn left and right to the marker post and re-cross the stile/bridge. Now turn ½ right to cross the field to the corner and through the hedge gap. Follow the left hedge line to the corner and on the same line cross the field. Go through the hedge gap and cross the field, aiming slightly left, to the hedge gap, to the road.*

*B. Cross the road, through the hedge gap and turn ½ left to the far corner and take the bridge/stile. Continue ½ left across the field to the corner and take the stile. Cross the field straight ahead to take the next stile. Now cross the field aiming for the right hand end of the white cottage and take the stile. Follow the footpath then drive to the road in Darlingscott.*

*C. Turn left along the road through the hamlet to the crossroads and turn left. Follow the lane as it turns right and then bends left. Look for the marker post on the right and take the gate to follow the fenced path. Take the gate into the field and follow the left hedge line to the corner, then continue straight across the field to take the next gate. Follow the same line through the narrowing field to take the gate, continuing to take the next gate. Cross the large field ½ left to exit to the road at the end of the small building.*

*D. Cross the road and take the gap at the side of the large gates. From the gates cross straight over the field to reach a marker post and a damaged bridge where, although it is probably safe, the easier option is to take the wide ditch crossing to the right. Turn left to take the gate and turn right to follow the hedge line and take the gate. Cross the field to the left of the bank then follow the curve right and take the stile, turning left to the road and join the 'Way'. The alternative route back to the start is to turn left along the lane and right at the crossroads. Follow the lane to the next crossroads and rejoin the 'Way'.*

## Section 29: Ilmington to Upper Quinton

We start in Back Lane from the church and quickly make our last steep climb on the 'Way'. The path undulates across the lower slopes of Nebsworth summit at 242m. There is quite a steep descent before we climb to a lane and pass the north-east corner of the deserted medieval settlement, and Ancient Monument, of Lark Stoke.

Historical England describes this site as a typical example of a Stour-Avon-Soar Clay Vales which would have become deserted by the late 15th century. The later, and separately listed, 16th century Lower Lark Stoke Manor House is not part of the scheduling. It is the relatively undisturbed archaeology recording the centuries of occupation of the settlement which, on the evidence of pottery finds, was occupied in Roman times. The website contains a mass of information of how the land was worked and managed including evidence of a chapel and burials.

We drop down the hill and follow a road to a cross-country path from Admington Lane Farm to the drive way of Meon Hall. Originally the right of way would have taken us almost to the Hall but was diverted. The hall is originally 16th century but restored and enlarged in the 19th century after a fire.

The last leg of the walk along the 'Way' circles the lower slope of Meon Hill. At the top of the hill is one of only two known mulitivallate hillforts in the County. Mulitivallate is, I discovered, the archaeological definition of a fort with at least three rings of defence. The fort extends over an area of 10ha and investigations through the best preserved perimeter sections have revealed that attackers would first have faced an outer 9m wide ditch then a rampart, a middle 16m wide ditch an inner rampart and another ditch.

The first archaeological dig in 1824 found 394 spit-shaped currency bars dated to the 3rd century BC. This hoard reflects the sites particular importance in revealing the advance that had been made in the adoption of an accepted, standardized currency. Subsequent investigations lead to the evidence of hut sites and an Anglo Saxon inhumation. From these 'digs' various finds have been discovered including Iron Age and Romano-British pottery shards, two spearheads, two bronzes, flint flakes, a shield boss and a metal band.

Given the hills early human pre-Christian habitation it is perhaps not surprising that over the centuries strange tales and legends have surrounded it. One of these is that the ghost of Celtic King Arawyn, who was the lord of departed spirits, hunts the hills at night gathering souls. If by chance you leave finishing this walk too late and dusk arrives, he rides a pale horse and has a pack of white hounds with red ears.

One true tale, which it has been suggested involved witchcraft, was the murder on St Valentines Day 1945 of Charles Walton, a 74 year-old farm labourer, who was well known and well liked. He was found on the hill brutally murdered with his own trouncing hook embedded in his throat and his pitch fork pinning his body to the ground. Witchcraft was suspected as the shape of a large cross was carved into his chest. The local police had no success with their investigations so Detective Superintendent Robert Fabian, of Scotland Yard, was brought in. This man inspired a 1950s television detective series, *Fabian of the Yard*, making him the first modern police, television hero. Despite his notoriety the case was never solved.

We continue to descend into Upper Quinton and turn right along Hill Lane to the Green and the end of the 102 miles of the Centenary Way. If you have not been following the circular walks you may wish to celebrate the completion of the 102 miles by finishing here. But, by following the return route it is only a little over ¾ mile to Lower Quinton's (GII) 17th century College Arms pub.

Across the road from the pub is the Grade I listed church of St Swithin, which was consecrated in 1238, it is an impressive building. Historically this village was part of Gloucestershire and except for Historical England's record of the listed buildings I could find no historical information on the village.

The route back to Ilmington, after leaving the road, follows a cross- country route passing close to the Jacobean period Grade II* Admington Hall. The onward path climbing the hill next to the hurdles in the hedges mark the estates equestrian interests.

The final approach to Ilmington crosses the perpetually 'boggy' area adjacent to the Newfoundland Well. This was a chalybeate spring discovered in 1684 by Dr William Cole. The oxford dictionary definition of chalybeate is 'a natural mineral spring containing iron salts'. Seemingly a Dr Samuel Derham, who was a promoter of the benefits 'of taking the waters' brought people to the village to enjoy the benefits of the water. The Lord of the Manor of the time had the well paved for public use but it is now in private ownership.

Church of St Swithin

## Walk Directions

| | |
|---|---|
| Joining points | Ilmington, Upper Quinton and Lower Quinton – kerbside parking |
| Pubs | Ilmington – the Red Lion and Howard Arms (P): Lower Quinton – The College Arms (P) |

1. In Back Street, with your back to the Church turn left and reach the junction with Front Street and turn right up the Campden Hill. After 155 metres take the footpath on the right up the steps and take the stile. Cross the field, take the stile and follow the right hedge and take the next stile. Cross the field ½ left, through an avenue of trees and through a hedge gap, Turn ½ left to the first of several marker posts which indicate the path across the field, through the valley. Take the gate and turn left, following the hedge and take the next gate. Continue between the fence and hedge to take the hedge gap left. Turn right to follow the path, descending to cross a brook and take the gate. Follow the field around to the left, passing Lark Stoke, to take a gate and turn right along the drive.

2. At the road turn right and at the bottom of the hill turn left along Park Lane. Continue along the road towards Hidcote, ignoring the right turn, to reach Admington Lane Farm. Pass the entrance drive and take the stile on the right. Follow the hedge line to its end and cross ½ left to the opposite hedge corner. Follow the left hedge to a marker post and cross the field ½ right to a marker post and cross the bridge. Turn left and right through the hedge gap and follow the hedge line. At a gate cross the field ½ right to the far corner, adjacent to the bungalow, and take the stile to the road.

3. Turn right and then left along the drive to Meon Hall. At the gates, adjacent to the green barn, take the gate on the right. Cross the field, following the marker posts and take the gate. Cross the field slightly left to follow a fence line and take the twin stile either side of a plank bridge. Turn right and take the stile and another plank bridge and stiles. Turn left, follow the left hedge and take a gate. Cross the field ¼ right to take a stile and continue between the trees to take a gate. Follow the path winding around to the left beyond the first house to take a stile. Follow the footpath between the buildings to reach and turn right along the road. Follow the road for a short distance to reach Upper Quinton and 'The Green' at the end of the Centenary Way!

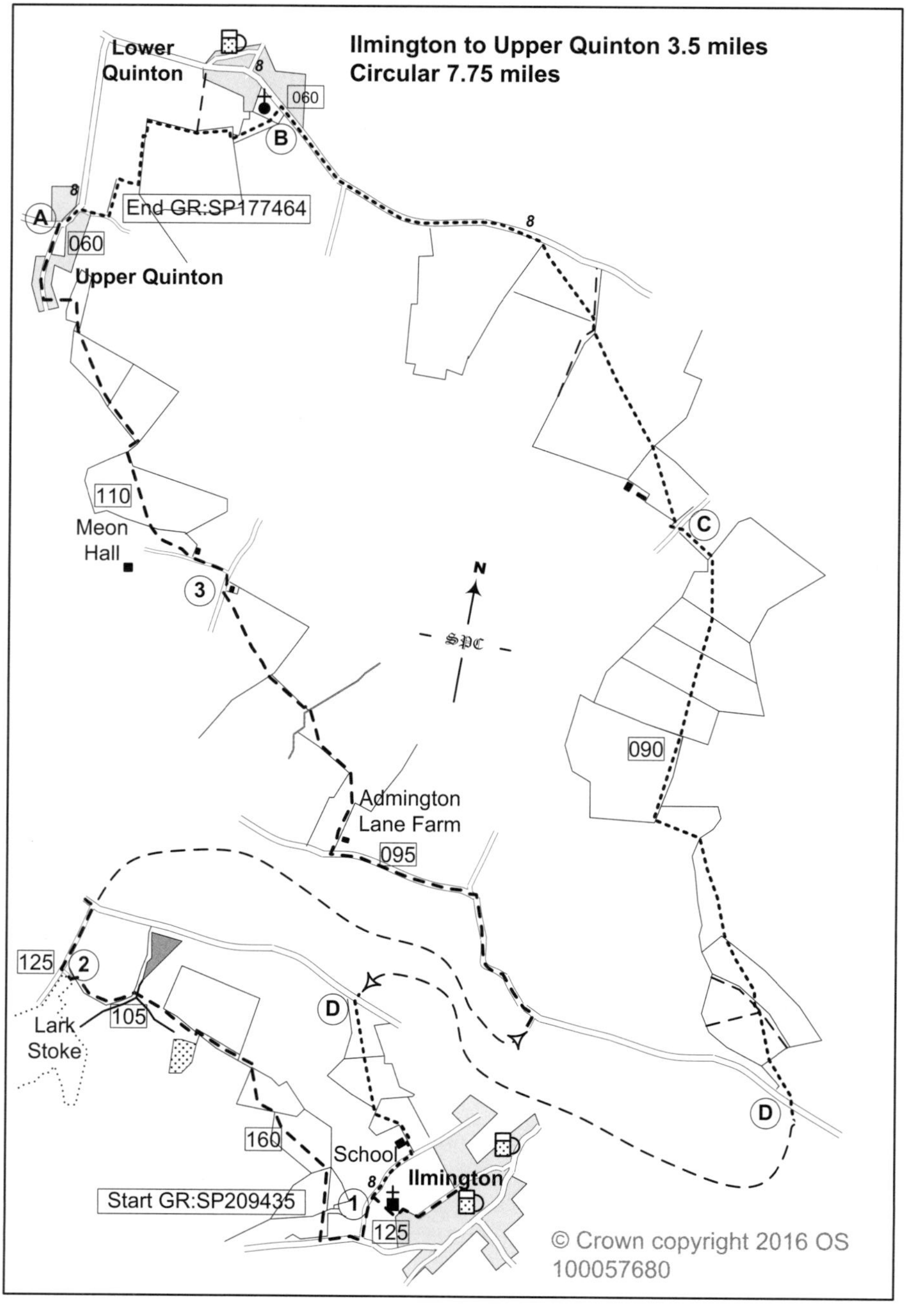
Ilmington to Upper Quinton 3.5 miles
Circular 7.75 miles
Lower Quinton
060
B
A
8
End GR:SP177464
060
Upper Quinton
8
C
110
Meon Hall
3
N
SPC
090
Admington Lane Farm
095
125
2
105
Lark Stoke
D
D
160
School
8
Ilmington
Start GR:SP209435
1
125
© Crown copyright 2016 OS 100057680

A. *To return to Ilmington continue along the road across the Green and turn right along Goose Lane. Continue until the road straightens and turn right along a drive either through the double gates or take the pedestrian gate at the side. Follow the drive and turn left along the right side of the high hedge. At the end of the hedge turn right across the field and turn left with the opposite hedge. Turn right through the hedge via two gates. From here the right of way should cross the field but since the farmer seems to have established a wide perimeter path that is the route that I have shown. Follow it to take a gate then another and cross the open area to the gate into the churchyard of St Swithins. Go through the churchyard and take the gate to the road.*

B. *Follow the road for about 1100 metres and, just beyond an unsurfaced lay by on the left, go between the posts, adjacent a bridge, into the corner of a field. Cross the field (crops) ¼ right to the end of the cross field hedge at a track. Turn right along the track for a few yards and cross the bridge. From the way mark post arrow (crops) cross the field ½ right - compass bearing 140° to the right of the two tallest trees and cross a bridge. Cross the next field on the same line, aiming for the house, to the end of the hedge. Turn right and left to follow a hedge and take stile to the road. Cross the road and take the stile to the left of the Humber Cottage drive.*

C. *Follow the right hedge and take the gate and turn right with the fence to continue on the same line across the field to take a stile. Cross the next two fields aiming for the hurdles in the hedge line and take the adjacent stiles. Continue on the same line to take a gate and follow the hedge line to take a corner gate on the left. Cross the field to take a bridge and stile and turn right. Aim for a point 70 metres left of the right perimeter to arrive at a way marked hedge corner. Turn left at the marker and right through the hedge gap. Turn left then take the ride right towards the electricity pylon. As the ride bends left take the gap in the hedge right and turn left. At the wide junction with two rides take the ride ¼ right. Follow the ride to cross a bridge and take stile. Follow the hedge line to a stile and cross the road.*

D. *Take the gate opposite and continue up the centre of the field to take the stile. Go left of the power pole, finding the best route to navigate around a potentially soft area, and take the corner gate. Take the next gate to the left and cross the field left of the school to turn right along the perimeter path. Take the gate to the path and turn left to Back Lane. Turn right along the lane to reach the footpath from the Church and the starting point.*

## HS2 Route Footpath Diversions

It is assumed that while construction work is in progress temporary diversions will be available

### Section 13 Bubbenhall to Stareton (South)

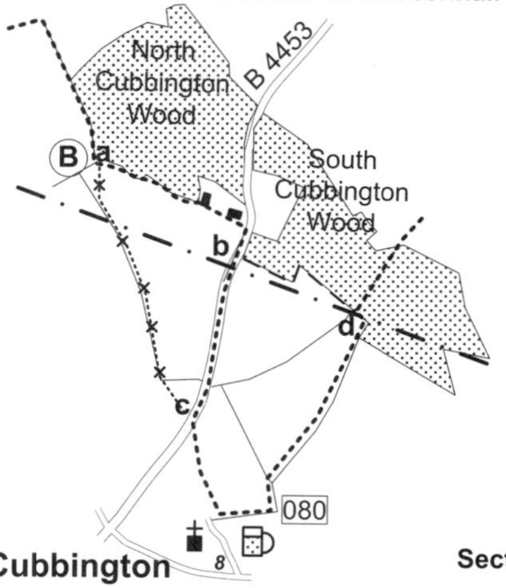


- Between points 'a' and 'c' the footpath is diverted between 'a','b' and 'c along the road, which will be the route to visit Cubbington.
- It is not known whether the permissive path between between 'b' and 'd' will remain.
- At 'd' there will be a footpath overbridge.

### Section 14 Stareton to Kenilworth Castle

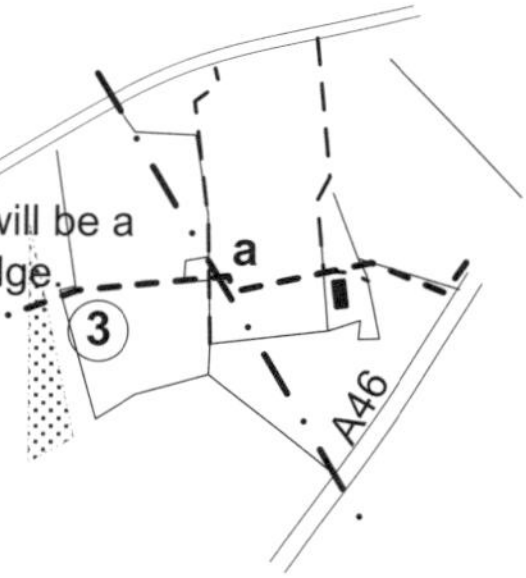


- At point 'a' there will be a footpath overbridge.

### Section 18 Newbold Comyn to Longhole Bridge

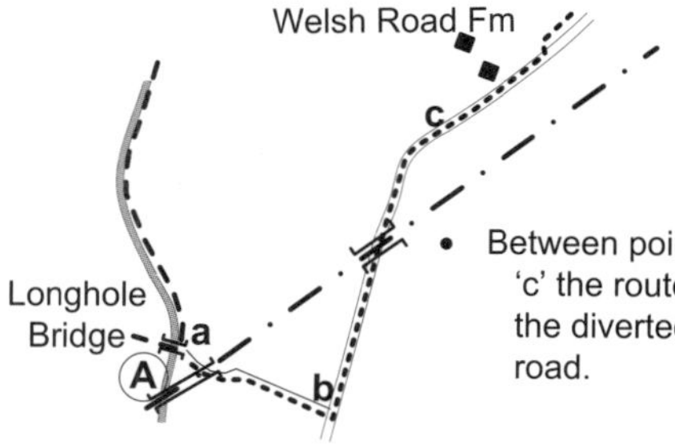


- Between points 'a', 'b' and 'c' the route will follow the diverted track and road.

## BUS ROUTES

For current timetable information visit www.traveline.org.uk

All of the route numbers operated in March 2017 providing services through the day on week days

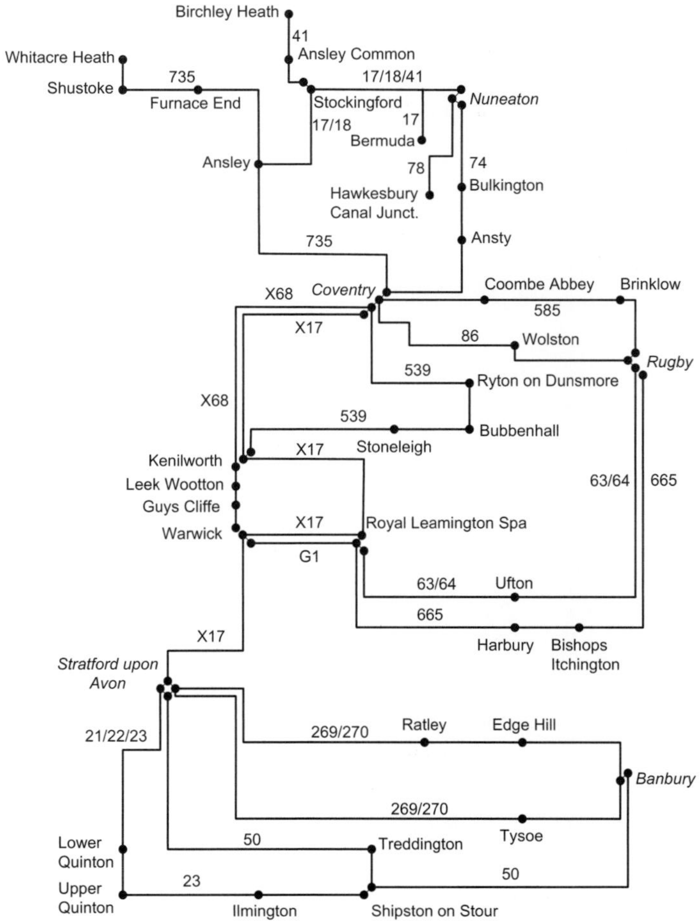

WARWICKSHIRE'S CENTENARY WAY & THE HEART OF ENGLAND WAY LONG DISTANCE FOOTPATHS
Milford Common
Cannock Chase
Lichfield
Drayton Bassett
Kingsbury Water Park
Whitacre Heath
Hartshill Hayes
Nuneaton
Ansty
Meriden
Coventry
Coombe Abbey
Rugby
Chadwick End
Ryton on Dunsmore
Bubbenhall
Kenilworth
Henley in Arden
Royal Leamington Spa
Warwick
Ufton
Harbury
Alcester
Stratford upon Avon
Burton Dassett
Bidford upon Avon
Avon Dassett
Long Marston
Upper Quinton
Ratley
Whatcote
Middle Tysoe
Ilmington
Shipston on Stour
Chipping Campden
Blockley
Upper/Lower Swell
Lower Slaughter
Bourton on the Water

# ACKNOWLEDGEMENTS

As with the *Heart of England Way* Guide the Centenary Way Guide has been a year long project. My wife Christine has joined me on many of the walks and we have enjoyed some excellent pub lunches along the 'Way'. Once again my thanks to her for providing all the back up, support and checking the written word. A sporting and walking friend of many years, Dave Higgins, enjoyed again (so he tells me) undertaking the mystery walker service. He has walked the routes, armed only with my guidance notes and maps, providing me with invaluable corrections and observations.

I would also express my appreciation for the support of Warwick Town Council, Shakespeare's England and Warwick Castle who have funded the mapping Ordnance Survey copyright fee.

Stephen and Christine on a wind swept Sun Rise Hill

## Primary Sources

In writing the travelogue of the walks the following books sat on my desk and provided invaluable background information: *Midlands Landscape Explained* - John Wright; *20th Century Defences in Warwickshire* - Steve Carvell; *Warwickshire Landscapes the Story So Far* - Michael Jeffs; *A History of Warwickshire* - Terry Slater; *Guys Cliffe Back to the Roots* - Bob Dixon; *Warwickshire Place Names* - Anthony Poulton-Smith and *Dark Ages Warwick & The Warrior Queen* - J R Watkin.

The websites of: British History Online, Warwickshire Railways, Historic England, Battle of Edgehill, the Battlefields Trust, Nuneaton History and Warwickshire County Council all proved to be an amazing resource.

# Also from Sigma Leisure:

**The Heart of England Way**
102 miles of linear walk or 225 miles of 32 linked circular walks
*Stephen P Cross*

A book both for the long distance and the leisure walker, The Heart of England Way, and 32 circular walks, takes the walker on a journey slicing through the quieter areas of the midlands countryside; The Heart of England Way starts in Staffordshire on Cannock Chase and crosses Warwickshire from north to south, with a little interruption from the eastern end of Solihull's rural fringe, and finishes in North Gloucestershire, providing a fascinating view through the back door of the regions history, people, buildings and landscape.

*£8.99*

**The Clough Walk**
from Nottingham to Sunderland
*Martin Perry and Geoff Smith*

The Clough Walk is a beautiful, exhilarating long distance walk that passes through the towns and cities associated with the illustrious career of Brian Clough both as a player and manager. Even people who profess to have no interest in football will have heard of Brian Clough but they may not be aware of his love for walking as an escape from the frenetic world of football management. The walk begins in Nottingham and ends on the impressive North East coast on Roker Beach, Sunderland and affords the walker the opportunity to visit football grounds and various memorial sites and statues along the way.

*£8.99*

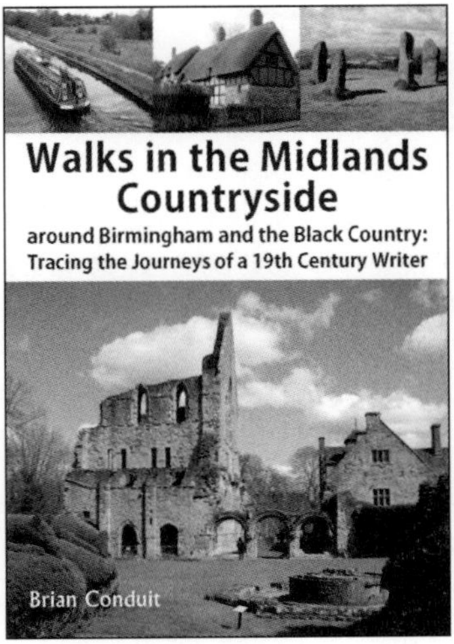


## **Walks in the Midlands Countryside** around Birmingham and the Black Country

*Brian Conduit*

In 1865 Elihu Burritt, a notable American peace and anti-slavery activist, was appointed the United States consul in Birmingham, at the time a rapidly growing manufacturing city and centre of a major industrial area. He travelling extensively throughout the Midlands, not just in Birmingham and the heavily industrialised Black Country but also in the rural areas that lay beyond the industrial belt in Warwickshire, Worcestershire, Staffordshire and Shropshire. Burritt was full of enthusiasm for everything he saw and his obvious love for the area shines through in the book that he subsequently wrote about his journeys. That book, published in 1868, was entitled *Walks in the Black Country and its Green Borderland*. These 20 walks take you through areas of the Midlands which, 150 years since Burritt walked this way, still contain some of the most varied, beautiful and interesting landscapes and some of the finest old towns and villages in the country.

***£8.99***

## **Country Walks around the National Forest**

*Brian Conduit*

The National Forest is an area of 200 square miles covering parts of west Leicestershire, east Staffordshire and south Derbyshire. The River Trent winds across the heart of it and for much of the way it is partnered by the Trent and Mersey Canal. This collection of twenty walks is not just confined to the boundaries of the National Forest but also includes a number of interesting and attractive areas on its periphery.

*£8.99*